The Dawning Age of

Cooperation

THE DAWNING AGE OF COOPERATION

THE END OF CIVILIZATION
AS WE KNOW IT
... AND JUST IN TIME

Gordon E. Moss

Algora Publishing
New York

Library of Congress Cataloging-in-Publication Data —

Moss, Gordon Ervin, 1937-
    The dawning age of cooperation : the end of civilization as we know it-- and just in
time / Gordon E. Moss.
        p. cm.
    Includes bibliographical references.
    ISBN 978-0-87586-873-8 (soft cover: alk. paper) — ISBN 978-0-87586-874-5 (hbk.:
alk. paper) — ISBN 978-0-87586-875-2 (ebook) 1. Social systems. 2. Cooperation—Social
aspects. I. Title.
    HM701.M67 2011
    302'.14—dc22
                        2011015028

Printed in the United States

TABLE OF CONTENTS

Preface: "You Cain't Get The'ah from He'ah"

I first heard that phrase while I was teaching at the University of Maine at Orono early in my career. You probably have heard it. It is the punch line of a folktale where a Mainer is playfully telling tourists they can't get to where they want to go from where they are. When I tell friends and colleagues what a cooperative America would look like, I often get a similar response: It would be wonderful, but it "just ain't gonna happen, maybe in a million years." It seems impossible to get "the'ah" from our current society that is pretty much the opposite of cooperative. The peace, harmony, and abundance of cooperation seem an unrealistic utopian dream. While these skeptics are correct that you can't produce a cooperative society out of the self-centered individualism and adversarial competition that underpin our current American society, it is possible to create within us the seeds of a new cooperative society and nurture it until it becomes our new way of life.

Our competitive individualistic American society is giving us exactly what it is designed to give us. If we don't like it—as many of us clearly do not—we must change the design of our society. Trying to get our society to be something different from what it is, such as more cooperative, by pushing and twisting it this way and that is as frustrating as it is futile. If Americans refuse to abandon their self-centered individualistic and adversarial competitive culture, they should stop complaining when our society gives us the same old problems and failures decade after decade. That's all it has to give. If we truly want a cooperative society, we have to design one. We have to build a cooperative culture and abandon our competitive individualistic culture, which cannot produce a cooperative society.

True cooperation will require Americans to step "out of the box," as we like to say, into a different world. It will be an experience similar to some of our fantasies where the characters step from our current world into a different one, such as Narnia through the back of the wardrobe. We will discover that life in the new world of cooperation is easy, engaging, and delightful. We will be shocked to see how hard our struggles with our old world are by comparison.

The transformation of America to a cooperative society will take many generations. But that is no reason to faint-heartedly abort the journey so early in its beginning. We didn't despair escaping the feudal world for an industrial one, or an aristocratic world for democracy. We can take it one step at a time gradually nurturing this emerging, still tender, new culture and the cooperative era will unfold for us. No need for military revolutions, nasty political battles, street fights, mass marches or any of the other romantic adventures we have come to associate with social change.

Cooperation is necessary for us to eliminate our maladaptive cultural habits that threaten our survival as a species. Cooperation is necessary for us to develop and enjoy the exciting high technology lifestyle, astounding explosion of information, and world-wide cultural community that are spreading over our planet. Cooperation is the gateway to the next level of human social evolution. It will be marvelous, and it is much easier to create than we imagine. Yes, we can "get the'ah from he'ah".

FROM TYPE A'S TO COOPERATION

I came to the study of cooperation later in life as a consequence of a search for the solution to social stress in America. We know that social stress is a general risk factor, like smoking, that increases our susceptibility to all kinds of diseases and mental problems. I have discovered that the source of most of our distress lies in our American culture. To permanently solve our massive stress problem, we will have to reformulate some basic operating cultural patterns of our society.

As a young man I was fascinated with the mind-body connection. I became a medical sociologist with training in both biology and sociology. My research focused on social stress and disease. Later, I joined with colleagues in Michigan to study the infamous hard-driving, time-urgent, impatient, hostile, and competitive Type A coronary-prone behavior pattern. The socio-demographics of Type As became a special interest to me as I searched for the sociocultural sources of Type A behavior. Research by others, including studies on twins, had shown that Type A behavior was learned.

My colleagues and I discovered much about the sociology of Type As. We found the distribution of the A and B coping behavior patterns between men and women was identical. In addition, urban versus rural living and religion showed little influence on Type A/B distributions. We learned Type A behavior follows a lifecycle curve, peaking during the pressured and burdened middle aged years of work and family rearing (Moss et al. 1986; Dielman et al., 1987).

I wanted to find the social sources of Type A behavior. I was looking for social groups that had high concentrations of either Type As or Type Bs for comparison. Surprisingly, we didn't find any. But sixty percent of our sample consisted of Type As. So, where were they all coming from? I concluded that rather than Type As and Bs being generated by different social communities, the sources of the Type A pattern are embedded in our basic social and cultural fabric. I concluded Type A behavior is the consequence of living in and trying to "succeed" in America's competitive individualistic culture.

That insight quickly showed me how truly distressing and unhealthy our daily competitive and individualistic social patterns are. That's when my research interest took a sharp turn. While self-help and counseling can relieve some symptoms and resolve some issues, any serious effort to eliminate the most important sources of social and psychological distress requires us to do away with the cultures of competition and individualism. It requires us to replace them with a new culture—one based on cooperation.

However, when I began designing research projects on work groups, I found that an adequate theoretical framework and solid measures of cooperation were lacking. We label all kinds of things "cooperation" that aren't. Our American history is lacking in good examples of cooperative social systems. It became obvious that research on cooperation and efforts to build cooperative organizations required fresh theoretical conceptualizations and models. Clearly, cooperation is not our natural habitat ... yet.

This book is a focused presentation of the results of my research into what true cooperative social systems and civilization would look like. Although we have not seen the like, there have been a few American efforts that have come remarkably close. I will introduce you to some. This book describes what true cooperation is, how it works, and how to create and maintain a cooperative culture and social system.

I will show you that cooperation is our future. It is even now struggling to emerge from our changing social garden. It is the right culture for a more stress-free society. It is the right culture for the world we are becoming.

ACKNOWLEDGEMENTS

One of the most enjoyable aspects of pursuing answers to research questions is working with fascinating people. I am very grateful to Ron Westrum who provided valuable information and insights over years of discussion and friendship, including the material on Section T of OSRD in Chapter 2.

In the 1990s in Ann Arbor, Michigan, I formed a cooperation work group with some friends and colleagues. Searching for true cooperation was a surprisingly uncertain and often frustrating process in those years. In our meetings, this group of business people, consultants, and academics examined many aspects of cooperation. We provided each other with information about our own efforts to produce more cooperative work places. We generated several consulting efforts and exploratory research projects.

The core group members were Bill Bottum, Jan Calle, Elizabeth Chapleski, Colleen Cooper, Larry Lippitt, Peggy Lippitt, Clay Mitchell, and myself. A number of other consultants and business people participated and contributed from time to time as well. Colleen Cooper, Larry Lippitt, and I researched several small companies among Michigan businesses, which were reputed to be cooperative. I remember those meetings and efforts fondly and with gratitude.

I have enjoyed the continued encouragement, discussions and friendship of Scott Fisher, who provided details for the material on Rensis Likert. I appreciate Bruce Gibb for his helpfulness on the business chapters and for the material on the "camp mode" in Chapter 16.

I am grateful for my editors Lavina Fielding Anderson, Carolee Ferguson Moss, and Allene Cooper. I especially appreciate my primary editor Colin Murcray who has patiently guided me through many necessary refinements, revisions and the publishing process with skill, humor and encouragement.

I'm grateful to Merry Henry who was for several years my patient sounding board and supporter. I am grateful most of all for my wife, Linda Macrae Moss who reads and improves everything with a sunny smile and nurturing companionship.

Introduction: A Stranger Called "Cooperation"

This book is an introduction to "true cooperation." True cooperation is a powerful new design for organizing human societies that provides the basis for a paradigm shift into a new, superior civilization. It can be adopted easily by smaller organizations, providing immediate benefits including relief from many of our current social stressors and problems. Part 1 presents the key elements of true cooperation and examines the outmoded competitive and individualistic cultural paradigms we must escape. Cooperation is the new paradigm our current, rapid-paced social evolution is pushing us toward.

Unfortunately, true cooperation is currently a stranger in America. There is nothing like it in our American culture. The cultural patterns and social behaviors we now label "cooperation" are many things but none are true cooperation. Bits and pieces of true cooperation are emerging here and there in response to the massive technology driven social transformation churning around us. I will show you some of those bits and pieces in Part Two. When it comes to mastering cooperation, Americans are starting from scratch. We are at risk of being left behind and declining as a society because our existing American social operating systems of competition and individualism are becoming increasingly incompatible with our high energy, high technology, interdependent, rapid information processing new civilization.

What is "Cooperation"?

Modern social scientists and our dictionaries offer one definition of "co-operation" as "two or more people working together for a common goal." However, there is no consensus on its meaning or on its practice. Common concepts of "cooperation" in America include compromising, getting along with others, benefiting equally, being helpful, following the rules even if you don't like them, democratic decision making, and giving mutual assistance to accomplish things we can't do alone. Working together on communal economic projects may be seen as cooperation, as well as coming together to deal with a natural or manmade crisis, (From an unpublished study by the author of popular conceptualizations of "cooperation.")

These common American views of cooperation focus on *individuals* rather than groups. "Cooperation," from this perspective, occurs when individuals choose to work together and sometimes make self-sacrifices for the common good. However, when individualistic Americans engage in a collective action such as some of those described above, it is usually not true coopera-tion, but a form of "mutual aid" (defined in Chapter 1). *True cooperation is not about individuals but is a characteristic of groups.* It is a particular way of organiz-ing and operating social systems of all kinds. The plan for cooperation must be contained in the culture. The initiative to cooperate begins with creating a cooperative "culture," with which you design and build a cooperative "or-ganization." Part 2 shows how to do this.

Time to Re-Conceptualize "Cooperation"

Scientific research on cooperation and the development of cooperative organizations in America are languishing because we have no sound con-ceptualization of "cooperation" that the scientific community can focus on and that can capture our imaginations and mobilize us to transform our society into a cooperative one.

A central and enduring quality of true cooperation is that it is group centered. It is focused on the group's operation and survival as a social sys-tem. The predominant "two or more people working together for a common goal" definition has several problems. It focuses on individual behavior— such as individuals coming together to accomplish something that each wants but can't do alone—rather than on group social organization. Just what we would expect from an individualistic culture. Further, an exami-nation of what forms this "working together" take shows that for some, virtually any collective behavior is cooperation. From this perspective most of what Americans do during the day when they are not acting alone is cooperation, such as running a business or university. But we are not a cooperative society; just the opposite.

The two most common mistakes, elaborated in Chapter 1, are equating collective actions by individualists—such as a food buyers co-operative or barn raisings in our pioneer era—and competitors—such as alliances to deal with a common enemy—with cooperation. I label them "mutual aid" to avoid confusing them with true cooperation. They fit the common definition of cooperation, but they are really just expressions of individualism or competition.

The many experiments on variations of the prisoner's dilemma game that constitute a large part of the scientific literature on "cooperation" also focus on individual behavior and decision making. At best they show how individualistic selfishness and/or competition sometimes produce conditions that press us to engage in mutual aid for our own wellbeing. They have nothing to show us about cooperation as a group property, located in the culture and social structure of social systems.

We have inherited some confusion about cooperation from our communal utopian era in the 19th century and our current efforts to form communes and intentional communities. Much can be said about this fascinating era and collection of wildly varying community-building experiments. Many of them sought escape from the "evils" of our burgeoning materialistic competitive capitalistic market economy, such as extreme economic stratifications, an excessive focus on accumulating property and manufactured goods, and the driven pursuit of achievement and "success." Some discovered true cooperation to some extent, such as the still flourishing Hutterites whom we meet in Chapter 3. Most lasted only a short time or transformed into common American farming or manufacturing communities. Many simply incorporated individualistic cultural practices such as democratic decision making, equality in status and wealth, and shared property held in common, into their cultures and called it "cooperation."

The communal ownership and use of property has come to be equated with cooperation for many Americans. From this perspective, if you want to cooperate, whether in a company or an intentional community, you must first pool your wealth, resources, and income or own the company in common. However, while doing so can eliminate many of the problems associated with our competitive market economy, it does not by itself produce true cooperation. More often it is individualistic mutual aid that emerges. The community's culture must contain the patterns for true cooperation for it to emerge, whatever the financial arrangements. Few of our communal utopias or current intentional communities were so blessed. *True cooperation does not require holding property in common.* Cooperation can work in those conditions but holding property in common is not mandatory or even desirable in many cases. The highest forms of true cooperative civilization will operate economically in more advanced ways that express what these pioneering community builders were dreaming. However, the vast majority of true cooperative organizations, especially in the early decades, will operate with a shared cooperative culture and whatever ownership patterns are current in that society.

To build truly cooperative social systems we need a fresh, discrete definition of cooperation. It must refer to only one form of group social behavior, which can be studied easily and put into practice with confidence. This more refined vision of cooperation must exclude or re-label the many noncooperative forms of behavior now under the umbrella label of "cooperation." Advancing this goal is a primary purpose of this book. You will be introduced to true cooperation, which will no longer be a stranger but a welcome friend and guide.

CREATING OUR OWN BREAK-OUT COOPERATIVE SOCIETY

American representative democracy was a break-out transformation society from the stagnated world of the aristocratic feudal era. A "break-out" society is a paradigm shift from an old society to new one. America has since undergone profound changes resulting from several evolutionary challenges: our explorations, battles over, and settling of the American continent, the innovation filled industrial revolution, and more recently the coming of the high-technology Information Age. Americans have demonstrated the ability to change and adapt to these and other challenges in our over two hundred year existence.

Our competitive capitalistic market economy and individualism-based democratic government have worked for us through these changes, if less effectively, fairly and with more commotion than we might have liked. But rapid human social and technological evolution has progressed to the point that a fresh qualitative transformation in societies is now required. It is time for a *new* break-out society. This is the way of the world: new societies being born and growing within the old, while the old passes away. We are now challenged to make a conscious self-transformation, to create our own new cooperative break-out society. Are Americans up to this, our greatest adaptive challenge of all?

The first step in major social transformations is always alienation from the old society. One major sign a civilization is declining is that it is no longer effective in solving its problems. Its repeated efforts fail because the dying culture does not have the necessary tools to deal with its current and emerging problems. The culture has been pushed beyond its capacities and many of the problems are self-induced products of the culture, such as economic inequalities in America. Many Americans have grown weary of our current society's failures and incompetence (many examined in the following chapters) and are thinking "surely there must be a better way."

The continuing evolution of human societies and our high tech, high energy lifestyle requires people and resources of countries, civilizations, even the whole planet to prosper and advance. Individualism and competition are incapable of coordinating and guiding the emerging complexity, specialization and interdependence. Only a culture of cooperation can usher in smoothly and adaptively this rapidly developing, new human era.

AMERICA AS A COOPERATIVE SOCIETY

Transforming America into a cooperative society produces the paradigm shift so many of us are eager to experience. The positive consequences for America if we become a fully cooperative society are so magnificent that it may look like a utopian fantasy compared with what we have now. The overview presented here, however, is no fantasy. It will take many generations and represents a very high level of development of true cooperation. This book will show you how to get started and why it can work so marvelously. Cooperation is comparatively easy to do. Surviving in our current conflict-burdened competitive individualistic society is what is hard.

Cooperation produces a society of plenty. Everyone will drive the "best" cars, live in the "best" houses, eat the finest pure foods, receive the best possible education and health care and so forth. Why? Because that is what a true cooperative society does, that is what it focuses on doing, day in and day out It is organized specifically to provide all with the requirements for adaptive survival. A cooperative America will take far less time and resources to provide us with the necessities of life. There will be no competing companies duplicating the same products and services. All participants have a "job" and they perform it to the best of their ability. In return, they are given everything they need. There are no poor, there is no asceticism, there is no glutting, there is no unequal distribution of wealth.

What we now call the institutions of "government" and "economy" will not be separate institutions. They will be blended into one set of social processes. Cooperative societies operate from a cultural consensus that is constantly being tested and evolving. Consequently, there are no competing interest groups. There is no need for committees, legislatures, or decision makers. Decisions are determined empirically, including trial and error testing, always with the good of the cooperative social system and its participants as references, not with a cacophony of opinions.

One huge body of correct information will be constantly tested. For example, the "best" diet will be known and practiced by all, with agriculture, food preparation, and distribution organized around correct knowledge. The time is well passed when individuals or families can take care of themselves alone, as they sometimes did during our frontier era. Now life is far too complicated. We need a whole society on our side helping us and telling us the truth. This cooperative intelligence far outstrips anything a competitive individualistic society can offer.

A cooperative society does all of this in harmony with the environment, because working with the environment is necessary for society's survival. There is more that a cooperative society will do, as the book will show you. One will begin to wonder why anyone would want to live the way Americans and other cultures do now when it can be so much better. Just remember that we are only now figuring all this out.

In the 1990s Bell Labs found that its most valued and productive electrical engineers were not those endowed with genius but those who excelled in rapport, empathy, cooperation, persuasion, and the ability to build consensus.

"20 Things You Didn't Know About Genius," Rebecca Coffey, *Discover*

October 2008, p. 88

Part 1. The Fundamentals of True Cooperation

Chapter 1. Individualism, Competition and Cooperation: The Basic Social Operating Systems

LET THE COOPERATION PARADIGM SHIFT BEGIN

We are living in fabulous times. These are times of astounding scientific discoveries that have altered our view of ourselves and the universe. These discoveries include, among many, the double-stranded helix of DNA, the nature of matter, the unity of time and space, the importance of biodiversity, and the mysterious dark (nonbaryonic) matter and energy that make up the bulk of the universe. These are also times of incredible technological innovations including electricity, rapid transportation, universal communication, and computers that are transforming how we live and what we can do. We are rushing through a window of awakening understanding and expanding capacities into a dazzling new world so different that it requires us to make massive changes in how we think, live and organize our societies. We are currently struggling to understand what is happening and to picture what is to become of us. What is happening is the greatest, most profound, transformation of human civilizations ever. We are launching into a quantum leap in human social evolution.

Unfortunately, our leap is not clean, graceful, or guaranteed of success. Inevitably, we are entangled in the cultural lag that always accompanies such civilization wide transformations and paradigm shifts. Different components of our societies transform at different rates. Our science and technology and related social patterns change first and often very fast. Our rapid adoption of cell phones, texting, twitter, and related innovations are examples. Others, such as our economy and governmental forms change at various rates but slower. And some, such as our traditional religions may change little or resist changing at all. This means that at any given moment there is a great deal of incompatibility and conflict between our social patterns that are changing at different paces and are at different locations in the process. Many of our current wars and conflicts are the reaction of old, traditional cultures lagging behind faced with threatening cultural changes, such as some religions, forms of government, and ethnic groups. Some current social patterns may turn out to work very nicely in our new world, such as our industrial era nuclear family as a functional unit within society. But at this point, it is difficult to predict which of our current social and cultural patterns will fit, adapt to, or be unable to survive in our emerging civilization. Especially since we can only see bits and pieces and swirling clouds taking shape in our future at this time.

Fortunately, the technologies spearheading our transformation are here to stay and provide the foundation for our still unfolding new civilization. These are electricity, rapid transportation, rapid and near universal communication, and computers. Electricity and other power sources are key limiting factors in our technological expansion and we are vigorously pursuing new sources. Electricity powers most of our advanced technologies. We already take for granted electricity, rapid transportation and communication, and our younger generations are comfortable with computers and related gadgetry. It is clear our new society will be characterized by these technologies; we are not going to give them up.

Despite the rapid changes and cultural lag we are experiencing, these technologies provide us with a stable platform for building new civilizations that will be around a long time. My grandparents, parents and I lived through different technological eras. We witnessed the first cars, planes, electrification of the nation, television, telephones, computers, cell phones and more. My grand children and great grand children and their children will all grow up in an electrical world with all of those same technologies, perhaps more refined and advanced. Those coming generations will all be living in the same technological world. This constitutes a new plateau in human technological evolution.

With the technology settling down, so to speak, the major needed changes shift to our cultures and the social systems we use to get things done. The really fundamental and "earth shaking" change yet to come is a paradigm shift from competition and individualism to cooperation as our basic sociocultural operating system. There are hints of the possibility of such an advanced social change already. These include the spread of modern technology throughout the world accompanied by ongoing international economic developments. Companies are operating in many countries, ownership of companies originating in one country are now frequently located elsewhere, and call centers in India and other countries handle service for America as well as other parts of the world. This is creating worldwide collaboration and interdependence (see for example, Friedman, 2006, *The World is Flat*).The hints also include the continuing and growing interest in how the Eastern Asian countries such as Japan and China operate with their more group-centered cultures (examples in Part 2, and see Reid, 2000, *Confucius Lives Next Door*, and Rehfeld, 1994, *Alchemy of a Leader*.) Increasingly the social consequences of our technological developments, such as our increasing interdependence to make it all work and the need to draw on the people and resources of the whole planet, are moving us quietly but firmly toward cooperation.

Currently, competition and individualism are America's two basic operating cultures. For our paradigm shift to cooperation to be successful, we must have a clear understanding of all three. We must be able to recognize them in our social systems. We will learn that true cooperation, for the most part, must stand alone. This means we need to learn how to weed out of our social systems individualism and competition, the sources of so many of our current problems.

BRIEF INTRODUCTION TO THE THREE BASIC SOCIOCULTURAL OPERATING SYSTEMS

Individualism, competition and cooperation are the three basic sociocultural operating systems. All human social systems large and small are built upon one or some combination of these three. This is true of families, tribes, businesses, religions, complex organizations, societies and civilizations.

The pattern of the three that characterizes a social system shapes and flavors all else that system creates. This includes their governments, economies, religions and recreations. Part One explores some of the particulars, which include democratic governments produced by our individualism and the market economy generated in our competitiveness. Individualistic societies produce religions where salvation or enlightenment is an individual project.

For a simple example closer to home, do members of a family (your family) go their own ways with little regard for each other or for the family as social system? They are individualistic. Do they compete with one another for resources, valued things, for dominance of the family, and the children for parent's attention? They are obviously competitive. Or, do they focus on making the family run well as a unit and enjoy being together and working on common projects? They are more cooperative. When one member of the family achieves something fine, do other family members ignore it?—individualism; put it down and make fun of it?—competition; or rejoice together as a family?—that's more cooperative.

Currently, Americans tend to explain such family behavior in other ways, especially personalities and "human nature," when the real explanation is their family *culture* of competition, individualism, or cooperation. After you have explained all you can by identifying which of the three basic sociocultural operating systems are being practiced in the social system being analyzed, *then* look for other answers. You will be surprised how much you can explain and predict with these three. It is also liberating to discover that many less desirable behaviors are culturally generated and can be changed by the members of a given group by consciously changing their culture, which, as this book will show you, is comparatively easy to do. Changing individual people is harder.

In turn, the other cultural elements of the social system shape and flavor the expression of a given basic operating system. For example what do competitors battle over in a given society: money and material wealth, popularity, aristocratic rank, the largest pile of yams (e.g. the Trobriand Islanders of Malinoski, 1961), piety, the finest or most statues (e.g. Easter Island, Diamond, 1997) or the most glorious tomb?

Knowing which basic operating systems are involved makes it easier to see what must change and what must be left behind in order to produce a successful paradigm shift to a better world. For example, you can't escape problems generated by competition, such as economic inequalities, if you don't understand the connection between competition and economic stratification. You might simplistically blame private ownership of property for unequal distributions of wealth. If so, rather than leaving competition behind as you should, you are likely to end up taking competition with you into the "new world" you construct, perhaps communal or socialistic. There, competition eventually produces economic stratification all over again and you have gained nothing (more details on the inherent problems of competition in Chapter 8).

Competition and individualism are not "the way things are"—fixed and final—for humans, they are products of our culture. Unfortunately, they are "The System" in America currently, but that's because we permit them to be. It is too easy to simply accept competition and individualism as the "natural" background of our lives and not challenge them as we should. All three of the basic sociocultural operating systems are cultural patterns. All cultural patterns for humans are human made. We can change them anytime we all agree to. This is one of the main points of this book and I will show you in depth what we are changing and why, and what we are changing to and how.

The foundation of our transformation to a cooperative society must rest upon a sound, fresh, more advanced scientific theoretical conceptualization of "cooperation." The rest of this chapter presents the results of many years of study, research and discussion with colleagues in search of this conceptualization. This more academic presentation may seem dry and even a bit tedious to read for some. Typically, the scientific style of presentation seeks to unambiguously and clearly present new ideas and findings. Here are the insights and definitions to guide our future efforts to build a cooperative civilization. They are the heart of the book and fully understanding them and how they can be applied is what this book is about.

MARGARET MEAD AND COOPERATION AND COMPETITION AMONG PRIMITIVE PEOPLES

The anthropologist Margaret Mead was one of the first to show us how individualism, competition, and cooperation occur together and contrast with each other in various societies. In the mid-1930's, Mead received a request from a committee of the Social Science Research Council. She was asked to survey the research on primitive societies for material that could be used as background for designing research on cooperation and competition in America. The conceptualizations developed by Mead and her students at Columbia University, originally published in 1937 in her book *Cooperation and Competition Among Primitive Peoples*, have been widely cited among Americans working on cooperation.

The committee gave Mead the following definitions of cooperation and competition to work with (Mead, 1976. p.8.):

"Cooperation: the act of working together to one end."

"Competition: the act of seeking or endeavoring to gain what another is endeavoring to gain at the same time."

Fortunately, Mead and her six graduate and post-graduate students quickly went beyond these overly general and inadequate definitions.

One of the first discoveries Mead and her students made was that cooperation and competition by themselves did not satisfactorily cover the practices observed in primitive cultures. A third category, "individualism," had to be added. Individualism was defined as "behavior in which the individual strives toward his goal without reference to others" (Mead, 1976, pp.16, 17). Mead also defined "true competition" as both "outdistancing all others and preventing the others from attaining the goal." This recognizes the adversarial component of competition. The selected primitive tribes studied were graphically arranged around a triangle of individualism, competition and cooperation to illustrate the degree each was mostly one or some combination (Mead, 1976, p. 461).

I adopt Mead's definition of individualism. I modify her definition of true competition somewhat but retain its essential tone. I reject the definition of cooperation given to her as much too broad, containing many things that are not cooperation. The most important ones I will show you. The new definition of true cooperation I will present draws on the considerable research in many disciplines on cooperation and related topics since Mead's time that shows the need for a fresh perspective with the focus on coopera- tion as a sociocultural pattern in social systems, rather than as a pattern that emerges among interacting individuals. Cooperation, as I'm defining it, is a characteristic of groups. Mead, perceptively, provided a foundation for this perspective.

True Cooperation is Culture Based

At the end of the study, Mead concluded individualistic, competitive, or cooperative behavior by individual members of a society is

> fundamentally conditioned by the total social emphasis of that so-
> ciety, that the goals for which individuals will work are culturally
> determined and are not the response of the organism to an external,
> culturally undefined situation, like a simple scarcity of food (Mead,
> 1976, p.16).

For members of a given society, being cooperative, competitive or indi- vidualistic is the result of the culture they live in, and is a habit, a taken for granted daily activity, learned from parents and other members of the so- ciety. This was certainly how Alexis de Tocqueville, the perceptive French observer of our American experiment a hundred years earlier in the 1830's and1840's saw individualism in America (see Chapter 6).

This insight reveals to us one of the most important criteria for recog- nizing true cooperation: individualism, competition, and cooperation are fundamental sociocultural patterns, part of the basic fabric of the society. They express major dimensions of the "social emphasis"—the culture—of a given society or organization. They shape differently how participants view the world and life and which goals and purposes they set their lives to pursue. The social systems individualism, competition and cooperation construct and the rules of the social "game" they will play are also different. For example, individualism encourages democratic organizations, competi- tion prefers control or dominance hierarchies, and true cooperation teaches operating all together as a highly coordinated problem solving organization.

Mead also provided the key to identifying and classifying two of the biggest categories of behavior erroneously labeled "cooperation." We now know that cooperation is a cultural pattern unto itself, it is not some collec- tive action of individuals.

DISTINGUISHING BETWEEN INDIVIDUALISTIC MUTUAL AID, COMPETITIVE MUTUAL AID AND COOPERATION

One of Mead's most important insights, one she unfortunately did not develop, distinguished between collective action and individual action within the sociocultural patterns of individualism, competition, and cooperation. Let's explore this distinction carefully. People can be individualistic, competitive or cooperative while acting either collectively or individually. That is, a person can act alone to produce a result that is cooperative, or people can work together collectively to obtain a result that is individualistic. Mead's (1976) example of a person cooperating while working alone: "So a man who hunts alone in the bush in order to contribute his kill to a communal feast is engaged in an individual activity inasmuch as he is working alone, but he is nevertheless engaged in a cooperative enterprise" (p.16). When individualists join together to operate a club, such as a ski club, that provides them each with cheaper products and services, such as ski lift tickets and trips, they are pursuing collectively an individual goal each wants for themselves.

Mead emphasized that not all individual actions are individualistic, or competitive, and not all collective actions—two or more people working together toward a common goal—are cooperation, in contrast to the definition of cooperation the committee gave her to work with. Mistaking collective action in general for cooperation is a common mistake in America. We think of that phrase, "two or more people working together for a common purpose…," and assume any time people do anything together they are cooperating. Mead says no; sometimes our working together is competitive or individualistic in purpose and form. We can now distinguish between individual and collective action in individualistic societies or organizations, between individual and collective action in competitive societies or organizations, and between individual and collective action in cooperative societies and organizations.

This distinction clears up a good deal of the fog concerning what is cooperation and what is not. Failing to distinguish collective actions engaged in by individualistic and competitive societies from cooperation is a major source of our misunderstandings about cooperation. *Individualistic collective actions and competitive collective actions are NOT forms of cooperation.* Cooperation is a different sociocultural operating system entirely. These collective actions do fit the "working together toward a common goal" definition of cooperation, and this demonstrates why that definition is so inadequate. It is a nearly universal practice in America to mislabel individual and competitive collective actions as cooperation. This practice is one of the reasons true cooperation has not developed appreciably in America. We assume we are cooperating when we are doing nothing of the kind; we are only engaging in individualistic or competitive collective actions. I have labeled individualistic collective actions "individualistic mutual aid" and competitive collective actions "competitive mutual aid."

Individualistic Mutual Aid

As Tocqueville so astutely observed (see Chapter 6), in individualistic societies, such as our own, individualists soon discover that there are a great many things they personally desire they can only get by working with others who also want it for themselves. These individualists then strive together to obtain this goal, which each will then use or consume by themselves. This produced the huge variety of voluntary associations Tocqueville marveled at in our new-born country; he would be astounded by how many there are now, over two million by one count (American Society of Association Executives, Private communication Colin Murcray, 2009). This is individualistic mutual aid. Even though these efforts may sometimes be very well coordinated and organized, and even produce permanent organizations (e.g. AARP—formerly the American Association of Retired Persons), they are not cooperative because the goal is individualistic. That is not to demean individualistic mutual aid, which is an extremely valuable tool for individualists. America could not be what it is or function without it. But cooperation is a totally different kind of social creature with very different goals.

Competitive Mutual Aid

Competitive mutual aid attempts to moderate the mutual damage all-out competition produces through agreements to curtail competition in certain areas. It provides protection from larger, more powerful competitors threatening them all. Competitors form cartels to control a market for their mutual benefit beyond what they could achieve alone. Competitive mutual aid is used to establish rules for competition, as in sports, and to form associations to pursue their common interests. Political lobby and public relations groups are examples. Gangs are generally competitive mutual aid associations with some individualistic mutual aid tossed in. These are all another form of American voluntary associations. Some have labeled this "coopetition," especially the agreement within competitive sports on the rules of the game and their enforcement (e.g. de Waal, 1996, p. 29), suggesting it is a form of cooperation. No, none of this is cooperation; it is competitive mutual aid in pursuit of competitive goals. It is very different from cooperation with very different goals and consequences.

This refined conceptualization recognizes that people living in individualistic and competitive societies do work together; they just don't cooperate. Sorting collective behavior into individualistic mutual aid, competitive mutual aid, and cooperation greatly clarifies the picture of what is and isn't true cooperation.

Individualism, Competition and Cooperation are Identified by Their Goals

Keeping in mind individualistic and competitive mutual aid, we can now more accurately describe how the *goal* of the activity can be used as the means of determining individualism, competition, and cooperation from each other. Mead and her students emphasized that whether an activity is cooperation, competition, individualism, or something else, such as helpfulness, is primarily determined by the reason people are engaging in the activity, by the nature of the goal participants are working toward. The goal or purpose has emerged as a primary means of sorting social actions into individualism, competition, cooperation, and actions that are something else.

In **individualism,** the goal of both individual and collective behavior is the benefit of the acting individuals themselves. Individualism is self centered. Individualists act, as Mead noted, without regard for the needs or welfare of others around them. When individuals can't get something each wants alone, they will join with others—individualistic mutual aid—so that all can get what each wants personally. Barn raising among our pioneers and early farming families provides a good example of how the goal determines whether the activity is individualistic or something else. The actual coordination of the barn building can be quite cooperative among people who have done this together several times, with the skills of the various workers well known and the division of labor established. Just watching, you might be tempted to say this is a cooperative activity. But because the goal is to build a barn for the use of one farmer and his family as they please, which is individualistic, and then build other barns for other families in turn, it is individualistic mutual aid. A typical goal for individualistic Americans is to make the best "deal" they can for themselves and, perhaps, for their families within our system while the rest of society fends for itself. Another is to make something of oneself and achieve something worthwhile. This does not require the defeat of someone else to be successful as competition does.

In **competition**, the goal is to win, to outperform all others and obtain the desired something of value that only one or a few can obtain while preventing all others from obtaining it, defeating them, and/or to dominate and control others. The second part of this goal, the dominance and control of others, is not often mentioned in definitions of competition, but it is frequently the primary goal of a particular competition. We see it in social animals with the battles between males for dominance of the herd and control of the harem, and in humans in dominance hierarchies such as aristocracies and being the "boss" at the top of a pyramidal organizational hierarchy, pinnacles reached through competition. While these goals can be subsumed in the basic definition of competition, I choose to highlight them because of their importance in understanding the shape of our competitive social systems and societies.

Competition is built around adversarial relationships, and imposes adversarial side-taking, contesting, and conflict on the social arena in which it is enacted. Competition produces losers and focuses excessively on winners. This struggle to win can be done alone, as a single competitor, or in groups like competitive teams and companies. Competitors create ranking systems for just about everything, rating competitors from best to worst. Success is judged by comparison of performances between individuals or groups. Competitors may form an alliance—competitive mutual aid—as noted above, to deal with a common problem, the potential damage to themselves of all-out competition, or a large competitor threatening them all. A typical goal of competitive Americans is to reach the pinnacle of a competitive stratification, to be the "best" at something, such as being the smartest in school, the most popular or prominent, the top athlete, the most beautiful, or to be the best in some professional endeavor, such as medicine or law, to go to the top universities and work for the best companies, or to be the richest business person.

Competition and individualism together produce the self-serving "interest groups" and the incessant "politics," so familiar to Americans, which are mostly disruptive, distorting or irrelevant to our society's adaptive efforts and wellbeing. Neither individualism nor competition is capable of thoroughly, effectively and reliably pursuing the adaptive common good of any social system. This is a prime source of the chronic discontent with our American government and society. It doesn't solve our problems or meet our needs.

In **cooperation** the goal is the adaptive survival of the social system. This is a group goal; a goal for the group as a social system. The participants are group centered, rather than self centered. The goal focuses participants' attention continually on the good of the whole and constitutes a common vision that also guides their decisions and choices. Participants work to make the group effective and to preserve its culture and the social roles and processes that constitute the social structure while making changes and evolving as required. Much of their attention is on the culture's contents and the daily social processes that constitute the substance of the social system, keeping them effective, accurate and improving. The cooperative social system is the participants' adaptive tool and they use it to provide themselves with their needs. Cooperation is the only one of the three operating systems that makes the social system itself the focus of activities and goals. Cooperation requires a very different world-view and approach to life than our competitive individualism does.

Since true cooperation is so rare in America, it is difficult to give an example that everyone recognizes, so let's take a hypothetical cooperative family. The family's goal is to preserve and advance their family, which exists to provide them with their survival and developmental needs. This means they all have roles to play and tasks to perform, sometimes projects together, to maintain their family. This means preserving the family as a culture and set of social roles and processes and enacting that culture and social structure. In the process the family provides the food, shelter, clothing, health care, education, talent development and other requirements of the participants and the family as an acting unit in society. It also means paying attention to relationships and social-psychological needs so that people are content, happily engaged in family activities, and do not abandon the family. A cooperative family organization is their choice for their adaptive tool, rather than going it alone or competing with each other for resources. The members identify with their family and enjoy the family dynamics and rewards they produce. Their goal is to use and preserve this dynamic social \system, which is their creation and home; sort of like their social "space ship" through a dangerous life.

True cooperation is not something that can be arbitrarily "painted," so to speak, on the surface of a competitive or individualistic system. "Teamwork," for example, between employees of competitive individualistic companies is not likely to be cooperative in the sense I am using the term. The "teamwork" is probably imposed upon the workers for competitive profit motive reasons such as higher productivity, lower worker turnover, fewer errors, and fewer jobs needing redoing. Such "teamwork" has more in common with the competitive athletic teams they are mostly modeled after and evoke, than with true cooperative workgroups. However, as we will see in Chapter 16, there are some workgroups organized around participative group management practices that do approach cooperative patterns.

In the 70 plus years since Mead published her work on cooperation, competition and individualism, our knowledge of these cultural patterns has advanced. We understand the cultural forms individualism, for example, takes in modern American society (Bellah et al., 1985;, see Chapter 7.). We have a better grasp of the consequences of competition for our society as well (see Chapter 8). While most of what Mead suggested is still relevant and appropriate, there is a problem with the over-broad and anemic view of cooperation prevalent in Mead's time that is still predominant in our own. The more robust model of true cooperation presented in this book corrects that condition and gives us a vibrant form of cooperation capable of great things including engaging us far more effectively in our own social evolution.

DEFINING THE CONCEPTS USED IN THIS BOOK

I will follow the customary practice of providing a clean one-line definition of the five basic concepts I'm using in this book. Each definition catches the essence of these concepts, which makes it easier to understand them and keep track of them when analysis gets complicated. However, each represents a distinctive and complex set of cultural patterns and social practices that are the subject of this book. These definitions follow Mead's insight that the goal and the way it is pursued are the prime defining quality of each.

Individualism: Pursuing personal goals without regard for others.

Individualistic Mutual Aid: The collective action of individualists pursuing a personal goal each wants for one's self but cannot obtain alone.

Competition: Pursuing a goal at the same time as others that only one (or a few) may obtain while working to prevent others from obtaining it.

Competitive Mutual Aid: The collective action or alliance between competitors to obtain a goal they cannot obtain alone.

Cooperation: Pursuing the group goal of adaptive success for the group as a social system.

Now we are ready to introduce the key elements of true cooperation. These elements are examined in more detail throughout this book.

INTRODUCTION TO THE KEY ELEMENTS OF TRUE COOPERATION

This list of key properties of true cooperation defines cooperation and provides a reference for keeping track of the necessary elements as we explore and develop our understanding of true cooperation and apply it.

COOPERATION IS A CULTURAL PATTERN

The patterns for cooperation are contained in the culture. They are part of the daily routine of that cultural community. The social systems are operated cooperatively. When creating cooperative social systems, we first create a cooperative culture, and then build our cooperative social system and train participants using those cultural blueprints. Mutual-aid between individuals as a result of some need or constraint is not true cooperation. True cooperation does not emerge from the competitive individualistic actions of individuals, though mutual aid often does. True cooperation is a characteristic of groups, not individuals.

CULTURE IS USED AS AN ADAPTIVE TOOL

Participants must understand that culture is humans' primary adaptive tool and understand what culture is and how to apply it, maintain it, and change it. Cooperative groups must be able to create a dynamic shared culture that is continually being tested, checked, and modified to keep it accurate and incorporating changes in the environment and adaptations to those changes. The cooperative culture is never fixed or final but ever evolving. Thus the culture becomes a living repository of everything the community collectively knows, their collective intelligence. They can each tap into it whenever they want. Using culture, which does not require genetic selection to change, makes it possible for human societies to adapt very quickly to changes in the environment.

CONSENSUS

There must be a consensus before cooperation can occur. Everyone in the would-be cooperative community or organization must agree that cooperation is going to be their basic social operating system and on how to do it. The cultural consensus is dynamic, meaning the contents are constantly changing and evolving as the cooperative community adapts. Participants must be constantly "tuned in" to each other and their community in order for the consensus to be coherent and current. Our communications technology greatly facilitates this. This consensus on a living culture produces a powerful state of oneness, of shared understanding of the world and its processes, of all being part of something bigger and more meaningful than individuals by themselves. Cooperation cannot occur in an atmosphere of disagreement, contention or confusion. Recruits must "buy in" to the cooperative culture and the consensus. The cooperative community thinks alertly and understands as one so they are able to act in an effective, unified manner.

RAPID ADAPTATION TO THE ENVIRONMENT AS A SOCIAL SYSTEM IS THE FUNDAMENTAL COMMON GROUP GOAL

This is the most critical piece in producing the powerful form of cooperation we need to make our paradigm shift. We can build whole societies upon it. It is not an individual goal; it is a goal for the social system. A fundamental fact of life on earth is that survival requires adaptation to changes and conditions in the environment. Culture, and the social systems that culture shapes, are humans' primary adaptive tools. They are unique to humans and an extremely powerful and effective evolutionary gift. Cooperation is pursuing together the group goal of adaptive success for the group as a social system. For America, it would be every one of us working together using the culture of cooperation to operate our society as an "organic" whole, with its complex division of labor, to adapt to the environment in order for society to survive as a social system, which in cooperation includes providing all of the survival needs of all of the participants as well. In this scenario, if America disintegrates, we all suffer. We lose our big, powerful, adaptive social system. It is in our personal best interest for America to proper as a *social system*. Pursuing this group goal transforms the society, or any other social system, into an environmental tracking device that is constantly adjusting its social processes, its social structures, to match changes and conditions in the environment and incorporate improvements. Pursuing this fundamental goal produces a division of labor and subsidiary goals for required tasks that provide the fundamental shape of the cooperative social system.

Specific Common Group Goals

In addition to the divisions of labor and tasks inherent in all cooperative groups, the purpose for which particular cooperative social systems are organized provides specific common group goals that further shape the division of labor and identifies the tasks to be pursued.

Group Centeredness

The group, the social system, the society is the unit of action in cooperation, not the individual. Individual members are group centered, focused on their role and membership in the whole. The good of the group comes first, rather than that of the individual as in individualism. Goals members pursue shift from personal, self-centered goals, to goals that benefit the group and its survival. For a simple example, do you pursue your own career whether or not it benefits the company or takes you hopping from company to company, or do you stick with the company, maybe even taking pay cuts at times, to help it survive? The focus of attention of the daily lives of group-centered participants in cooperation is on the contents of their culture, their collective intelligence, and keeping it accurate, and on the social processes that are the substance of the social systems, performing them competently and continually refining and improving them. Members identify themselves with their cooperative community and are devoted to it. This contributes to the oneness of living cooperatively and the group's adaptive effectiveness.

COMPETENCE

The most competent people available are assigned tasks and roles within the cooperative social system. In cooperative societies education and training seek to develop participants' talents and provide them with a variety of skills and bodies of knowledge. Whoever is the best qualified to do a task is assigned it at that time. There is a competence threshold required of all participants that must be crossed before true cooperation can take off. As the levels of competence increase and refine, including in divisions of labor and specialties, the benefits to the social system of cooperation increase.

A POSITIVE COOPERATIVE SOCIAL CONSEQUENCE NETWORK

All of the cooperative group participants together use agreed upon rewards and punishments to shape and maintain the cooperative social system and the culture according to the group consensus. They thereby create a behavioral consequence network that sustains the daily performances of the cooperative social system. The continual flow of rewards for performance and corrections where needed provide guidance and motivation. The emphasis is on rewards, positive responses. This creates a highly rewarding experience for cooperative people, with their good qualities and performances continually and reliably rewarded. Approval is the primary reward. Other rewards of value in that culture are also used. This contributes to high self-esteem, quality performances, and contentment with the cooperative group. People are appreciated for who they are and what they do. This is in contrast to individualists generally ignoring and competitor's negative—punishing—responses to other's good performances. Constant attention is paid to the pattern of rewards and punishments applied and its consequences for the shape and functioning of the social system, the dynamic culture and the participant's well being. These rewards and punishments are not used to advance individuals' personal goals by manipulating others, as in competitive individualism, but to advance group goals. It is this consequence network that drives, shapes and energizes the daily activities of cooperative social systems. (See Chapter 13.)

SOCIAL STATUS AND MATERIAL WEALTH RANKINGS ARE MINIMAL

The social status and material wealth rankings of great value to competitors especially, and individualists pursuing self-aggrandizement, are irrelevant, even bizarre, from the point of view of true cooperative societies. The accumulation of large amounts of personal wealth, especially as markers of social status, is neither meaningful nor necessary in true cooperation. That's not what the cooperative life game is about. The material and social status differences between cooperative social system participants will be minimal, in part because all are working competently and receiving comparable rewards, in part because such stratification has comparatively little value in group-centered cooperative systems. Such differences in status as occur are the result of rewards for highly competent and outstanding performances in the service of the community only. Property is valued and used differently in cooperative compared with competitive and individualistic societies. In cooperative social systems that are communal or approaching it, material goods are seen as tools to be used for the good of the community, not private property. Shared property, however, is not required for social systems to cooperate. The primary motivation in cooperative social systems and societies does not come from the pursuit of personal gain but from the social support, approval and acceptance of the other participants and the survival benefits provided by social system.

COORDINATION HIERARCHIES REPLACE DOMINANCE HIERARCHIES

There are few levels of hierarchy, with the focus on "where the action is." The dominance hierarchies of competition are dysfunctional and maladaptive in cooperative societies and social systems (see Chapters 5 and 16). Multilayered hierarchies of control with a dominant person at the top do not occur in cooperation. The fluid cooperative social dynamic could not be more different from the "by the book" and "through the channels" exercise of control, limitation of decision making to a few at the top, and the superior-subordinate relations of competitive dominance hierarchies. Hierarchy in cooperation will be one, two, perhaps three layers that serve to coordinate activities. The most competent people in cooperation are generally "on the line"—where the actions and reactions between the social system and the environment occur, often rapidly—and are the ones best able to judge the situation and make decisions concerning the most adaptive action. There is no need for levels of control or decision making above them, the dynamic consensus and positive consequence network provide guidance and "control." It is competent people working cooperatively to keep society functioning smoothly, often making changes "on the run," so to speak, as needed to minimize adaptive delays.

Cooperation is Ethical and Moral

Cooperative communities are by their nature moral and ethical. What we usually consider moral and ethical behavior results from group centered concerns. We don't hurt others because they are at one with us in our community; hurting them hurts our community and there by hurts us. Cooperative people understand that they are interdependent, all needing the skills and performances of all others for the social system to function effectively. Cooperative people share a common community, a consensus, and shared goals that foster good fellowship. Cooperative social systems will practice the golden rule, be honest, civil, and trustworthy routinely. Those raised in cooperative communities internalize the cooperative norms and values and feel guilt when they break them; they are self-controlling. Cooperative social systems and communities require far less "law enforcement" than do competitive individualistic communities. Treatment of deviants and law breakers in cooperative communities tends to focus on retraining, restitution and reincorporating the party back into the community. Punishment—retaliation—for wrong doing is not the paramount concern. At the same time, cooperative social systems and communities do not tolerate such unethical behavior as free-riding, cheating, theft, assault, fraud and the like. They may well expel from the group offenders who seriously disrupt the cooperative effort.

Cooperative Social Systems Benefit All of the Participants

Cooperative social systems are created by their participants to provide themselves with the considerable benefits offered. While the focus is on operating the cooperative social system as an adaptive tool, one of the major consequences is the reliable and abundant fulfillment of individual participant's survival needs. It is like an organism which is much more effective in adapting than each individual cell would be on its own. While cooperative companies and smaller organizations are limited in how many of their participants' survival needs they can meet, especially in the early phases of a society's adoption of cooperation, mature cooperative societies and civilizations are organized to fulfill those needs. In fully cooperative civilizations and societies, all cooperative participants receive all of their survival needs including food, health care, housing, education, transportation, recreation, and so forth routinely and directly as a reward for their participation. Cooperative groups are secure and well cared for and able to adapt their behavior quickly and appropriately. It is the best plan for the long term survival of the human species.

To apply the more general and theoretical perspective of true cooperation presented in this chapter to the concrete world, the next two chapters examine two social groups that illustrate how true cooperation works. Neither completely practice true cooperation, but are close enough to show us how it could be done. One is a work group of scientists, technicians and engineers and the other is a society of self-supporting communal colonies.

Wallace Stegner, a famous author and advocate for conservation in the American West in his book, *The Sound of Mountain Water* (New York: Doubleday, 1969, pp. 37-38) said:

> Angry as one may be at what heedless men have done and still do to a noble habitat, one cannot be pessimistic about the West. This is the native home of hope. When it fully learns that cooperation, not rugged individualism, is the quality that most characterizes and preserves it, then it will have achieved itself and outlived its origins. Then it has a chance to create a society to match its scenery.

This sentiment applies to all of America.

Chapter 2. Cooperatively Creating the Most Secret Weapon

Since our culture lacks a clear definition of cooperation as a property of social systems, people sometimes stumble on to it or parts of it without realizing what they have done. The group of scientists and technicians in the following example are a case in point. They did, in fact, create a rapidly adapting information processing cooperative research and development organization. It wasn't pure, but it was amazingly close and it illustrates how productive these cooperative social systems can be.

The Organization of OSRD

Efforts to cooperate in America are frequently triggered by crises that jolt us out of our competitive individualistic pursuits for a time and press us to cooperate, or at least engage in mutual aid. Seventy years ago, the terrors of being thrown into a world war with foes who were skilled at inventing and developing cunning new weaponry of ever increasing destructive power was as scary a crisis as can be imagined, and Americans responded.

Before America entered the Second World War, a group of concerned scientists saw that the United States was woefully unprepared technologically to fight the modern form of warfare that Germany and its allies were waging. We would have been fighting with the weapons of World War I. So they met informally to discuss ways science could contribute toward preparing America to succeed if and when we entered the war. They were especially concerned with the rapid development of new weaponry. These informal gatherings grew into the National Defense Research Council (NDRC) and then evolved into the Office of Scientific Research and Development (OSRD). Both were under the direction of Vannevar Bush, a former vice president of MIT, and had the responsibility to develop new weapons. NDRC-OSRD sponsored projects created or contributed to many of the war's major new weapons, including radar, the bazooka, guided bombs, many kinds of rockets, guidance systems, and war related medical research and drugs (Westrum, 1999, p. 17; Westrum, private communication 2002; Baldwin, 1980, pp. 49-56).

Vannevar Bush recalled, "There were those who protested that the action of setting up N.D.R.C. was an end run, a grab by which a small company of scientists and engineers acting outside of established channels got hold of the authority and money for the program of developing new weapons. That, in fact, is exactly what it was" (Westrum, 1999, p. 16). In this manner they were able to separate themselves from the intrusiveness of "established channels" and military and other competitive individualistic bureaucracies. They felt a need to separate their cooperative organization from the rest of American society in order for it to flourish. This type of separation turns up repeatedly in our history among groups attempting cooperation.

"The most important invention of the war was OSRD itself," according to Ron Westrum, a sociologist of technology. He noted that OSRD was not only successful in developing and contributing to crucial new weapons, but also in contributing a "style of operation and habits of thought" that some of its work groups practiced and passed on (Westrum, 1999, p. 17).

Creating the Deadly Fuse

The particular OSRD task group we're examining is Section T, directed by Merle A. Tuve. Section T had responsibility for the development of fuses for antiaircraft shells, artillery shells, rockets, and bombs. Most of the work was done at Johns Hopkins University's Applied Physics Laboratory at Silver Springs, Maryland. Starting with only four people, the laboratory expanded to more than 700 in 1944 (Baldwin, 1980, p. 104). Ralph B. Baldwin's (1980) book, *The Deadly Fuze (sic): The Secret Weapon of World War II*, provides us with a firsthand account of this effort.

The military had placed development of this new fuse among its top priorities for new weapons development. The statistics for naval antiaircraft guns, for example, were pathetic. According to one count, only one plane was shot down per 2,500 shells fired. American ships were vulnerable to attacks from land and carrier-based enemy planes, and thus were limited in where they could go and what they could do. Gunners could attempt to track and anticipate the path of an enemy bomber plane, which was difficult enough, but then the shell had to explode when it was close to the plane, not below or above it. Hitting these planes dead on with contact fuses was extremely difficult. Time fuses were a poor improvement, being mostly guesswork.

After considering a number of alternatives, Section T scientists and engineers selected the proximity radio fuse as the most promising option to develop. The fuse, set in the nose of the antiaircraft shell, sent out a radio beam, similar to radar. When this beam reflected from another object—the target plane—back to the radio's receiver, it triggered the fuse that set off the explosives in the shell, thus spreading thousands of steel shards in a particular configuration.

Section T had to solve a number of technical difficulties to develop the fuse. These included creating vacuum tubes (transistors had not yet been invented) small enough to fit into the nose of the shell. The vacuum tubes also had to be tough enough not to break from the shock of being shot from cannon or by the terrific centrifugal forces of the shell spinning many times a second. Developing an adequate battery was also a problem. Nevertheless, against high odds, the fuse was successfully developed, manufactured in large quantities, and distributed to our armed forces and those of our allies.

The fuse played a very important role in the defeat of the Germans and Japanese in World War II. These successes include the Battle of the Bulge in Europe when our forces used radio proximity fuses in artillery, and in protecting American warships from Japanese bombers and kamikaze planes in the Pacific. In the latter theater, the shell was so successful that American warships could pursue land-based Japanese planes to their bases on shore. Antiaircraft guns using shells with the fuse emplaced to protect Antwerp's important harbor from Germany's "buzz bomb"—jet-powered unmanned flying bombs destroyed an astounding 92 percent of the flying bombs encountered, preserving the harbor. General George Patton expressed his enthusiasm for the proximity radio fused artillery shells in a letter to OSRD. He wrote, "the new shell with the funny fuze [sic] is devastating.... I think that when all armies get this shell we will have to devise some new method of warfare. I am glad that you thought of it first. It is really a wonderful achievement" (Baldwin, 1980, p. xxxi).

The development of the fuse was shrouded in heavy security, which was never breached by spies or enemies who recovered parts of unexploded shells. A self-destruct mechanism destroyed fuses on shells that were not triggered by proximity to a target. The enemy's few efforts to investigate rumors about the shells failed. This fuse was one of the most important and best-kept secrets of the war. Even now, few people appreciate its significant role in the allied victory in World War II.

The cooperation within Section T demonstrates that true cooperation is possible in our country. This style of operation sometimes carried over into other organizations and work groups by Section T's participants after OSRD was disbanded (Westrum, 1999). It is unfortunate that in studying this group we are limited to records of brief descriptions, observations, and anecdotes by the participants. Nevertheless, these brief glimpses reveal social patterns that could not have come from anything but cooperation at the group level. These participants were not aware that they were practicing cooperation, but they knew they were doing something special.

THE SOCIAL DYNAMICS OF SECTION T

Dr. Merle A. Tuve, the head of Section T and wartime director of the Applied Physics Laboratory of Johns Hopkins University, offers an intriguing social interpretation of why they were so successful. In a foreword to Baldwin's book, Tuve attributes their success and, indeed, America's victory in the war to what he calls the "efficiency of the democratic principle" in "directing the efforts of organized groups of people" (Baldwin, 1980, p. xiii). Tuve calls this "democratic principle" the "collaborative principle" of organizing group effort and the "democratic or collaborative sharing of control" and defines it this way: "Tell the group what the needs are, make the goals conspicuously clear, and invite them as individuals to contribute in the best way they can" (Baldwin, 1980, pp. xiii, xv). He continues:

> A boss using the democratic principle does not depend on just giving orders from above. He asks his men, his workers, *to participate* in the efforts toward goals he sets. This means that they help him with the whole job; they don't just do what someone else tells them to do. This system of asking people to help with the whole job was what I used in running the proximity fuze development. We were each of us accepted as persons, not just workers. We were interacting flexibly, but each one had a clear role to play at any one time. Nobody

stayed fixed in his or her assignment, and when troubles arose we encouraged each other and proposed a dozen possible solutions. It worked so well, the whole team took hold so vigorously, that during most of the work I had to struggle hard to keep abreast of them (Baldwin, 1980, p. xiv; emphasis Tuve's).

Tuve described the social patterns that emerged: "The web of human ties and shared experiences was so intense that it was difficult to analyze what was really happening at the time" (Baldwin, 1980, p. xvi). Tuve believes that free-flowing criticism and suggestions between bosses/leaders and participants, as well as among participants, are a key to efficiency and productiveness.

Baldwin felt the concept of "team" dominated Section T. "Hierarchy was fluid, and so were assignments. What needed to be done at the time was paramount, and any unoccupied person who could do the job was given it" (1980, p. 82). Even if the task was not directly related to the person's academic training or status, he would work on it.

Baldwin notes that making Johns Hopkins University the contractor for Section T's housing and work was important. It turned out to be a crucial step in allowing cooperation to emerge.

> Making Johns Hopkins the contractor created conditions of freedom and stimulation that made for highest creative achievements. There was no waiting for weeks for committee meetings or decisions, no longer any hindrance to uninterrupted progress from idea stage to production and use. Tuve had practically complete freedom to run his job. Even within the laboratory, *the minimum of organization and hierarchy was permitted. The fluidity of personnel was characteristic of the situation. Each man did the job for which he was best fitted. One day he would be directing his associates. The next day he would be one of the associates under the direction of the man he was directing yesterday. This was true in all stages of development and production, with the organization itself changing as needed.* A man in charge of a project might find himself replaced by a notice on the bulletin board setting up a new organization, signed by a characteristic "This is it!—M.A. Tuve" (Baldwin, 1980, pp. 104-105; emphasis mine).

The laboratory social patterns are typical of cooperation. Cooperation in many cases is the coordination between competent people with no supervision or hierarchy. In other cases, the most competent coordinate and guide the cooperative effort. It the case of the fuse development, the range of competencies required was broad and also highly specialized. Consequently, as the work progressed or problems emerged, those trained and competent in the current area of concern directed and coordinated their coworkers' activities. As new tasks emerged, the leadership rotated to the scientist or engineer who had the needed expertise. The leadership was fluid depending on changing adaptive requirements and not derived from fixed roles as in typical bureaucratic hierarchies.

One scientist, Dr. Wilbur Goss, described how Tuve dealt with the cooperative process of constantly replacing leaders and other employees with those more competent to do what was required:

> When he first put me in charge of the Mark 45 fuze developments....
> He warned me that he wouldn't expect me to last out the job—that
> I would be replaced whenever anyone else could do the job better.
> But then he reminded me that this was war, and that in a war there
> were casualties of war. And if I were to be replaced he wanted me to
> regard myself as a casualty of war and be proud that I had given it my
> best effort (Baldwin, 1980 p. 105).

In true cooperation, the most competent people available are always given the job, just as Tuve was doing. However, handling those who are replaced is done gently and with support. If the cooperative enterprise can provide meaningful new assignments, the person is reassigned. If not, the good of the larger community must come first, as Tuve clearly understood. In this case, success in producing the fuse was critical for our survival as a country. In communal cooperative communities, such as the Hutterites, whom we meet in the next chapter, the replaced person remains a member of the community in full fellowship, receiving other duties or retiring. In all cases, the replaced people can take comfort and pride in the success of the group from which they also benefit.

Of the overall fuse project Baldwin said, "It was a team project with leadership in Section T but with cooperation and help from scientists and engineers in other universities, industrial laboratories, and manufacturing plants. Overall was the enthusiastic stimulus from, and cooperation of, the military authorities under the protective umbrella of military secrecy" (Baldwin, 1980, p. 59-60).

ELEMENTS OF COOPERATION IN SECTION T

Now let's take a look at the elements of cooperation in these descriptions. The fundamental common group goal of all cooperative social systems is the creation of a rapidly adapting information processing social system. This includes continual effort to maximize the match between the group structure and the current and changing environmental conditions. It also includes fulfilling its specific tasks and the common group goals it was organized to pursue. Section T accomplished all of this surprisingly successfully, but it was accomplished without the participants having a clear idea that they were cooperating. As we saw above, Tuve tried to articulate what was going on with his "democratic principle" notion, and clearly had a handle on it. But without a body of literature and scholarly vocabulary on cooperation for him to draw upon he was unable to get very far.

In addition to the fundamental goal of creating an adaptive system, every particular cooperative group is organized by its participants to serve a specific purpose or goal. The larger goal breaks down into a number of component goals and related tasks required to fulfill this purpose. In Section T, the work was organized around a larger goal: developing the fuse, getting it into production, and into combat. Specific tasks to reach this larger goal emerged in each stage of progress. These specific tasks provided the current common goal for each work group within the larger cooperative Section T.

Competence and the free flow of information are also key elements in cooperation. The fluid flow of energy, attention, information, and people to where the "actions" is, is typical. People are not locked into a bureaucratic role that limits what they can do, to whom they can talk, and to whom they must "report." The focus is on the goal and getting it accomplished. This is how Section T functioned. The workers in the lab were all selected for their competence in a needed area. Those who were competent in the current task worked on it. Each person also developed helpful skills that could be used in a pinch under the direction of someone who was competent. Information flowed freely around the laboratory. Everyone was allowed to take part in developing new ideas and solving problems.

In cooperation, "leadership"—or more accurately coordination and direction—falls to whomever is best suited by experience and expertise for that phase of the project. In cooperation, there is as little hierarchy of control and formal organization as possible. However, in Section T, Tuve, rather than the work team, often made decisions himself. Such concentration of authority is not typical of cooperation, though it is not totally incompatible with it. In true cooperation, leadership shifts constantly among the work groups as needed. The membership and social structure of the work group are fluid, depending on the requirements of the task, the state of progress toward completion, any problems encountered, and the expertise required. All of these elements were present in Section T and its laboratory work groups in most respects.

In group centered, cooperative groups, members do not compete for credit or recognition. Achieving the common group goal together is paramount. This is in direct contrast with self-centered individualism and adversarial competition. The spirit and practice of interpersonal competition and personal individualistic pride are replaced with the satisfaction in accomplishing the goal as a group. Enjoying the mutual support and appreciation of others is also typical of cooperative social systems. Keeping competition and individualism out of the cooperative social system is critical for success. According to Baldwin, there was little competition for credit for inventing and producing the valuable proximity fuse. All involved recognized the achievement as the result of their cooperation. Section T accomplished this in part by isolating and insulating the group from the larger competitive individualistic society as much as was possible. Many cooperative groups and communities have isolated themselves for the same reason.

Cooperation is the pursuit of a common group goal by a social system, and the social patterns of cooperation must be built into the group culture. The principles of cooperation were integrated into the basic sociocultural operating system of Section T and its laboratories. In sum, these principles are: creating an adaptive social system, making specific groups responsible for specific tasks, placing the most competent people on specific tasks, allowing for the free flow of ideas, information, and energy, making leaders out of the most competent person at that time, enjoying mutual support, and accomplishing the group goal.

The values and norms guiding cooperative interaction and activities must be understood, articulated, shared and accepted by all. There must be a dynamic cultural consensus that changes whenever the information processing and testing of the group's culture and techniques indicate that it should. It is clear that participants in Section T understood how cooperation works. They understood the culture of cooperation—and engaged in it with gusto.

The creation and dynamic evolution of cooperation in cooperative organizations and societies requires a well-developed cultural blueprint. Otherwise our episodic encounters with cooperation will remain ephemeral, fading in the mist before we can grasp them. That is what this book is about: spelling out what cooperative culture is, what it contains, and the ways it is maintained and changed. Part Two is devoted to developing this cultural blueprint.

Chapter 3. The Hutterites: A Cooperative Hybrid

The proximity fuse research and development group in OSRD, described in the last chapter, was created for a purpose and disbanded when they had fulfilled that purpose. They are an example of cooperation in a work group. The Hutterites show us a different form of cooperation. They are a self-supporting, mostly self-contained, permanent community cooperating as a social system.

The Hutterites are a successful product of the many efforts to create communal utopias in America during the 19th century. Several groups sought to establish permanent new communities and a "better" civilization. Most of these utopian experiments lasted only a few years, some only months. Very few survived for a generation or more. The Hutterites are one of those survivors. They are prospering and growing among us still, over 130 years after coming to America and establishing their first colonies in South Dakota. They discovered the piece that was missing in many failed idealistic efforts. They developed cultural-based organizational cooperation which can adapt to changes in their natural and social environment, allowing them to prosper where virtually all other communal efforts have failed.

The Hutterites are a remarkable and seemingly paradoxical blend of a rigid Sixteenth-century Christian religion and a cooperative, continually adapting, economic community. They have created a hybrid. In this chapter, this duality is examined for what we can learn about cooperation from it. As with Section T of OSRD, this is a form of cooperation that works in the real world.

The Hutterites emerged during the Protestant Reformation in the sixteenth century. Fifteen twenty-eight is their traditional founding date. They were part of the Anabaptist movement originating in southern Germany and Switzerland, which also produced the Amish and Mennonites. Their Christian beliefs include adult baptism, separation of church and state, and pacifism—refusing to bear arms or fight in wars. While they pay their taxes and obey the laws, they do not vote or participate in political activities and are conscientious objectors (Hostetler and Huntington, 1996, p. 55). They are a deeply religious community that found it necessary to live in physical and social isolation to escape the negative influences of our competitive individualistic materialistic society, which they believe is influenced by Satan.

The Hutterite colonies in North America have grown from 3 in South Dakota in 1874, to 96 in 1951 (Infield, 1955). In Minnesota, Montana, North and South Dakota, and Washington in the United States, and Alberta, British Columbia, Saskatchewan, and Manitoba in Canada there were 424 colonies in 2001. Their colonies average about a hundred people (Kraybill & Bowman, 2001, p. 22). When they get above this level, they split and start a new colony in a new location. Typically, the colony life-cycle of population growth and the splitting off of new colonies averages 14 to 15 years, but may be slowing. They keep their colonies small because they have found it best matches their agricultural and small-manufacturing life style and creates sufficient work and responsibilities to keep everyone efficiently occupied. This group size has also been found to be conducive to cooperation.

The anthropologist Gertrude E. Huntington (1997), observed: "A vigorous, growing population of communards, the Hutterites combine unchanging religious beliefs and changeless social structure with flexible utilization of modern technology and economic adaptability" (p. 319).The Hutterites are able to harmonize their fixed traditional religious and social patterns with rapid changes in their agricultural and economic practices because they distinguish between their spiritual world—which is governed by God and eternally correct and changeless—and the material, secular, world—which requires adaptive responses to meet the colony's survival needs. Huntington (1997) sees this duality as one of the Hutterites' secrets of success,

> . . . throughout their long history, they continue socially and religiously traditional, submissive to the authority of their own group, which they see as the eternal kingdom of God. Simultaneously, they are assertive and progressive in economic matters and in their dealings with the transitory, secular world (p. 325).

This seemingly incompatible blend of rigidity and adaptability works because their religion gives them the continued motivation and conceptual framework for communal living and cooperation (details follow). They then allow their rapidly adapting cooperative interface with the environment—their farming and other economic endeavors—to transform as required. While this duality works for the Hutterites, it is obviously not recommended for the pure cooperative social systems we will be building. The Hutterites's success, however, illustrates the adaptive power of cooperation.

GETTING THE WORK DONE COOPERATIVELY

For the Hutterites, the colony is where the action is. The colonies decide what they will raise on their farms, what other businesses they will engage in, and how their money will be used and the details of how they live. The colonies are thus able to operate as independent cooperative units on a daily basis with minimal intrusion from their overarching Leut. The Hutterite colonies are organized into three independent "Leuts" named after their original leaders: the Schmiedleut, the Dariusleut, and the Lehrerleut. Each Leut provides coordinating and administrative services to member colonies. This arrangement is ideal because it makes each colony an adaptive social unit. The colony is at the interface with the changing environment and can adapt very quickly in response to changes and needs. It does not have to deal with a huge bureaucratic organization dominating it and complicating decision making and actions. This is typical of true cooperative social systems. Even large complex cooperative organizations will be organized similarly into task units operating where the action is, at the interface between the organization and its environment.

The Hutterite cooperative culture leads to the selection of leaders with different qualities than competitive individualistic organizations favor. Hutterite leaders are selected, not for their charismatic dazzle, aggressiveness, take-charge dominance and bold self-confidence, as in many individualistic and competitive groups, but for their competence, sense of community and common purpose, and humility. Hutterites frown on aggressive, assertive personalities in general, and overly dominant personalities are unlikely to ever be selected for the top positions (Kephart, 1982, p. 286). Cooperation isn't about leadership; it's about a community operating as an adaptive unit, a whole. Such hierarchies as occurs in pure cooperative social systems are for coordination and are fluid, as we saw with Section T of OSRD (elaborated in Chapter 5). The colony hierarchy serves to coordinate economic and secular matters, as well as other functions.

The Hutterites exhibit their form of cooperation most clearly in their work organization. The daily work of the colony is carefully organized into an effective division of labor with selected colonists, mostly men, in charge of each of the areas of responsibility or "departments". The minister, colony boss (manager), and farm boss organize the daily work. The German school-teacher is in charge of the school. An English teacher is hired from outside the colony usually through the local public schools system. The English teacher typically teaches what is taught in public schools including math, some social studies and science. (Hostetler & Huntington, 1996, p. 107-108).

The farm boss plays a major role in all agricultural operations. Although major decisions are generally made by the group, the farm boss is responsible for the work assignments, the tempo of the work, and the schedule for planting and harvesting, and the like. He is considered the technical expert on farming. A good farm boss reads the farm journals and obtains up-to-date information from commercial companies. He understands such things as market values, cost-price ratios, and the efficiency of labor-saving machinery (Kephart, 1982, p. 295).

One Montana colony, for example, subscribed to *Progressive Dairymen*, *Poultry Digest*, *Hogs Today*, *Montana Wool Growers*, *National Wool Growers*, *Tool Crib*, and the *Billings Gazette* for news (Wilson, 2000, p. 106). These would be used by the farm boss and by specialists in charge of various departments.

This is what we would expect in cooperation, minimal hierarchy, with the farm boss' main focus the coordination of the work. The farm boss typically does not tell the hog man, the chicken man, the wheat man and other specialized bosses/supervisors how to do their jobs, though he will be knowledgeable about them. He deals with the larger view of the colony's farming operation and how all the parts fit and work together.

Competent, married, baptized, men are selected and "assigned to specific areas of responsibility—cowman, beekeeper, shoemaker, plumber, goose man, and so on. Each of them is the 'boss' of their respective area." Although some job assignments are seasonal, "most are long-term, if not for a lifetime.

Occasional rotations occur, depending on personal skills and the needs of the colony" (Kraybill & Bowman, 2001, p. 38). These areas of responsibility, often thought of as "departments," include supervising other colonists working in that area as required (Hostetler & Huntington, 1966, p. 32). Additional colony jobs for men with responsibility for a department include dairyman, electrician, shop man, and carpenter; the list varies with the kind of work a given colony is engaged in. These specialized bosses might have full-time assistants or apprentices (Kraybill & Bowman, 2001, p. 39). The department bosses are expected to be competent and keep current with needed skills and new information, which can include taking courses and training outside the colonies. Early retirement among men, often late 40s or early 50s, is common, allowing younger, stronger, men to serve as bosses/supervisors and making it easier to change adaptively. While this works for cooperative Hutterite colonies, and is one way to do it, it is still a compromise with the ideal. A pure cooperative organization places the most competent people at any given time "in charge" of directing current operations, as was the case with Section T of OSRD, with none permanently occupying the position.

There are few comparable long-term or permanent positions for women. The most important is head cook. Sometimes a woman is head gardener of the vegetable and herb garden for the kitchen, though in some colonies the German teacher takes this area of responsibility as well. A tailoress is in charge of distributing cloth among the members. Most women work at domestic chores such as cooking, baking, and canning, on a rotating basis. Responsibility for supervising this work is also rotated among capable women. Women generally work in groups when they bake, can, cook, butcher chickens, do gardening work, and care for domestic animals for colony use (Hostetler & Huntington, 1996, p. 36). This division of labor by gender works for the Hutterites, but a true cooperative system would utilize the talents and abilities of women and men equally because the full utilization of all the community's talents maximizes its adaptive capacity.

Hutterites learn young how to work and how to take responsibility for community tasks. School children from six years old serve as baby sitters, work in the gardens and fields, and assist with the care of the farm animals and the like.

In a pure cooperative organization, the participants and leaders are the most competent available at the moment for those tasks. There would be few fixed organizational roles and seldom would participants be permanently—or for many years—assigned to them. The more fluid flow of action and responsibility exhibited in Section T of OSRD is closer to the cooperative ideal. Still, the Hutterite style of organization has many qualities of cooperation in general. All of the job boss assignments are "on the line" responsibilities for an area at the interface of the colony and the natural agricultural environment. This front line is where most of the work of adapting to conditions and changes in the environment occur. The Hutterites commonly use the latest in equipment, including tractors and harvesting machines, as well as air-conditioned, automated and computer monitored facilities for the care and cleanliness of their animals. Hutterite men learn about the areas of specialization as they grow up and work in the colony. The bosses have a highly skilled and dedicated labor force to draw upon as needed.

THE HUTTERITES'S AMAZING PRODUCTIVITY AND CREATIVITY

A characteristic of cooperative organizations is their high level of productivity and the quality of their products and services. Cooperative organizations announce themselves in part by this level of quality and productivity. This is one of the main reasons people create cooperative organizations. This is true of the Hutterites.

The Hutterites's daily cooperative dynamic comes from everyone having assigned responsibilities and specializations in the colony division of labor, including floating and rotating labor pools, to do whatever is required at that time and season. Colonists perform several different jobs during the day, with each one scheduled to dovetail with others. The colonies are small enough that everyone knows what the colony must do that day, how all the assignments fit together, what each individual must do, and how that task contributes to the colony's welfare. The day's and week's work are planned and scheduled. Some jobs are routine and repetitive and are automatically scheduled for certain times of the day or week. Everyone does his or her job at the assigned time. This high level of harmonized coordination is a hallmark of cooperative social systems.

The Hutterite colonies demonstrate the high levels of agricultural and economic proficiency and innovativeness expected of cooperative social systems. They routinely out-produce other farmers on the same amount of land. This high productivity is one of the major rewards for practicing true cooperation for the Hutterites. They believe in and relish hard work (Hostetler & Huntington, 1996, pp. 46, 47). It is an expression of their dedi-cation to God, the focus of their activities, and keeps them happy, engaged, and out of mischief. While the economic basis of Hutterite colonies has tra-ditionally been large scale agriculture, small manufacturing companies and offering services for sale to the outside community have been added.

The Hutterites's cooperative efforts produce an amazing amount of work and output.

> In 1990 a specific Hutterite colony in North Dakota with a popula-tion of thirty-four adults and thirty-seven children had a hog barn that held 1,200 hogs, two chicken barns that together housed 44,000 chickens, a pullet barn for 20,000 pullets, and a cow barn with 50 dairy cows and an addition for calves. The colony raised grain for their livestock and had their own storage elevators and feed mill. They worked three truck garden plots and raised potatoes on two quarters of irrigated land. The potatoes were stored in a building they owned in a nearby town. The colony had its own electric shop, carpenter shop, blacksmith shop, and garage. High quality equip-ment was purchased in the United States, Canada, and Germany. All equipment is serviced in the colony. For seven years the colony ran a grain salvage business that took them throughout the upper Midwest. They continue to take demolition jobs in their immediate area (Huntington, 1997, pp. 338, 339).

According to Hostetler and Huntington, (1996, p. 46), "The Hutterites produced a large percentage of agricultural commodities in the states and provinces where they live." In Manitoba, for example, "they produced 31 percent of all hogs in that province, 17 percent of all laying hens, 20 percent of turkeys, 62 percent of ducks, and 95 percent of Manitoba's geese."

In addition to being very productive, the Hutterites as they coopera-tively adapt develop a variety of new products and inventions. Huntington (1997, pp. 339, 340) illustrates their adoption and creation of innovations:

> Hutterites constantly exchange information among colonies and have been pioneers in introducing new farming practices. The two-litter-a-year hog cycle was introduced into Manitoba by a Hutterite colony. Colonies keep computerized records, striving to produce twenty-five weanling pigs per sow per year. Specialty potato pro-duction in Alberta was pioneered by a Hutterite colony. Hutterites continually experiment with different seed varieties, some-times be-ginning with as little as an envelope of gift seed. They have used the most modern milking machines for years. In their processing, milk never comes in contact with the air. It goes directly from the cow to refrigerated bulk tanks from which the milk company picks it up. Hutterite dairy parlors may be completely computerized, with the

total milk production and amount of feed given each cow recorded and adjusted daily. Cow barn floors may be flushed mechanically several times a day by automated machines. The effluent is held in a large lagoon until used to fertilize the fields. The Hutterites construct their own buildings, make their own furniture, manufacture some of the farm and kitchen equipment, and maintain and repair everything they use.

This kind of engaged productivity is typical of cooperative communities. All are working together with their attention and efforts focused on current projects and problems, sharing ideas and solutions and delighting together in their successes and innovations. They all benefit together from their various efforts, all of which contribute to the adaptive vitality of the colony. There are no internal competitors trying to sabotage one another's efforts and no individualists going off to do "their own thing," free-riding on the rest of the colony's work. There is constant positive feedback for contributions and sharing in the particular delights and challenges of various projects. Everyone belongs and is a useful part of a whole, they are all one, and it is fun. The Hutterites thoroughly enjoy one another and visiting and playful teasing are favorite activities.

The Hutterites are also expert mechanics and clever inventors. Hostetler and Huntington (1996, pp. 54, 55) observed that Hutterites can repair and rebuild just about anything including massive tractors and large trucks and other huge farm implements. They utilize scrap metal from city dumps for all kinds of creative projects.

> New equipment may be used for several years, then repainted, reconditioned and sold, or used equipment may be bought, and skilled Hutterite mechanics may improve and adapt it to colony needs. This applies to modernizing hog and poultry barns, including installation of feeding and egg-gathering equipment. Hutterites often improve the existing models of farm machinery or adapt them to their purposes. One mechanic constructed cabs of plexiglass for the grain combines long before farm implement companies sold them on the market. Another made an attachment to a combine that prevented the stones from entering the cylinder, thus protecting the machine from considerable damage. Cultivators adapted to dry-land farming are made by colonies in Canada. Specialized machines such as hydraulic rockpickers and tractor cabs are manufactured by colony shops (pp. 54, 55).

Concerning the innovative dry-land cultivators: "The Noble Blade, widely used by Canadian colonies, acts like a gigantic knife slicing the soil at a depth of about five inches. This method of cultivation, an alternative to the disc plowing, reduces wind erosion" (pp. 54,55). And, "A capping knife for extracting honey from honeycombs was made by a colonist and was later patented and produced by an outside firm" (pp. 54,55).

These efforts are examples of the Hutterites's ability to develop competencies that contribute to their self-sufficiency and adaptive success. Their many inventions, innovations and creative uses of resources result from their attention to areas needing adaptive responses and then producing effective solutions. That is exactly what cooperative adaptation is all about. This is all part of the fun, excitement, novelty and reward of cooperating. It is an engaging way to live life.

There are those who believe that competition and prospects for personal gain are the best stimulus for creativity and inventiveness. I don't agree, and neither does Henrik Infield. Concerning the argument that "profit was the only effective incentive for production," Henrik Infield (1955) said in his *Utopia and Experiment: Essays in the Sociology of Cooperation*, "Which argument could be easily disposed of by reference to the fact that it was by no means the inventive but rather the exploitative mind that was stimulated by profit only ... inventiveness was much less hampered in cooperative than in competitive society" (pp. 90, 91). The Hutterites illustrate this observation. Their inventiveness is an element of the way they live, a continual process, with the rewards coming from their community members' positive reinforcements, primarily. It would be tough for purely competitive individualistic organizations using money and hierarchical status as rewards to match it, especially for the "price." In later chapters we will see how competition frequently blocks and undermines many adaptive and inventive developments and that support, approval and acceptance of peers and coworkers is a very powerful reward and motivator for creativity and innovation. The enormous creativity and productivity among Hutterites clearly is not motivated by eagerness for personal gain or competitive superiority in accumulation of rewards, but by the social and material rewards of belonging to and participating in a cooperative colony as one.

Establishing a Colony of Heaven

Let's review the elements of cooperation we have observed so far among the Hutterites. They have a culture based form of cooperation focused on

The Hutterites' self-images derive mainly from their cooperative colony life. As Huntington (1997) notes: "An essential part of the Hutterite concept of self is the individual's identification with the colony, which" is "highly functional for the maintenance of community" (pp. 335, 336). To the Hutterite, "we" refers to their colony, their community (Kephart, 1982, p. 288). They describe themselves, when asked, as having hundreds of friends.

At the same time, as Huntington (1997) points out, "they strongly believe that each person has the freedom to decide whether or not to belong to or stay in the community. Individual responsibility rates very high both in deciding one's own destiny and also in protecting and maintaining the group" (p. 335). Individual choice and free will are not lost in Hutterite group centeredness.

I expect this level of identification and oneness with the community, as well as an expectation that individuals will assume responsibility for their contributions to the cooperative community and for their own actions, to be found in all cooperative cultures and communities. In later chapters we explore this oneness and self-identification with the cooperative group in more detail. These two are essential elements of cooperative groups, contributing to social cohesion and consensual focus on the common group goal(s). They are also immensely rewarding personally, as we shall see.

I don't think it is necessary to make so much of self-sacrifice or of the "crushing" of the individual to the will of the community as the Hutterites do. I rather see cooperative community as a welcome escape from individualism and competition where people can live and work very effectively in harmony and good fellowship for the benefit of all. There is no self-sacrifice in cooperation as I envisioned it. Rather, there is the swap of an uncertain and often negative self-image for the far more positive, secure, and rich one that cooperation provides.

MATERIAL COMMUNALISM

Hostetler and Huntington (1996) said of the Hutterites: "Living communally is believed to be the divine order of God, who from the beginning created all things for common use. Through private possession, it was man who brought disorder into the world by his grasping and greedy spirit" (p. 12). The Hutterites' communalism has been successful both as a religious and as an economic practice. As a result, Huntington (1997) can say: "With the exception of the Roman Catholic religious orders, the Hutterites exceed in numbers and wealth all other communally organized movements in the history of North America" (pp. 320, 321).

Communalism—ownership of property by the community—and cooperation have a mixed relationship. Sometimes cooperation and communalism go together and work very effectively, as in Hutterite colonies. Sometimes cooperation occurs alone, without communalism, and works better without it, such as in Section T of OSRD. And there are cases of communalism without cooperation, which occurred frequently among 19th century communal groups and also in modern intentional communities. Among the most famous secular efforts to create a communal/socialist community were the Fourierist communities, such as the famous Brook Farm in Massachusetts favored by many Transcendentalist American intellectuals in the 1840s including Hawthorne, that were a response to Fourier's belief "that an entire economic system based on the anarchy of free competition was wrong" (Guarneri, 1997, p. 159). Unfortunately, the social organization of these appealing communities was not cooperative. Other communal communities lacking cooperation were based on religious principles, such as the "St George" form of the Mormon United Order (Arrington, 1966, pp. 327-331). (The Mormon's "Orderville" form of the United Order was more cooperative and more successful.) Individualistic democratic efforts to produce equity in material wealth and avoid competition are a common basic operating system in other cases in America. Twin Oaks is a thriving modern example of a communal community operating democratically (Kinkade, 1997).

Some communards expected a more cooperative community to automatically emerge from communal living, but the two are not linked in that manner. It is important to remember that communalism is not necessary for true cooperation, and the presence of communalism does not mean the group is necessarily cooperative. That has to be determined directly. However, it is also clear that cooperative communities, societies and civilization that are self-sufficient and able to provide for most of their survival requirements are most effective if organized communally, as the Hutterites are. If America becomes a cooperative society, I expect we will also become communal. The Hutterite version works very well and illustrates one way it can be done. In a later chapter, we see what a cooperative communal America might be like. One of the big differences is I expect communal cooperative Americans to enjoy an abundance of high quality products and services without the self-sacrifice or asceticism common in religion based communal societies in the past and practiced by the Hutterites.

In Hutterite colonies, money is deposited in a commercial bank in a common account operated by the business manager, though other adults are permitted to use it to make small cash purchases as needed. Individual Hutterites do not receive a salary and pay no income taxes, although the colony is taxed. All of the members' needs are filled by the colony (Kephart, 1982, p. 294). As Huntington (1997) dryly puts it: "Fringe benefits have been worked out long ago, and no energy is wasted discussing wages" (pp. 319-320).

The Hutterites reject the concept of private property.

> To a Hutterite, property is something to be used, not owned. It follows then, that there is no such thing as affluence within the [colony]. It is true that the Brethren buy the best types of farm machinery and use various labor-saving devices. But these are [colony] properties and as such are presumed to further the group cause. As for individual aggrandizement, the Hutterites will have none of it (Kephart, 1982, p. 293).

The Hutterites do recognize personal belongings or property. Personal property is defined as: "Something given to me from the colony for me. Once it has been given, it is mine to use" (Hostetler & Huntington, 1996, p. 58). Personal property includes clothing, mementos, a locked box to keep personal items in, and so forth.

Among the Hutterites, "austerity and simplicity are consciously accepted by the individual as a necessary way of life" (Hostetler & Huntington, 1996, p. 62). This austerity is derived from their religious beliefs. The Hutterites live with fewer and more modest personal possessions than cooperation requires, although they are gradually utilizing more modern appliances in their apartments to make their lives more comfortable and convenient. The dualism between their conservative Christian Anabaptist faith and their cooperative secular adaptation is expressed in the clothes and living conditions of Hutterite families on the one hand, and their spending on farm equipment and resources on the other.

Hutterite men's work garb, for example, is not much different from that of other American farmers. Women's wear, however, is similar to the dress of sixteenth-century Europe peasant women: "an ankle-length skirt, separate bodice, long apron, low-heeled black shoes, and the familiar polka-dot head scarf." Most of their clothing is homemade including underwear and shoes (Kephart, 1982, p. 290). Homes are generally apartments in a long building with other families, often built like a duplex. Furnishings are simple and mostly homemade, comfortable but not fancy. In contrast, their agricultural equipment is top-of-the-line; "nothing is too modern if it benefits the colony" is the Hutterite attitude (Kraybill & Bowman, 2001, p. 38). The Hutterites believe that God requires personal austerity as a form of self-denial and self-sacrifice, but they also fear that any personal accumulation of material wealth will inevitably lead to individual desires for more and introduce competitive struggling to have more and "better" things than others in the colony.

This kind of cooperative communal living greatly streamlines and simplifies the colonies' internal economic practices and material distributions, just as it would for a cooperative communal society. There is no need for money or record of "credits" earned. One does not have to acquire sums of money before he or she can acquire food, clothing, housing and other necessities. There is no motivation or reward for accumulating money or material possessions since members are provided all they need as a routine consequence of membership. They get housing, clothing, food, and so forth as needed automatically as part of the communal cooperative social process. They don't need savings, insurance, or retirement accounts. The adaptive cooperative communal community provides all the needs of the Hutterites—or for some other such society—as a consequence of what it does; it is organized to do this, it is one of its primary purposes. As we will see when we look at American society in this light, huge amounts of time, energy, and material are saved and large numbers of complex organizations become irrelevant, freeing participants to concentrate on their collective survival and adaptive needs. This vastly reduces the amount of time, labor, concern and resources necessary for quality daily living.

Communal ownership of property to be used by and for all eliminates a great deal of wasteful duplication of equipment, such as lawn mowers, snow blowers, and tools, our American way requires each household to own. Many things American households have to do for themselves, such as repair and maintenance of dwellings, are taken care of at the community level by the Hutterites.

The Hutterites, personal restraint serves another purpose: the accumulation of capital needed for the expensive process of branching regularly, buying land, updating equipment, capitalizing new business enterprises, paying for professional services such as modern medical care and legal counsel, paying taxes, and meeting other needs for their collective well-being.

Though the Hutterites are frugal in most personal areas, they spend a good deal of money on our modern American doctors, dentists, opticians and other health care specialists and clinics. They are careful about what they eat but will consult with a professional dietitian if they feel the need. Not surprisingly, given their life style and health care, they are in very good health. Seriously ill Hutterites can select their own doctors and hospitals, including such prestigious ones as the Mayo Clinic. Research shows there are virtually no suicides, drug addiction, and very little abuse of alcohol even though alcohol use is permitted. Sexual problems are almost unheard of. Cases of serious mental illness, as with physical illness and aging, are handled within the framework of the colonies (Kephart, 1982, p. 292). As Huntington (1997) observed: "No government today spends money for Hutterites who are unemployed, disabled, aged, or retired. No Hutterites are homeless street people or permanent residents of mental institutions. None are malnourished, battered, or born with drug addiction or fetal alcohol syndrome" (p. 338).

This is the level of care and support for all the colony's members to be expected from a truly cooperative communal community. It is a major reason to pursue such a society. It is also one of the utopian dreams that keeps running through human societies, like a wishful sigh. I'm showing you it is possible and how to do it.

ON THE PERSONAL CHARACTERISTICS OF HUTTERITES

Are there personality traits that work especially well in cooperative communities?

I was amazed to discover that the Myers-Briggs personality inventory had been administered to Hutterites. It is one measure many of us are familiar with that can reveal the type of people Hutterite socialization produces. "Hutterites are somewhat more extroverted than introverted on the Myers-Briggs personality indicator. They are sensing rather than intuitive, feeling rather than thinking, and judgmental rather than perceptive." The standard description for the ESFJ type reads:

> Warm-hearted, talkative, popular, conscientious, born cooperators, active committee members. Need harmony and may be good at creating it. Always doing something nice for someone. Work best with

encouragement and praise. Main interest is in things that directly and visibly affect people's lives (Hostetler and Huntington, 1996, p. 94, as per original).

From the popular Kersey and Bates (1984, pp. 192-194) book on the Myers-Briggs test we add a few more characteristics of the ESFJ. Their values contain clear shoulds and should nots, and they like a routinized, scheduled, and correctly executed work and home situation. They take their roles in the community seriously. They are prone to take the blame for things that go wrong in their social system and can become depressed as a result. They need to be loved and appreciated. They are soft hearted and sentimental, observing birthdays, anniversaries and the like with gusto and flourish. They are wonderful with people, and are the most sociable of all the Myers-Briggs types. The ESFJ is found in 13% of the American population.

This is just the type of person the Hutterites would want for their cooperative colonies, and they have succeeded in producing them through their socialization practices and enactment of their culture.

I expect that fully cooperative societies will socialize their members to be skillful, sensitive and compassionate in interpersonal relationships and to be trustworthy, diligent, creative, and responsible people. Whether they will tend to be ESFJ types or something else we'll have to wait and see.

In Admiration

The Hutterites are widely recognized as being cooperative. The sociologist Henrick F. Infield explored utopian communities worldwide, many of them first hand, and judged the Hutterites of North America to be the only full-fledged cooperative community. They practiced what Infield (1955) called "all-inclusive or comprehensive cooperation" (pp. 25, 92). The Hutterites "had, long ago, crossed the border that divides competitive from cooperative living, and were satisfied to stay there for all days to come," he said (Infield, 1955, p. 90). The sociologist William M. Kephart (1982) summarized, "of the scores of communistic groups that have appeared on the North American scene, the Hutterian Brethren are far and away the most successful.... The Hutterites have not only succeeded but are truly in a class by themselves" (p. 279).

Laura Wilson (2000), an admiring observer and photographer of the Hutterites said: "Whatever the faults of the Hutterite way of life, whatever its limitations, it recognizes and responds to the human longing for community and a higher purpose. The Hutterites' faith, which is both demanding and compassionate, nourishes their spirit. There is nothing indifferent or impersonal about colony life" (p. 140). Adds a thoughtful Hutterite: "If there will ever be a perfect culture it may not be exactly like the Hutterites—but it will be similar" (Hostetler & Huntington, 1966, p. 128). Infield (1955) enthusiastically commented:

> Watching them, it all looked so simple, each of them worked steadily at the assigned job, and tried to do it as well as he knew how.... They were gay and satisfied; they were obviously not scared of life, and death could not hold much fear for them. If any human being deserved that name, they certainly had a claim to being called happy" (p. 90).

Kraybill and Bowman (2001) observed that the Old Order Anabaptists, the Mennonites, Amish, and Hutterites, are not only fascinating societies within our own, they are beginning to attract the attention of disenchanted Americans. Americans are taking a closer look at these Anabaptists as an alternative to a failing American culture. If they look closely enough and discover the Hutterites, they will also discover cooperation, exactly what they need to rejuvenate and transform American culture.

Nature also has some lessons on cooperation for us. The next two chapters look at cooperation among social animals and show us a number of useful insights and social techniques we can adopt in our own efforts. One could make the case that animal social evolution is moving toward cooperation, just as our own social evolution is.

Chapter 4. Nature's Lessons On Cooperation

To understand ourselves, we must understand and accept our place in the natural processes of life on Earth. We are beginning to grasp the interdependent whole that is our living planet and the need to live within it constructively for both our own survival and that of many other species. As we look at life on Earth now and in the past, we see a bewildering array of life forms that have lived for various periods of time. Some, like sharks and horseshoe crabs, have been around in their well-adapted and essentially unchanged forms for hundreds of thousands, even millions of years. In other animals, new varieties are continually emerging. Evolution is a restless process going many directions or standing pat, producing a kaleidoscope of life.

We have ignored or misunderstood critical components of our place in this living whole. That ignorance prevents us from successfully harmonizing with our natural environment and fully realizing our own potential. We humans are a unique and stunning product of evolution. We are a new order of creature that is young and not yet fully adapted to its condition and capacities. We have a number of new qualities that are major evolutionary advances. We have a high level of intelligence far above any other species that includes astounding tool (and weapon) making skills. We have the capacity for complex communication from speech to computers. And we have cultures with which we produce complex social systems that are extraordinary social adaptive tools. No other creature comes close to us. What we don't collectively understand yet is: "What is it all about?" We haven't *got* the big picture yet.

From the point of view of our evolutionary origins and biological home, *it* is all about adapting to the ever-changing environment using our unique intelligence, communications, and culture. Adaptation is the "name of the game" for all life on Earth. This is the basic "meaning" and "purpose" of life for us and the reference point for all we do. We humans are currently running riot across the planet dominating and destroying it. We are immaturely overwhelming our world as we delight in, and too often misuse, our superior and unique adaptive tools. We are only beginning to ask, "Is this action adaptive for us, other species and our environment in general?" If not, it shouldn't be done. If we don't know whether it is or not, we have the cultural means in science and our technologies to find out. Our evolutionary gifts are "designed" to give us the capacity to assess our ongoing condition and respond adaptively rapidly and intelligently.

We are only partially and unevenly utilizing our gifts; indeed, we are still figuring out their nature, such as the power of culture. We have yet to seriously collectively assess whether individualism and internal competition are adaptive sociocultural systems for humankind and, if not, what would be superior. We layer other "meanings" for life onto the vaguely perceived adaptive one, such as religious beliefs that this life is a test, a training ground, a way station to eternal joy and glory in the afterlife, or that life is about the competitive pursuit of individual wealth, status and earthly glory. Effective adaptation is absolutely the basic, must do, requirement for our continued survival, ever evolving advancement, and the successful "pursuit of happiness."

While there has never been another social species like ours on the Earth, evolution has produced and continues to produce social species, a few of which actually cooperate. The three basic social operating systems of individualism, competition and cooperation are common among social animals. They also engage in individualistic and competitive mutual aid, and have interspecies forms of mutual aid as well. Our human competitive individualism is pretty ordinary among social animals, including the vertebrates and mammals of our evolutionary family tree. True cooperation is rarer among animals. Ants, in particular, have evolved cooperative social practices that we can adapt to help us use our social systems more adaptively than we do.

This chapter provides an overview of the evolution of social behavior and our place in the process. Our sociobiology provides amazing adaptive capacities on the one hand and serious obstacles to becoming truly cooperative, especially on the national and world-wide levels, on the other. Understanding where our strengths are and the nature of the obstacles is necessary if we are to overcome them.

THE FOUR PINNACLES OF SOCIAL EVOLUTION

E. O. Wilson (1975) in his classic, *Sociobiology: The New Synthesis*, shows us there are *four* pinnacles of social evolution among animals. There are two pinnacles among invertebrates: the colonial invertebrates and social insects, and two pinnacles among vertebrates: nonhuman mammals and humans. Comparing ourselves to the other three pinnacles reveals some of our sociobiological strengths, weaknesses, uniqueness and similarities in mastering cooperation. We will be able to see our own tapestry of social behavior more clearly as we observe other species and see their various social patterns and their consequences. The pinnacle in each case is or approaches cooperation, not competition or individualism. Cooperation is the ultimate pinnacle of social evolution among social species.

THE COLONIAL INVERTEBRATES

The colonial invertebrates include some familiar creatures such as the corals and the siphonophores like the Portuguese man-of-war with its gas filled float, looking something like a jellyfish. From Wilson's (1975) point of view the colonial invertebrates have come close to producing perfect societies.

The Siphonophora order, according to Wilson, has developed the highest level and most cooperative social systems among animals. Wilson (1975) gives the example of a *Nanomia*, which is at the same level and similar to the Portuguese man-of-war.

> At the top of each *Nanomia* (colony) sits an individual modified into a gas-filled float, which gives buoyancy to the rest of the colony strung out below it. Nectophores (specialized zooids) act like little bellows. They squirt out jets of water to propel the colony through the water. By altering the shape of their openings they are able to alter the direction of the jets and hence the path followed by the

colony. Through their coordinated action the *Nanomia* colony is able to dart about vigorously, moving at any angle and in any plane, and even executing loop-the-loop curves (p. 383).

Individual zooids have specialized for ingestion and distribution of nutrients, including long branched tentacles used to capture prey and also to defend the colony. Sexual medusoids produce new colonies through gamete formation and fertilization. Other zooids, bracts, have specialized in protection of the colony by becoming scale like shingles. New zooids for the colony "are generated by budding in one or the other of two growth zones located at each end of the nectophore region" (pp. 384).

Each zooid can act, at different times, independently, as a member of initiative-taking coordinated groups, or as part of the colony as a whole, just as individuals in a true cooperative human society would. Each nectophore, for example, has its own nervous system but "remains quiescent except when aroused by excitation arriving from the rest of the colony." When the rear portion of the colony is touched the forward nectophores begin to contract and then others join in with coordination conducted through nerve tracts. These colonies are so well coordinated for movement they can do loop-the-loops. Several gastrozoids may collaborate in capturing and ingesting prey independently of directions from the rest of the colony. Nutrient distribution involves the coordination of the whole colony. The gastrozoids and the palpons, which are auxiliary digestive organs, pump digested food along the stem to the rest of the colony with the whole colony participating in the peristaltic movements that flush the digested material quickly back and forth along the stem (Wilson, 1975, p. 384-6). Wilson (1975) feels "The achievement of the siphonophores ... must be regarded as one of the greatest in the history of evolution. They have created a complex metazoan body by making organs out of individual organisms" (p. 386).

Human cooperative social systems will be similar to *Nanomia* colonies in their high degree of division of labor and specialization and organism-like coordination and responsiveness as a unit, all benefiting each zooid in the colony. We will see this capacity of individuals to take on different morphologies—physical shapes—to meet the needs of the colony again with the ants. We see here the development of high levels of competence by individuals—including through physical specialization—to fulfill their adaptive function for the colony as a whole, and to take initiative as a task group for the benefit of the colony. Along the continuum from "free and self-sufficient" individuals to societies "indistinguishable from multicellular organisms," these *Nanomia* colonies are clearly at the organismic end.

Comparing colonial invertebrate colonies with human cooperative societies reveals some fascinating and important contrasts. The high level of specialization, division of labor, and individual competence achieved by the *Nanomia* colony is very effective but for a given colony it is also fixed. Specialized zooids cannot reverse the process and change into some other specialized organ. Thus challenges and changes that a given colony cannot meet with its current form cannot be successfully handled.

Humans, on the other hand, are the most flexible and adaptable species when we do it right because our cultures can be changed any time environmental changes and conditions require. Our intelligence allows us to substitute our constantly evolving technologies and techniques for the invertebrates' morphological specializations to serve specific tasks. Our way is *much* faster; we don't have to wait for genetic evolution to make the needed changes. Human individual intelligence—not found in *Naomi* zooids—is a plus because we are able to take responsibility for various tasks and act upon them for the good of the whole, are able to comprehend the dynamics of large scale activities, learn large bodies of information and change our behavior as warranted. However, individual intelligence can be a maladaptive negative when humans refuse to develop the competence through training necessary to perform skillfully and/or to share the consensus necessary to act for the good of the community. When humans are competing and pursuing individual benefits while battling others over how the community should operate, we have an adaptive nightmare. The *Nanomia* colonies—if they were intelligent—could only marvel at our self-destructive commotion. Getting our societies and communities to work right—adaptively—is a constant challenge for humans, while the *Nanomia* colony floats happily along in complete harmony.

One of the most common concerns individualistic Americans have about cooperation is that a cooperative society will be like a *Nanomia* colony, with each person's role fixed and prescribed narrowly so they are just little cogs in a big machine. They don't want to lose their "self" in what they imagine is a cold, mechanical role. However, cooperative human societies require a great deal of intellectual and emotional engagement and participants must be able to adapt, change, learn new skills, and solve problems continually. Each person is a critical and valued specialized component of the cooperative whole. Cooperative oneness has great social, psychological, physiological, and emotional benefits as chapters in Part 2 detail. Your "self" is much more vibrant, distinctive, and positive in cooperative societies. These same worried Americans seem unaware or untroubled about being exploited cogs in the wild and ruthless machinery of our competitive market economy and individualistic democracy. In our current society, we are "consumers," "employees," and "citizens" who are too often exploited, made "losers," and left to fend for ourselves when we are no longer valued, cannot perform, or our resources have been exhausted. Our competitive societies trap you in a social game that you must play to survive, robbing you of your individual freedom to live any other way. Why are you not complaining if you abhor being a cog in a dehumanizing steamroller machine?

SOCIAL INSECTS

Of all the social species, the social insects at the pinnacle, the ants and termites, have the most to teach us about cooperation. Like humans, ants and termites have to coordinate the behavior of large numbers of physically independent individuals. The lessons they have for us constitute a major portion of true cooperation as I'm defining it and presented in Chapter 1. These lessons are examined in more detail in the following chapter. They include the ants' focus on adapting to the environment as a cooperative social system, the critical importance of competence in participants, using the social system as an environmental tracking device, optimizing the adaptive fit of the social structure to the ever changing environment, and the shape of coordinating hierarchies in cooperation. The cooperative ants and termites reinforce the importance of a common group goal and "consensus" in establishing the division of labor and in coordination of participants.

Our comparative advantages and disadvantages in relation to the social insects are similar to those with the colonial invertebrates such as the *Nanomia* colony. We have culture and can change anytime, making it possible to adapt very fast. The ants must await evolution's natural selection for adaptive changes in their morphologies and behavior, for the most part. We can change in a single generation. But they have a built in consensus and division of labor. We have to constantly struggle for consensus and fail more often than we succeed. Our divisions of labor may or may not be effective, efficient, or even complete. The ants and termites have clear divisions of labor, often with a wide range of morphological specialization in addition to the familiar queen, worker, and, soldier ants. The European ant *Colobopsis truncatus* has a highly specialized caste with plug shaped heads that they use as a gate to the nest, making them the door ants. A Celebes ant species has a caste whose members are "virtually 'walking heads'" specialized in the milling of seeds. The development of defensive specialization such as exploding abdomens has also been observed. The honeypot ant of the American southwest collects nectar from desert plants and "honeydew" from homopterous insects it farms "and stores them in the crops of the repletes, nestmates specialized to serve as food storage receptacles." These ants' crops are huge extended sacs longer than the rest of the ants' body (Wilson, 1975; Holldobler and Wilson, 1990, esp. pp. 178-9, 298, 332-334, and plate 8).

Ants and termites communications are always direct and clear; our communications are often confounded by different languages, vague, garbled or inaccurate content, competitive efforts to control access to needed information, and other problems.

The comparatively limited communications of the social insects, coupled with their morphological specialization and some simple "programming" nevertheless produce some amazing feats of coordination. When the famous army ants bivouac at night from their marches, for example, between 150,000 and 700,000 workers will form a huge—up to a meter across—construction of their own bodies by linking together their strong tarsal claws and forming chains and nets in interlocking layers into a solid cylindrical or ellipsoidal mass under which the queen, immature, and other colony members are sheltered (Wilson, 1975, pp. 424-425). The army ants can also be formidable foragers. Acting as coordinated teams they can take down larger insects and even small mammals. Something like our Plains Native Americans and the buffalo hunt.

Coordination within the colonies of various ant species produces ant "agriculture" with ant "farmers and ranchers" rearing aphids, mealybugs and other homopterous insects in their nests and feeding off their "honeydew" anal secretions. They grow fungi or yeasts that they gather and carry into their nests. Among some ants the art of gardening has been highly developed and includes "manuring" of the fungi with fecal droplets rich in chitinases and proteases.

Just as astounding are the coordinated construction skills of the termites *Macrotermes* and other African fungus-growing termites. Wilson (1975) describes their huge mound nests:

The labyrinthine internal structure of these termitaries has been designed in the course of evolution to guide a regular flow of air from the central fungus garden, where it is heated and rises by convection, upward and outward to a flat, peripheral system of capillary-like chambers, where it is cooled and freshened by proximity to the outside air. In the *M. natalensis* the architecture is so efficient that the temperature within the fungus garden remains within one degree of 30 degrees C and the carbon dioxide concentration varies only slightly, around 2.6 percent (pp. 11-12).

These enormous constructions are not built by direct communication. Each termite is "programmed" with the competence to respond to each stage with a discreet action. Even if one constantly removes one set of termites and puts a fresh set in, the work progresses properly. Experiments show that their actions are based on very specific clues, such as two columns needing to be joined by an arch. This is similar to what computer scientists call "dynamic programming." At each step the result is assessed and the precise program for the next step out of several available is activated. "No termite need serve as overseer with blueprint in hand," Wilson marvels (1975, p. 12). However, the termites are stuck with the architectural patterns programmed into them. They cannot change the plans by choice when environmental changes occur, they must wait for evolutionary constraints to do the job. Many colonies would likely perish before needed changes became the preprogrammed norm.

Control of sexual reproduction is a key factor in the social insects' cooperative success. Among social insect species that have multiple competitive reproductive females, cooperation is not achieved. When only the queen reproduces and the rest of the colony provide the necessary support efforts for survival of the young and their incorporation into the colony, then cooperation can occur. Reproduction among human mammals where all of the adult females and males are fertile and females can conceive at any time requires some special social norms for cooperative civilizations and communities. This is one of the sociobiological obstacles we humans will need to overcome in order to become fully cooperative. Currently, people have babies whenever they decide they want to, an individualistic decision without regard for the consequences for the larger society. Or they may engage in "unprotected" sex as they choose and unplanned babies are a consequence. Or a particular racial or ethnic community may decide as a competitive strategy to increase their presence and power in a society by out reproducing others in that society. This latter can also occur as a happenstance consequence of unrestrained individualistic sexual and reproductive behavior in a racial or ethnic community. Cooperative communities, acting with a consensus and common goals, will coordinate their childbearing for the benefit of all and the cooperative society.

One interesting if minor similarity between us and the social insects is our current dependence to some degree upon "elites." Here "elite" is not a status designation. Among social insects, all individuals even within the same caste are not equally active or productive. "Some individuals, referred to by entomologists as the elites, are unusually active, perform more than their share of lifetime work, and incite others to work though facilitation" Wilson noted (1975, p. 549). The remaining ants or bees are "consistently sluggish" and their lifetime output of energy and services to the colony or hive is a small fraction of that of the elites. I would not describe the average human as sluggish, however, we can be energetic in pursuit of our own goals. We do have human "elites" who express themselves in many ways including organizing community action groups, starting and operating various organizations, creating and inventing useful devices and practices, motivating others to action and quality performances, and so forth. Here is the "leadership" quality Americans highly prize.

Once an insect species evolves into what Wilson calls "eusociality," cooperation from our perspective, it can continue to advance in colonial organization by increasing the numbers and degree of specialization of the worker castes and by enlarging the communication code colony members use to coordinate their activities. Wilson suggests the social insects' evolutionary pattern is toward an ever-increasing number of specialized insect castes until there is one for each task. This progressive differentiation and complexity with its increased demands for integration, including more precise and complex communications, is the hallmark of all evolving and growing societies, including human. It is evidence of an ever more refined fit between the social species and its environment, including an ever improving capacity to track the changes in the environment. In humans it is marked by a constantly expanding culture with more and more information, technology, divisions of labor and specialization. Of the ant's evolutionary trend, Wilson (1975) declares, "It is fair to say that as an ecological strategy eusociality [among social insects] has been overwhelmingly successful" (p. 399). As cooperation will be for us.

Nonmammalian Social Vertebrates

Now we come to our own evolutionary family tree. Non mammalian social vertebrates are not one of the pinnacles of animal social evolution but we need to appreciate them in order to understand our own evolutionary roots. First we will look at the level of social evolution among nonmammalian vertebrates and then the mammals. In general, among vertebrates, true cooperation is found only in rare cases among humans. Individualistic and competitive behavior predominate and with them individualistic and competitive mutual aid. Elements of cooperation are found, however, among the most socially advanced mammalian primates and canids, indicating the general direction social evolution is taking among these animals. Among all social vertebrates, competitive dominance hierarchies have always been the predominant form of social organization, from the chicken's famous pecking order to humans' warlord-style dictatorships.

The sociobiology of our vertebrate, including mammalian, relatives has nothing to teach us about how to cooperate. But it does show where we came from as we evolved and why we have so much to learn before we achieve cooperative societies. Our ancestors didn't provide us with much help. This is another obstacle we must overcome on our path toward cooperative societies. Also, some of the presented social behavior patterns are frequently given mistakenly as examples of cooperation. Learning to recognize these social patterns as mutual aid and not cooperation is an important advance in our understanding of what is and is not true cooperation. It is also helpful for us to understand where we are in our own social evolution. If we master true cooperation, it will be an evolutionary break-through for mammals and vertebrates in general.

Schooling Among Fish

Fish schools are a good example of the advantages of simply banding or aggregating together in larger numbers. While most animal species operate in a two dimensional plane, fish—and flying birds—operate in three dimensions as they swim through the water—or fly through the air—giving their social organization unique features. Fish schools have no leaders, as we think of them, and appear to have no dominance hierarchies. Whichever fish are in the front when the school turns in a given direction become the "leaders." We have all marveled at the beauty and precision of the movements of large schools of fish as they wheel and reverse directions, catching the light in various ways, giving us an ever changing spectacle. These movements and formations, however, vary and are determined by whether the school is traveling, feeding, resting, or defending itself, and the hydro-dynamics of water itself.

One advantage to the fish in schooling is energy conservation. Like birds flying in formation and racing cars tailgating, fish, too, space themselves in the school to take advantage of the dying vortices of water turbulence around their neighbors, utilizing the energy expended by school mates to make swimming easier and even coasting short distances. In cold water schooling helps keep the fish warmer. They tend to be more compact in the front and scattered in back due to the lower levels of oxygen in the water. They are tightest in formation when well fed. To move as a well-coordinated unit, the school is generally composed of fish of the same species and about the same size. Fish too small will be too slow and move in patterns that are suited for its smaller length; fish too large will be too fast and swoop too wide.

Defense is another reason to school. The school as a whole, with its multitude of eyes, lateral lines, and other sensory organs can detect preda-tors more quickly and respond more effectively than the individual fish can. Most schools of fish spring away as a unit at a sharp angle to the original course when attacked or alarmed. Some will form a circle around the preda-tor. Just sheer numbers provide important survival value for individuals in the school; predators can only grab one or a few at a time leaving the rest—especially those in the center—of the school alive. The rapid movement of the school can confuse and over excite predators. In some cases schools will shrink tightly to provide fewer points of contact and make discerning indi-vidual fish more difficult. Experiments have shown that pike are less suc-cessful when attacking schools of perch than when pursuing solitary perch. As one might expect, it doesn't take long for the individual fish to "figure out" that the center of the school is the safest place; there is a constant "roll-ing inward of the vanguard" as the school progresses.

The individual fish can improve their success in feeding by schooling. They can pool their discoveries and previous experiences when their food is unpredictably distributed. This outweighs the disadvantages of competi-tion among school members over food. Some predators, who have no fear of predation themselves, school when searching for food for this reason. Newcomers to the school take their searching cues from the rest of the school and learn to contribute quickly (Wilson, 1975, pp. 438-442).

Schooling, as befits basic vertebrate self-centeredness, is primarily individualistic mutual-aid involving energy conservation, protection, and location of food. It might be considered competitive mutual-aid when individual fish ordinarily competing for food school in order to find food in the first place.

Of Frog Choirs and Pelicans

Here are some charming additional illustrations in passing of individualistic and competitive mutual aid among our nonmammalian vertebrate relatives. Male frogs form choruses to attract mates. These choruses are far louder—as you have no doubt noticed if you live near frog ponds—more continuous and last longer than single males can sustain, improving each male's chance of mating. Some species have rather well organized choirs, such as the *Similisca baudini*, composed of four pairs of males, each pair acting as a duet, alternating, and all eight singing a different note (Wilson, 1975, pp. 442-444).

This is mostly competitive mutual-aid since frogs competing for mates band together to act in a way that increases dramatically the chances of any and all of them finding mates. What happens when the females show up? As we might expect, there is a dominance hierarchy among frogs in the chorus with the dominant male initiating the singing and enjoying the most success in mating.

Pelicans may form a half-circle at the mouth of a bay, and then swim together toward the shore, herding the fish before them, feeding on the trapped fish. This can be both individualistic and competitive mutual aid. Cranes practice a more coordinated form of mutual-aid. Cranes, like many bird societies, keep sentries to warn them of danger. If a hunter succeeds in surprising and flushing them into flight, they will not return to that spot without first sending out a scout to reconnoiter. If that scout returns and presumably communicates everything is all clear, a party of scouts is sent to confirm, and then a second party of scouts to make doubly sure (Kropotkin, 1987. pp. 36, 38).

Mutual aid is a powerful adaptive tool. It is worth considering, as Kropotkin (1987, p. 26) suggests, how ducks, which practice mutual aid in their flocks, fare so well and occupy so many areas of the earth despite the fact they are delicious fare for many predators and not well suited for aggression or self-defense.

Nonhuman Social Mammals

The nonhuman social mammals form the third pinnacle of social evolution according to Wilson. Mutual aid among social mammals takes several common forms. They engage in individualistic mutual aid, for example, to rear the young, aid the hurt, sick or disabled, and to hunt. Although they are generally competitive when it comes to consumption of food and captured prey, some species reserve food for the young and needy. They engage in competitive mutual aid to improve their competitive success against other animals of the same or different species, as in protecting their territory, or forming alliances and cliques to improve or maintain their rank in the competitive dominance hierarchy, and to defend against predators that threaten them all. These are not examples of cooperation even though considerable skill in coordination may be required, such as in the hunt. (It is important to remember that not all forms of social coordination are cooperation. Bureaucratic hierarchical coordination, such as is common in American government and most of our large businesses, is not cooperation.)

There are many remarkable forms of mutual aid among nonhuman social mammals. We will look at wolves as an example of the higher levels of social coordination found among these species that exhibit elements of cooperation. We will look at chimpanzees when we explore the emergence of empathy, morality, and elementary cultures.

Remember that any group organized around a competitive dominance hierarchy is not cooperative, no matter how amazing the level of coordination and accomplishment may be. All the nonhuman social mammals I'm aware of operate with a competitive dominance hierarchy. Females dominate in some species such as elephants, hyenas, and meerkats. Males dominate in most species such as deer herds, wolf packs, lion prides, and chimpanzee troops. The dominant animal gets first choice of resting places, mates, food, and leads and disciplines the group. Battling for dominance and higher rank in the hierarchy is an ongoing social activity among social mammals, including competitive humans. It is also important to remember that cooperation is a *group* property. Individuals do not cooperate, groups cooperate. There is no such thing as a "cooperative" individual.

Wolves

Farley Mowat (1979, 140-145) tells one of my favorite stories about wolf pack life. It's a story about how wolves train their pups to hunt and shows the level of coordination and planning they are capable of. The wolf pack Mowat was observing was composed of mother, father, four pups, an "uncle," and an unidentified male that had recently attached himself to the family. The alpha male, father, roused the female from a nap, and together they rounded up the other two adult males and the four pups and headed out to where a herd of about 200 caribou were moving leisurely through a broad valley. On a ridge above the valley, the wolves formed a circle and howled together. Then the female, the uncle, and the other male headed down through the herd of caribou that paid no attention to them. Father stayed on the ridge with the four pups. The three adults picked their way casually through the herd to the mouth of the valley and then turned and spread out and started herding the caribou back toward the ridge where father and the pups waited concealed.

Now the caribou knew something was up and became anxious. The three wolves were good at keeping the caribou moving back in the direction they had come from, herding them expertly, allowing a few to spill over the wings of their drive. When they were close to the ridge the three adults focused on a smaller herd of a dozen does and seven fawns. They herded this little group on the run close by the father and pups' hiding place on the ridge. The father and the pups jumped from concealment upon the surprised and thoroughly frightened herd of does and fawns, and took up the chase. Meanwhile the three adults jogged up to the ridge, laid down, and rested while watching the pups.

Once each of the four pups picked out a caribou to attack; the father slowed down and just watched. The pups were all running full out, giving it all they had and trying to deal with the caribou, which were zigging, zagging, and generally confusing the pups. The pups turned out to be no match for the caribou who dodged and out ran them, leaving the pups to drag themselves panting back to the ridge to collapse. The whole scenario was a planned and well-orchestrated hunting exercise for the wolf pups. This pattern of ambush and the well coordinated planning of the hunt are common in wolves (Wilson, 1975, p. 505).

In this particular exercise, we see some elements of cooperation. The wolves had a temporary group goal of giving the pups a lesson in caribou hunting. They had a consensus on what they were doing and how to do it. There was a division of labor and each wolf performed the given role. However, the operation was initiated and supervised by the alpha male as part of his role in the wolf pack competitive dominance hierarchy.

Self-Awareness, Empathy, and the Roots of Moral Community Among Chimpanzees

Self-awareness is another major evolutionary development—along with intelligence, complex communications and culture—that distinguishes humans from other animals. Self-awareness changes the landscape of social interactions considerably. It may come as a shock to many that we share self-awareness with the chimpanzees and the orangutans. We probably shared it with others of the *Homo* genus now extinct as well. Chimpanzees and orangutans appear, for the moment, to be the only other animals besides humans who are self-aware. The primatologist Frans de Waal cautions that other species may be more self-aware than we realize because they use other senses to distinguish self and others, such as smell—dogs and cats—and sound—bats.

De Waal (1996) described a set of experiments among primates using mirrors that revealed the dramatic differences in responses to seeing one's own image between primates that are self-aware and those that are not (pp. 66-71). When most primates, such as monkeys, are given mirrors to look into, they treat their reflection as a "stranger of their own sex and species," according to de Waal (1996, p. 68). Orangutans and Chimpanzees, however, are aware that what they see is themselves. They make faces. They hold the mirror so they can see other parts of their bodies such as their behinds and genitalia. They hold up objects around them to see how it looks in the mirror, checking between the object and the mirror. They may adorn themselves with various things such as vines and vegetables, evaluating their appearance in the mirror. In one telling experiment, chimpanzees were unknowingly given a dot of paint on the face just above the eyebrow. "Guided by their reflection, chimpanzees and orangutans—as well as children more than eighteen months of age—rubbed the painted spot with their hand and inspected the fingers that touched it, recognizing that the coloring of the reflected image was on their own face," de Waal reported (1996, p. 68). Other primates and younger human children failed to do this. Of significance for cooperation, cognitive empathy appears at about the same time as mirror self recognition in human children (de Waal, 1996, p. 70).

One of mankind's key qualities is self-awareness or reflexiveness, the ability to see oneself as an object with properties, experiences, feelings, and behaviors. It is the source of our self-image and self-esteem. We are aware of self, other, separateness. It is the key to our ability to be empathic and sympathetic with others. We are able to see ourselves in them, to know how we feel in those situations. It also contributes to human's sophisticated levels of social interaction. We are able to understand and anticipate others' actions in given situations, shaping our behavior to accord with—or take advantage of—theirs. And it makes our behavior predictable to others. This is essential for the complex social systems we have developed to function well and remain stable.

Self-awareness is also an underpinning of our morality. Most of what we call "moral" has to do with paying attention to the consequences of our actions for others, for the community, and often for the environment. We have to see ourselves as others do and evaluate our actions from the point of view of members of our family or group and the consensus of our community—what George Herbert Mead called the "generalized other." The Golden Rule—Do unto others as you would have them do unto you—captures beautifully the special social capacities that self awareness grants us; and also tells us to use those capacities constructively.

There is also a negative side to our self-awareness. Chimps—and humans—often use the knowledge of other's behavior to trick, attack, or in other ways harm them. De Waal (1996, p. 85) also describes "harm-joy" behavior in chimps and humans, where we laugh and find joy in other's misfortunes. A more benign example is our enjoyment of slapstick comedy.

At the same time that there are many conflicts and often violence among chimpanzees, they also have well-developed social patterns for reconciliation that de Waal finds lacking in human societies (de Waal, 1996, p. 193-208).

Self-awareness is one of the most important reasons the chimps—and not wolves, macaques, or gorillas—are at the peak of the third pinnacle of social evolution.

What Noble Savage?

De Waal is troubled—as I am—with our individualistic society's lack of grasp of the social whole. He expresses disdain for our Occidental culture's "long standing love affair with personal autonomy." Based on his years of primate studies, de Waal (1996) rejects with disgust our society's individu-

alistic notions of autonomous humans who are rational and mutually disin-
terested parties constructing contracts and relationships (pp. 166-173). De
Waal sees the philosophical foundations of our individualism as a ridiculous fantasy totally incompatible with our primate nature and origins.

> A morality exclusively concerned with individual rights tends to ig-
> nore the ties, needs, and interdependencies that have marked our
> existence from the very beginning. It is a cold morality that puts
> space between people, assigning each person to his or her own little
> corner of the universe (p. 167).

In a wonderful insight, de Waal (1996) recognized that morality is an
expression of community.

> Human morality can be looked at as community concern made ex-
> plicit to the fullest degree. The higher a species' level of social aware-
> ness, the more completely its members realize how events around
> them ricochet through the community until they land at their own
> doorstep (p. 207).

HUMANS

We humans occupy a pinnacle all by ourselves according to Wilson
(1975, p. 380).

> Human beings remain essentially vertebrate in their social struc-
> ture. But they have carried it to a level of complexity so high as to
> constitute a distinct, fourth pinnacle of social evolution. They have
> broken the old vertebrate restraints not by reducing selfishness, but
> rather by acquiring the intelligence to consult the past and to plan
> the future.

Humans make long-remembered contracts. We are "preoccupied with
kinship ties to a degree inconceivable in other social species" (p. 380). Gene-
alogy is a passion with many humans and their societies. We have a "unique
syntactical language" that allows us to exceed all other species in our power
of communication. Our rich and vast cultures and complex organizations
are powerful marvels. Despite all of this, as Wilson points out, we have yet
to escape some of the social limitations of being vertebrate mammals.

Humans Are Cooperation Challenged Vertebrates

As we can see, cooperation in various forms and degrees is natural. It
has emerged repeatedly during evolution among the social invertebrates,
such as the ants, termites and *Nanomia*. We can see elements of cooperation in the social behavior of the most advanced mammals. Unfortunately
for us, cooperation—cooperatively organized groups and colonies—has not

yet evolved within our evolutionary branch. Not only do vertebrates lack cooperative social groups, they have produced fewer highly social species overall compared with the invertebrates (Wilson, 1975, p. 380). Instead, we humans are stuck with the common competitive dominance hierarchy style of social organization of our mammalian relatives.

Consequently, if we humans are to become truly cooperative, we are going to have to take the initiative, use our intelligence, and construct cooperative cultures ourselves. The amazing thing is we can; our evolutionary gifts of intelligence and culture are just what we need to do the job. We are not going to have to start from scratch trying to figure out what cooperation is all about, either. The cooperative invertebrates show us a number of key cooperative components we need. We examine the cooperative gifts to us from the invertebrates in the next chapter, and take an in depth look at culture and other necessary social tools for constructing true cooperative social systems in Part 2 . Now, let's take a look at the challenges our unprogrammed intelligence presents us.

The Challenges of Unprogrammed Intelligence in Humans

"Intelligence," as biologists use the word, is a capacity. It is not content, and here lies the "rub" as Shakespeare would say. Intelligence is found to some degree in a variety of vertebrates, such as some birds, dogs, cats, elephants, dolphins and chimpanzees, and some invertebrates, such as octopi. To have "intelligence" means to be free of genetic programmed behavior or early hardwired behavior in the sphere intelligence is operating. "Intelligence" means the animal can learn from its experiences, remember what it has learned, change its behavior accordingly, and anticipate what is going to happen. The animal's "picture" of the world is not fixed but changes with trial and error testing of what it has learned and incorporates new experiences. Intelligent animals can change their behavior patterns anytime their learning indicates. The species that adapt fastest to changes and opportunities in the environment are the species that survive and prosper. Intelligent species can change very fast compared with those species that are not intelligent, hundreds of times faster than those dependent upon the natural selection of more effective behavioral genetics for their adaptation. Coupling our high level of individual intelligence with a well-tuned culture and cooperation would make us the most amazingly successful adaptive species ever.

There is a "but" in this otherwise glorious picture of intelligence for humans. We have intelligence and we can learn and change and adapt very fast.

But intelligence does not give us automatically accurate content. We can misinterpret what we see. We may make incorrect connections between cause and effect. We may develop habitual ways of dealing with things that may have worked once upon a time but don't any longer. Humans can adapt faster and more successfully than other species on a much broader environmental horizon *only* to the degree our information is accurate, is constantly checked and modified to remain accurate, our coping patterns are correct and continually updated, and to the degree we skillfully execute those coping patterns. Sometimes we do well, sometimes we don't, and sometimes we are disastrously wrong. And too often we are bull-headedly determined not to change those erroneous ideas. For humans, intelligence is a mixed blessing. We have fumbled and bumbled our way to our present condition of being on the brink of both self-extinction and adaptive glory.

It is enough of a challenge to try to accurately fill our empty human heads with correct information and useful coping patterns and skills generation after generation, but we are currently struggling to do this through the destructive social battlefield of our individualism and competition. Both create confusion and conflict over what is and what to do about it, for control over the means and benefits, and over which "authorities" to listen to or reject. The debate and battles for preeminence of one's ideas and beliefs are added to the battles for dominance and control of the material world. The vigorous battle over global warming is a good example. The solution is to replace competition and individualism with cooperation. We must work together rather than against each other. Our science and technology can then guide us in creating and maintaining a constantly self-correcting body of information, techniques, and skills. All we have to do is just change our intelligent "minds" and do it.

Nature's cooperative gifts to us come primarily from the social insects, the ants and termites, but also from the larger perspective of adaptive, evolving life on Earth. The following chapter details these gifts that make it possible for humans to begin cooperating in this generation. Who knows how long it would have taken us to figure out how to truly cooperate on our own. We would likely be stuck on individualistic and competitive mutual aid and dominance hierarchies for a long time to come.

John Steinbeck in *The Log from the Sea of Cortez* (N.Y.: Bantam, 1971, p. 218) made a wonderful observation:

> ... all life is relational.... One merges into another, groups melt into ecological groups ... And the units nestle into the whole and are inseparable from it ... one can come back to the microscope and the tide pool and the aquarium. But the little animals are found to be changed, no longer set apart and alone. And it is a strange thing that most of the feeling we call religious, most of the mystical outcrying which is one of the most prized and used and desired reactions of our species, is really the understanding and the attempt to say that man is related to the whole thing, related inextricably to all reality, known and unknowable. This is a simple thing to say, but the profound feeling of it made a Jesus, a St. Augustine, a St Francis, a Roger Bacon, a Charles Darwin, and an Einstein. Each of them in his own tempo and with his own voice discovered and reaffirmed with astonishment the knowledge that all things are one thing and one thing is all things.

Chapter 5. Natures Gift: Elements Of Cooperation

Nature and the social insects in particular give us some essential elements of cooperation we can adapt for use in our social systems as cooperative adaptive tools. Since we humans have so little experience with cooperative cultures and social systems, we are fortunate to have these evolution and time tested techniques to add to our own. These tools show us how to think about and use our social systems adaptively, as our unit of action for coping with life and living. They help us move beyond our current fixation with personal advancement, competitive triumphs and self aggrandizement to work together as a functioning social unit.

When I was searching for the elements of cooperation, one of the biggest problems was finding a truly cooperative common group goal. It had to be one that could be used by any and all groups wishing to be cooperative, even whole societies. I could not find one among the many American corporate mission statements, communal communities, research findings and other sources I examined. In retrospect, that shouldn't have been surprising. Why would I expect to find a key component of true cooperation in organizations operating in a competitive individualist society? I didn't appreciate the Hutterites or the scientists of Section T of OSRD until after I discovered the common group goal I was looking for. Then I realized they each had a version of the adaptive cooperative common group goal suited to their culture and purposes.

My focus on adaptation came only after I finally turned to sociobiology and the study of social animals. Then I was able to step out of the "box" of our American competitive individualistic culture and see that the proper use of our cultures and social systems is to adapt to our ever changing environment. This purpose, this goal, is built into the nature of things. We've just been oblivious to it. All of the American groups and organizations I looked at—with the exception of the Hutterites and Section T of OSRD—lacked insight into the social system as a cooperative adaptive operation. Instead, they reflected the commercial, competitive capitalistic and democratic values of our society.

The Fundamental Common Group Goal

The essential first step toward creating cooperative human societies is recognizing there is a fundamental common group goal for cooperation that is the same for all cooperative social species. This goal is inherent in the nature of evolving life on Earth and clearly states the purpose of any cooperative community. *The common group goal is continual adaptation to conditions and changes in the environment as a social system.*

This goal is incorporated into the definition of cooperation I gave in Chapter 1: "Pursuing the group goal of adaptive success for the group as a social system." The cooperative social system is organized to operate as a unit to maximize the adaptive wellbeing of the participants composing it and to evolve and adapt as social system. This is true whether the group is a colony, clan, community, organization, society, or an entire civilization. All of the individual participants in a cooperative social system embrace this goal as the guide to their daily behavior, social interaction, and decision making. It is the foundation of their consensus.

There are common, shared, goals in individualistic mutual aid and competitive mutual aid that guide individual behavior in those efforts, but they are not group goals, they are personal, individual, and interest group goals that happen to be the same, shared, for the moment.

How do we do this? How to we pursue this common group goal of adaptive success as a social system? The social insects, especially the cooperative "eusocial" ants (as E. O. Wilson labels them), give us four key techniques: 1) utilizing the group as an environmental tracking device, 2) continually optimizing the match between the group's social structure/social processes and the environment, 3) recruit competent participants and enhance their performances, and 4) using coordinating hierarchies with few layers instead of multilayered dominance hierarchies. We explore each of these in turn.

Cooperative Groups Act as Environmental Tracking Devices

A key element in the fundamental group goal of cooperative social systems is the accurate and continual tracking of what is going on in the environment. Wilson (1975) observed, "Social behavior, like all other forms of biological response, is a set of devices for tracking changes in the environment" (p. 144). Tracking means picking up correct information from the environment and acting effectively—adaptively—on that information. Wilson places animals' responses to the environment on a continuum from biochemical reactions in their cells that take microseconds to social devices that can take as long as a generation or more to respond. The social devices include modifying genetically determined behavior, which can take generations; refining morphological specialization, such as the development of newborn ants into new variants of workers, warriors and queens; and learning new behavior through socialization or directly from the environment. The latter is by far the fastest.

Our human social tracking devices and their uses are very uneven, too frequently contaminated by personal ambition and competitive struggles. On the one hand, we have scientific research, new technologies, and various efforts to monitor trends and changes in our environment that are effective trackers. The Centers for Disease Control works hard to track diseases in our country. There are monitoring services watching weather, earth quake and tsunami threats. We routinely monitor our industrial production and economic trends. We are watching extinction threats to various species in many places in the world.

On the other hand, we have trouble coordinating our tracking efforts and responses effectively. Instead of cooperating, we tend to compete with one another, including debating who is right about what changes have occurred and what to do about them. The vigorous debates over global warming are an example. Battles over which species to save and how much to spend are ongoing. We are also too often preoccupied with self-centered pursuit of our own well-being and comfort and don't pay attention to changes in our environment, leaving the well being of society as a whole unattended. We too often wait for crises to jolt our attention back to our environment and what is going on in the larger world instead of tracking and anticipating problems. (Anticipation of what is going to happen is a mark of intelligence.) The subprime mortgage market and derivatives generated economic crisis had to smash us hard before we decided to pay attention and try to regulate these activities, something we should have done in anticipation of just such a boom—bust tragedy. A fully cooperative civilization would not have a subprime mortgage market or derivatives and similar financial gimmicks. In one form of mature cooperative society, there is no "economy" as we think of it, and no internal use of money, thus there are no financial institutions. Participants are given homes and other necessities as part of the cooperative adaptive process. (See Chapters 17 and 18 for details.) We are not using our society as an environmental tracking device effectively and that is costing us extravagantly as we fail again and again to anticipate and adapt promptly to serious environmental—internal and external—changes. This tracking includes keeping track of changes in and actions by various societies and cultures around the world.

We humans also have a bad habit of preserving cultures and their social systems even though they are no longer tracking effectively. Some of our religions, political ideologies, customs, economic systems, and forms of government are examples. These maladaptive efforts to preserve outmoded cultures and social systems are often justified in the name of "tradition." Sometimes the effort is to preserve the competitive dominance and wealth of the current people in control. This freezing of cultural communities instead of allowing continual adaptive transformations contributes to the decline of civilizations and the well-being of participants. Tracking devices either track effectively or gradually die out, eventually selected out of the evolutionary flow. Cooperation will use our intelligence and culture to get us on and keep us on track.

Optimizing Group Social Structure for Adaptive Success

The information collected by the cooperative community acting as an environmental tracking device is applied to the community's culture and social structures/social processes. Changes are made to produce and maintain a match between the group's social structure and the environment to optimize adaptive success.

E. O. Wilson (1975) points out that the primary "goal" of the individual cooperative social insect or other colonial invertebrate is "the optimization of group structure" (pp. 380-382). This goal seeks to improve and maximize the adaptive and survival success of the species by optimizing the current fit between their social structures, their social processes, and the ever changing environment. This is a fundamental component of the cooperative group goal.

The evolutionary trend among cooperative "eusocial" ants Wilson described (see Chapter 4) with ever more refined and complex morphological specialization to fill environmental niches is an example. The modification of how many of which specialists are bred and nurtured among the ants, such as more workers or fast track development of soldiers, is another example of responding to changes and conditions in the environment.

If we had the ants' "goal," we would be constantly aware of how well our social processes are working and ready to adapt where needed for the advancement of the colony as a social system. Japanese management techniques, such as "kaizen," include paying attention to the processes involved in producing particular products or services in an effort to constantly improve and refine them and make them more effective. (See Chapters 11 and 16 for more details.) The employees are often improving the social structure/ environment fit by so doing. In cooperative social systems, this would be done "on the run," so to speak, as part of the daily social operations. This is one of the skills and responsibilities required of cooperative group participants. No committee meetings, no administrative decisions, no legislations, just adaptive action by skilled participants.

The Hutterites' continual adaptive responses to their economic activities, including more refined machinery, advanced seeds and breeds of livestock, and efforts to keep abreast of the latest developments in farming and markets are an example of a human community working to optimize their social structure/environment fit. The scientists of Section T of OSRD had very fluid responses to changes in the problems and level of development of the fuses, easily changing the focus of effort, the "leaders" or coordinators, and the specialties of the participants as needed. That kind of easy and effective change in social structure/processes as required to fit the ongoing situation is characteristic of cooperative social systems.

Unfortunately, the typical human has no concept of what an optimized group structure for cooperative, adaptive human groups would be like. Such group structure as emerges among social vertebrates is usually the result of individual competition for dominance and control. This is generally true of human groups as well. Individualistic and competitive Americans, even in our advanced complex civilizations, rarely pay attention to optimizing group social structure for our collective adaptive survival and that of our society. Many of us have a hard time even seeing group social structure clearly and knowing what to do with it when we do. (This was one of the goals of teaching introductory sociology when I was a professor, to help students see this, to become aware of what is all around them. It was a challenge for many.) (Part 2 provides more detail and examples that show what social structure is and how it is used, changed, and maintained.)

The daily news provides us with running accounts of the "mismatches of the day," so to speak. Some of our social structure—environment mismatches are chronic. These include our health care needs and what our society is providing, the survival needs of Americans and our system's inability to provide adequate housing, food, and other necessities reliably for all, mismatches between the levels of education and training our changing economy needs and our educational programs, mismatches between what our citizens need to know and what they are being taught at home and at school, mismatches between population growth and carrying capacity of our environment, mismatches between what our society teaches us to desire and what the environment can provide such as fresh sea food, sources of energy, enough lumber and metals and other materials for our products, mismatches between clean water supplies and what our growing high-tech societies require, mismatches between what we need from immigrants and what we are getting and how to deal with it, and on and on. If we watch the news on our ongoing wars, we find slow responses by our military to conditions and changes in the enemy's actions. The long delay between the appearance of deadly roadside bombs and the provision of vehicles armored adequately to protect our soldiers was costly in human lives and typical of the way our American social systems operate.

It is hard to find an example of prompt and effective adaptive changes in social structure in response to environmental changes in our society. It takes some getting used to, but our society was not socially constructed to solve problems. Chronic mismatches between changes in the environment and our society's responses are inherent in our adversarial competitive and self-centered individualistic sociocultural system. It cannot be "fixed," only abandoned for something better. This alone is reason enough to abandon our competitive individualistic culture and make the paradigm shift to true cooperation.

It is important to remember that there is no one social structure that is "one-size-fits-all." If you set up a complex organization bureaucratically, rigidly, and hope to be a rapidly adapting social system, you are in for a lot of disappointment. The social structure itself must change in response to environmental and conditional changes for adaptation and ongoing optimization of group structure to occur.

COMPETENCE AND THE TAKE-OFF THRESHOLD FOR COOPERATION

THE ROLE OF COMPETENCE IN COOPERATION

Cooperation by itself is no guarantee of success; the individuals cooperating must be competent for the cooperative social system to be effective. Bert Holldobler and Edward O. Wilson (1990, p. 356-357) in their Pulitzer Prize winning definitive book, *Ants*, describe a mathematical curve relating individual ant competence to the success of the ant colony. Below a certain level of individual competence, ants working together accomplish less than ants working alone. In a very simple example, two not very competent nurse ants trying to move the same larva may find themselves pushing and pulling against each other and generally accomplishing less than one ant could by itself. As individual competence improves, however, there is a critical point on the curve when working together dramatically improves the colony success over what it would be with each ant working independently. At this higher level of competence, "colony-level [natural] selection favors cooperative behavior" over independent behavior for each ant (Holldobler and Wilson, 1990, p. 356, insert mine).

Research shows that the ant colony can come together and cooperate successfully *only* above a certain level of individual competence. Individual competence is a prerequisite for adaptive cooperation. At the same time, once a certain level of individual competence is reached, cooperation can greatly enhance the capacities and success of the group compared with acting alone.

As humans, we would expect that the more competent and highly trained people are, the more they will benefit from cooperating compared with acting individualistically. The participants must all be well trained and competent or cooperation is not likely to occur or be successful. It has been commonly assumed that living communally and trying to be more "cooperative" will automatically produce success. But one of the main reasons intentional communities fail is that the participants do not have the competence—the skills—to produce a self-supporting community. Competence and cooperation are inseparably linked. Among the Hutterites, the most successful cooperative communal society in America at this time, great effort is expended to acquire and maintain competence in assigned areas of responsibility. They are, in fact, frequent innovators in farming techniques and machinery. (See Chapter 3.)

Alexis de Tocqueville, the famous 19th century French observer of America's formative period, whom we meet in the next chapter, observed that individualism worked fine in early America as long as people had the competence to provide for themselves the rather low-tech tools and equipment, and the survival skills they needed. They didn't really need to cooperate at the more advanced level we're exploring. Minimal individualistic mutual aid was sufficient. But as technologies emerged and advanced, specialization was required and working together in an interdependent division of labor became necessary. Training and finding enough skilled workers to fill all of the positions in our continually expanding division of labor is an ongoing problem in America. This makes it harder to produce cooperative organizations and a cooperative society.

THE TRANSFORMING BLEND OF COMPETENCE AND COOPERATION

The nature of the ant colony actually changes once this threshold of competence is high enough for cooperation to take off. The colony becomes something much more than the sum of its parts and can accomplish things not possible by a collection of individual ants. The individual ant, depending upon species, may have a repertoire of only 20 to 45 separate acts it can perform. When these actions are all put together in a colony involving a large number of competent workers, "the whole pattern that emerges is strikingly different and more complicated in form, as well as more precise in execution" than that of ants acting individually, according to Holldobler and Wilson (1990, p. 358).

> The cooperative ants have even anticipated occasional failure of some members in the way the colonies are organized. They have developed a redundancy of ants with appropriate skills and functions within each task system; an approach engineers call 'series-parallel operations,' so that breakdown in one unit, or ant, will not cause failure of the whole (Holldobler and Wilson, 1990, p. 356-357).

Clever little creatures, aren't they?

In our human social experiments, the profoundly different and more effective social patterns of the social insects' cooperative social systems are found extremely rarely and then are relatively short-lived. Competitive individualistic Americans practicing mutual aid such as our voluntary associations have a hard time even comprehending true cooperation. Most of us are going to have to experience it to fully understand. Once we get started with cooperation, it is going to take on a life of its own. New, more complex and effective social patterns and competencies will emerge and transform our communities as they evolve toward their full, yet unknown, cooperative potentials. Who could have predicted that electrifying the country could lead to the technological miracles it has in just a century. Cooperation will be like that.

At this level, cooperation produces a very fast responding interdependent social system. Much like an organism, it cannot have weak links, lazy or irresponsible participants, incompetents, or free-riders undermining coordinated efforts. Perhaps it's easier to see in a machine like an automobile. We can all appreciate that a well built and engineered car with top of the line components will run better, longer, safer, and be fun to drive. Start switching in low quality, inadequate, poorly engineered, worn out parts and the performance of the whole is diminished considerably. But when all the parts are high quality and in place, wow!

COOPERATION AND SOCIAL HIERARCHIES

During this time of rapid social change into the Information Age, there is a trend away from the pyramid shaped, multilayered hierarchies commanded from the top down that Edward Lawler, a prominent professor of management and organization (1992, p.25), calls the "control-oriented approach." These characterized our industrial companies after the Civil War and peaked in the 1950s and 1960s but still predominate. As organizations engaged in information creation and processing by experts become more widespread, flatter forms of organization with fewer levels of hierarchy and different coordination patterns are emerging. The ants are already where we seem to be heading. Their cooperative organization of competent participants does not require the tight control and supervision provided by multilayer hierarchies.

According to Wilson (1975, p. 11), social species have two forms of hierarchies, those with and without dominance. The hierarchy without dominance coordinates activities to achieve the goals of the cooperative colony as a whole. Which hierarchy a social species uses is an indicator of how advanced they are. At the lowest level is the simple dominance hierarchy such as most social mammals practice. The dominant male or female rules the pack, troop, or herd primarily with force. At the highest level are the social species with a nondominant hierarchy used solely to coordinate the cooperative activities of competent individual members in complex ways, such as the social insects. Human societies are dominated by dominance hierarchies. Coordinating hierarchies without dominance are still comparatively rare and never pure. The scientists of Section T of OSRD come closest to this ideal. The Hutterites are mixed, with their religious organization and much of the community division of labor organized around a dominance hierarchy with their preacher at the top.

DOMINANCE HIERARCHIES

Dominance hierarchies are described by Wilson (1975, p. 11) as "in ordinary sociobiolgical usage, the dominance of one member of a group over another, as measured by superiority in aggressive encounters and order of access to food, mates, nesting sites and other objects promoting survivorship and reproductive fitness." Note that the "survivorship" and "reproductive fitness" promoted by dominance hierarchies are those of the dominant animal(s), of a particular individual or of a few individuals near the top, not of the animal social community as a whole. They are based upon competition.

Dominance hierarchies are found in all noncooperative social species, usually centering on aggressive efforts to control access to food, sex, reproduction and territories (Wilson, 1975, p. 279-297). The highest social insects with queens and sexually celibate workers have solved the problem of competition for sex and reproductive advantage, and thus have eliminated one major source of dominance hierarchies in animal societies. The "queen"—despite our anthropomorphic label for her—does not rule or dominate the mature nest; she has morphologically specialized to become the reproductive unit. Dominance hierarchies are virtually the only form of social organization exhibited by many social species including the mammals. Once the dominance hierarchy is settled, a particular band, flock, pack or herd seems to be more or less at peace, until threats to the dominant male or female are made by younger members or threats to the hierarchy are made by newcomers.

Clearly, these dominance hierarchies do not emerge in nature as a means for coordinating complex colony actions. They are not well suited for coordination since their purpose is to maintain individual advantages for the dominant animal(s). They are not designed to solve group problems. While some coordination of group activities generally occurs within dominance hierarchies, the quality of the coordination will always be restricted by the element of dominance. Dominance hierarchies generally do not develop around competence rankings. They are the result of competitions, with the strongest and often most ruthless competitors succeeding. Task oriented coordination suffers if the dominant animal(s)' skills are inadequate and the adaptive success of the social group declines. Dominance hierarchies are not able to track the environment nearly as well as coordinating hierarchies, as the social insects have discovered. Dominance hierarchies are paying much more attention to the internal competitions and social dynamics required for the few to maintain and enjoy dominance.

Dominance hierarchies are generally pretty raw competitive individualism. The "losers" at the bottom of the hierarchy may find themselves getting little of the food, the worst resting places, with little opportunity to reproduce, getting ill and left behind, thus excluded from the herd or band. This is the kind of animal behavior that human admirers have used to justify no-holds-barred competition with presumably only the fittest surviving and ruling the resulting dominance hierarchies such as Social Darwinism that flourished for a time in early industrial America. Such philosophies can only be justified if people also embrace one of the central myths of the culture of competition that competition selects and elevates the "best." Competition only elevates the "best" if the competitive rules and criteria make those competencies the focus of selection. More often it is the best and roughest *competitor* who wins. There are far better ways to encourage people to develop competencies and reward them and integrate them productively into society than through competition generated contests and dominance hierarchies.

It could be suggested that dominance hierarchies involving access to sex and reproduction, as they all do, tend to select "mean-genes" that favor and provide the physical size, strength, "cunning" and other characteristics for aggressive, ruthless, self-centered, dominance behavior.

Mutual aid for particular tasks, such as capturing prey and defense and perhaps den or nest building, is common among the members of the dominance hierarchy. Cooperation does not occur. Remember, "cooperation" as used in this book refers to coordinated activity to further a group goal, such as the adaptive optimization of the group structure. I know of no examples of nonhuman mammalians—and few human mammalians—working to improve the adaptive vitality of their social structure.

Competitive dominance hierarchies can form long chains of descending rank order, such as the famous chicken pecking order wherein the top chicken can peck all others and is pecked by none, the middle chicken gets pecked by the half of the flock above it and can peck the other half below it, and the poor bottom chicken can peck no other chicken but gets pecked by all others. Wilson (1975, p. 23) sees dominance hierarchies, such as the chicken pecking order, as the consequence of aggression among the members of the social unit, the flock in this case. This internal aggression and competition is endemic in virtually all vertebrate, mammalian, and human social groups. The chickens put up with it because they can survive better in a flock than alone. This is, of course, the reason any social animal species submits to a dominance hierarchy.

Dominance hierarchies are still the primary form of social organization among human societies. It should, then, be no surprise when those on the top—presidents, CEO's, etc.—use their position to benefit themselves, often grossly, without regard for how this affects the organization they "run" or the quality of the services and products they produce. You can't create cooperative organizations out of a competition generated dominance hierarchy.

COORDINATION HIERARCHIES WITHOUT DOMINANCE

Hierarchies without dominance are common among social insect colonies and occur marginally among the more socially coordinated mammals such as higher primates and social canids. The most advanced of these animal societies, excluding humans, are usually organized at one or two hierarchical levels made up of individuals tightly connected by relatively few kinds of social bonds and communicative signals (Wilson, 1975, p. 11). These "coordination hierarchies" exist solely to coordinate large numbers of individuals to maintain the entire community or colony.

The nondominant ant colony hierarchy looks something like a human organization turned upside down. "Often [human] hierarchies are run by a central command structure, in other words a 'boss' at the top, but this is not necessary and in fact does not occur in ant colonies," because "the highest level of the ant colony is the totality of its membership rather than a particular set of superordinate individuals who direct the activity of members at lower levels" observed Holldobler and Wilson (1990, p. 355). The *highest* level of the ant colony is the *whole colony* itself, with all of the individuals as an acting, coordinated whole. The stimulation for action starts at the colony level, moves "down" to the caste or group of specialists who will take care of the task, and then "down" to the specific individuals who then carry out the concrete actions required. Wilson calls this a hierarchy of "decomposability" from the whole nest to various task related castes to specific individuals. "Groups of workers specialize as castes for particular tasks, and their activities are subordinated to the needs of the whole colony" said Holldobler and Wilson (1990, p. 355). These specialized castes don't act as chains of command independent of other castes or groups of workers. They don't have separate divisions or departments. They act as a whole at the colony level. Unlike human organizations, the ants use competent specialists to respond to the colony needs as required in a fluid manner.

Ant communications focus on the coordination that more cooperative human organizations strive toward but rarely achieve, such as the "open door" policies of some managers. An individual ant is likely to communicate with any other according to need. "They are open at all times to influence by most or all of the membership of the colony," report Holldobler and Wilson (1990, p. 355). Communications are not hindered by the many levels of hierarchy or parallel hierarchies, as in human organizations. There are multiple pathways of communication from one part of the colony to all others or to the part of the colony that needs to respond, such as from the nursery to the foragers requesting more food of a particular type. This communication seems to ripple through the colony and the response ripples back, such as information or the requested food from the foragers. Holldobler and Wilson (1990, p. 345) call this "pulsative activity," an integrating technique that synchronizes the behavior of the ants through the exchange of relevant information that is current and accurate enough for "critical reliability" in the colonies' actions.

Keeping the whole colony, organization, or community attuned to what's going on and participating in the environmental tracking process is important for cooperation. It is very difficult to do in human groups with our dominance hierarchy styles of organization. Whenever would-be American cooperative groups exceed face-to-face size we tend to lose the capacity to keep the whole group in tune through quick communications. Yet, the ants can do it with huge colonies of individuals, hundreds of thousands. Modern technology holds the promise for creating these quick, ongoing organization wide communications necessary for true cooperation among human organizations. Internet sites or networks could be created that allow individual participants to tune in to what is happening anywhere in the company of consequence for participants' current decision making and actions. As an example, some auto companies show what is happening on the assembly line at various stations on multiscreen TV's so workers can tune their work to one another.

Ants do not recognize each other as individuals or personalities, but rather as nest mates, and in terms of their size and shape denoting their special functions. This makes it easier to determine who can do what and to coordinate actions rapidly without the intrusions of personality differences and "clique" formation that so hinder human hierarchies or the need for "bosses" or supervisors. The closest human organizations come to this is in emergency organizations—hospitals, police, military—with uniforms and badges to identify authority and specialization in emergency situations where the actors may be strangers. But even there, the first act is often to establish who is the ranking authority or boss.

What this all means for the ants is they can "blanket a large area in quick response" as a whole colony, or take the initiative as subunits in the non-dominance, coordinating hierarchy of the nest acting locally as required for the good of the colony (Holldobler and Wilson, 1990, p. 356). Not all actions are colony wide. Specialist castes and individual ants can act for the good of the whole quickly on their own. There is no need for the ants to consult with or await the direction or approval of hierarchical authority. There is no need to wait for committee or legislative decisions. Each ant and ant caste is constantly checking to make sure things are going as they should for the colony's benefit in each ant caste's area of specialization and tracking responsibility. When action is required they have the authority to act with the responsibility to do so quickly and effectively. This is what cooperatively working for the common good is about.

For example, an individual foraging ant—or small group of ants—may come across a food source, such as a small animal carcass. That ant—or group of ants—evaluate the food source in terms of its richness and appropriateness for the needs of the colony, and then lay a pheromone trail to the food that communicates its quality. This is an individual—or small group of specialists—acting alone cooperatively for the good of the colony. Other foragers will follow the trail, perhaps reinforcing it with trails of their own, and harvest the needed nutrients.

In reproduction a complex pattern of information such as pheromones and food type guides the feeding of the queen and treatment of the larvae. This ensures that more, less, or the same number of eggs are laid and treated to become minor workers or to more rapidly develop into major workers or a new queen, as needed. Reproduction and replacement of specialists is not allowed to proceed willy-nilly as in America and human societies in general, but is carefully coordinated to the current makeup and needs of the colony and current environmental conditions. Coordinating reproduction with the current needs of human society is one of the most difficult tasks we will have to master on our road to true cooperation. With modern birth control techniques, it is now possible to match reproduction with current community adaptive needs. Making reproduction a cooperative community planning effort will take some getting used to, but the results will be very beneficial for our adaptive well being.

Pure mutual coordination between competent specialists to do a task required for the good of the whole community—as the ants do—is virtually impossible for competitive individualistic humans in a dominance hierarchy. On the other hand, with the right levels of competence it is quite easy to create an organization with a coordinating hierarchy that operates cooperatively. And it can be fun and exciting to do. The scientists working on the proximity fuse in Section T of OSRD are a successful example. In these cooperative efforts, no dominance hierarchy control is necessary or tolerated. Supervision only occurs to coordinate the efforts of competent specialists and groups of specialists into a coherent action, not on making sure each person "does it right." The job gets done "right" because only highly competent specialized workers are permitted to do the job. These individual specialists and specialized group activities produce a living, coherent whole, functioning as a rapidly adapting, information processing social unit. There are many organizations that could adopt this approach now. Some are heading in that direction as later chapters illustrate.

These four elements provide us with powerful tools for creating cooperative social systems of all kinds. Applying them we can produce new kinds of organizations very different from the ones we are now using. What emerge are highly coordinated, rapidly adapting social systems in which everyone has a place and contributes. Since human communities and organizations are culture-based, they can be changed as fast as we figure out what is happening and how to respond. A cooperative social system is constantly processing information coming in from the environmental tracking activities, checking internal operations, assessing how effectively the current environment is being handled, and assuring that the survival needs of the participants and social system are being met.

CULTURE AND EVOLUTION

Before leaving the topics of sociobiology and evolution, we need to be aware that human biological evolution has not stopped. Indeed, there is a powerful new selective force working on us that can produce changes in as little as 10,000 years. Very fast by evolutionary standards. That force is human culture. We are shaping our genetics with our cultures and the civilizations we build from them. Gregory Cochran and Henry Harpending

(2009) provide examples and some details in their book *The 10,000 Year Explosion: How Civilization Accelerated Human Evolution.* One example is the emergence and spread of genes to produce enzymes that allow human adults to digest milk. Only infants were able to do that in pre-agricultural humans. But the domestication of cows, goats, camels and other milk giving animals has naturally selected humans for the capacity to produce lactase and lactose tolerance. The transformation is not complete, however, as there are still people unable to digest lactose. What kind of humans are individualism and competition selecting? I shudder to think. What kind of humans would a cooperative society produce over time? Now that has possibilities.

Chapter 6. Tocqueville's Prophecy

"Individualism" in one form or another, probably unnamed in most cases, has been with humans throughout our history. In this and the next chapter we examine the unique cultural forms of individualism that emerged and have evolved in the United States from our founding. Alexis de Tocqueville, as far as I can tell, was the first to describe and call attention to this American cultural pattern and gave it the mane, "individualism."

THE DISCOVERY OF AMERICAN INDIVIDUALISM

In April 1831 when the young American republic was barely fifty years old, a slight, sensitive, and eager 26 year old French aristocrat, Alexis de Tocqueville, and his close friend Gustave de Beaumont, set sail from Le Havre for New York City. Their official mission was to study the successful American penitentiary system, which was experimenting with occupational training, for the Ministry of Justice. The prison study was not Tocqueville's real reason for planning a nine-month trip across the Atlantic; it was an excuse to be relieved of his duties as a *juge-auditeur* (roughly approximating our assistant district attorney) to conduct a study of the exciting American experiment in equality and democracy that everyone was discussing. During Tocqueville's visit to America he spent months interviewing people from most of the states then in existence and from many walks of life, from leading politicians and business men to slaves, laborers, and farmers. From these interviews emerged an understanding of a new attitude toward life that generated our belief in equality and democracy. He labeled this attitude, "individualism" (Tocqueville, 1840, p. 202).

Tocqueville had mixed feelings about this startling new life style. Individualism encouraged us to value all individuals equally and to give them a voice in government producing our democracy. (It would take over a century of ferment before all Americans would have that voice and the vote.) Tocqueville admired much that our fresh form of democracy and novel pursuit of equality were producing. However, there were other aspects of our individualism that deeply concerned and dismayed him. Tocqueville observed that when Americans acquired enough education and fortune to satisfy their wants they acquired a self-important aloofness. "They owe nothing to any man, they expect nothing from any man; they acquire the habit of always considering themselves as standing alone, and they are apt to imagine that their whole destiny is in their own hands" (Tocqueville, 1840, p. 206). Our individualism was something new and bold, but also a worrisome threat to the fabric of society:

> *Individualism* is a novel expression to which a novel idea has given birth. Our fathers were only acquainted with egotism. Egotism is a passionate and exaggerated love of self, which leads a man to connect everything with his own person, and to prefer himself to everything in the world. Individualism is a mature and calm feeling, which disposes each member of the community to sever himself from the mass of his fellow-creatures, and to draw apart with his family and friends; so that, after he has thus formed a little circle of his own, he willingly leaves society at large to itself (Tocqueville, 1840, pp. 202-203, emphasis Tocqueville's).

This severing of ourselves from the community makes "every man forget his ancestors,... hides his descendants, and separates his contemporaries from him; it throws him back for ever upon himself alone, and threatens in the end to confine him entirely within the solitude of his own heart" (Tocqueville, 1840, p. 206). One can imagine Tocqueville's passionate disapproval as he wrote, "individualism proceeds from erroneous judgment ... it originates ... in the deficiencies of the mind" (Tocqueville, 1840, p. 203). How could we, a people so admirable in so many ways, *do* that to ourselves?

Voluntary Associations: The Unique American Form of "Cooperation"

Tocqueville soon realized that if Americans were going to produce any kind of a viable society, given this intense individualism that separates us from our fellows, we would have to simultaneously invent a means of facilitating the collective efforts needed in any society such as barn raising, school building, political action and the like. He found our solution: voluntary associations. Early Americans formed them on a more or less *ad hoc* basis to serve a wide variety of special purposes. To this day voluntary associations remain our predominant form of more cooperative collective action. As unique at that time as the individualism that created the need for them, the bewildering variety of voluntary associations he discovered could be compared to America today. Tocqueville observed (1840):

> The political associations which exist in the United States are only a single feature in the midst of the immense assemblage of associations in that country. Americans of all ages, all conditions, and all dispositions, constantly form associations. They have not only commercial and manufacturing companies, in which all take part, but associations of a thousand other kinds—religious, moral, serious, futile, extensive or restricted, enormous or diminutive. The Americans make associations to give entertainments, to found establishments for education, to build inns, to construct churches, to diffuse books, to send missionaries to the antipodes; and in this manner they found hospitals, prisons, and schools. If it be proposed to advance some truth, or to foster some feeling by the encouragement of a great example, they form a society.
>
> I met with several kinds of associations in America, of which I confess I had no previous notion; and I have often admired the extreme skill with which the inhabitants of the United States succeed in proposing a common object to the exertions of a great many men, and in getting them voluntarily to pursue it.
>
> The English often perform great things singly; whereas the Americans form associations for the smallest undertakings. It is evident that the former people consider association as a powerful means of action, but the latter seem to regard it as the only means they have of acting.
>
> Thus the most democratic country on the face of the earth is that in which men have in our time carried to the highest perfection the art of pursuing in common the object of their common desires, and have applied this new science to the greatest number of purposes. Is this the result of accident? or is there in reality any necessary connection between the principle of association and that of equality?

> Amongst democratic nations ... all the citizens are independent and feeble; they can do hardly anything by themselves, and none of them can oblige his fellow-men to lend him their assistance. They all, therefore, fall into a state of incapacity, if they do not learn voluntarily to help each other ... if they never acquired the habit of forming associations in ordinary life, civilization itself would be endangered.
>
> Unhappily, the same social condition [individualism] which renders associations so necessary to democratic nations, renders their formation more difficult. . . (pp. 220-223; punctuation and style as per original)

This is a remarkably perceptive description of one of our central and enduring problems in America: the constant tension between individualism and the need for cooperative collective actions.

Tocqueville saw clearly that our individualism creates an absurd situation. This self-centered cultural operating system we've built our society upon undermines our social structures such as government and communities so they cannot meet our needs in an organized and predictable way. We often have to create voluntary associations ourselves when a need arises, and then go out and persuade others to join us. Our individualism gets in the way of forming and effectively operating our voluntary associations. Individualistic Americans make fickle members. They come and go as they please, participate when and how they please, and pay their dues if they please. With such transience it's hard to maintain cohesion and whole hearted commitment.

Meanwhile, no one and no association is paying attention to the good of the whole society. Tocqueville pointed out that a better integrated society would be able to provide for more of its citizen's needs effectively, making the formation of so many voluntary associations unnecessary. Individualism prevents us from taking advantage of the adaptive power of a more community focused culture that organizes us into an effective cooperative unit working together for the benefit of all. Our self-centeredness loads way too much responsibility for our personal and collective well-being onto individual Americans. Such an insistent, stand alone approach backfires on us by making it much harder for each individual to survive and prosper than is necessary.

Tocqueville's description of voluntary associations also illustrates our predominant form of more cooperative effort in America, which I label "individualistic mutual aid." As Tocqueville pointed out, our individualistic mutual aid involves people voluntarily coming together to pursue a goal of common interest to them. Usually the goal is something each wants for themselves but cannot obtain or produce alone. They need the help of others to do it. A classical example was a barn-raising in our agricultural era. Several farming families worked together to build each farmer a barn on his property in turn. After the barns were built, every farmer owned one that was his to use as he pleased. Another example would be farmers in a region forming a co-operative to store and market their produce and/or to act as a political advocate. Individualistic mutual aid is just one of a variety of forms of collaboration available to human societies and is characteristic of societies such as ours.

Americans using individualistic mutual aid have accomplished a great many worthy projects in America and continue to do so. However, individualistic mutual aid has serious limitations, especially when it comes to providing a well coordinated society-wide cooperative system. Ominously, we are witnessing a steady decline in voluntary associations, beginning around the 1960s (Putnam, 2000), as ever more extreme expressions of individualism in our younger cohorts further undermine our social fabric. (See Chapter 7 for elaboration.)

MASTER "THE ART OF ASSOCIATING TOGETHER" OR LOSE IT ALL

Early American pioneers with their agricultural lifestyle and comparatively simple technology were able to provide for themselves most of what they needed to survive. This made it possible for an early American "to sever himself from the mass of his fellow-creatures, and to draw apart with his family and friends," perhaps to stand alone as a rugged individual and survive just fine. The self-reliant mountain men and pioneer families played major roles in the building of our country—including our mythology.

However, even in Tocqueville's time the pattern of the future was clear. The growing complexity of societies and the developing technologies meant an end to our self-reliant independence. He said, "It is easy to foresee that the time is drawing near when man will be less and less able to produce, of himself alone, the commonest necessaries of life" (Tocqueville, 1840, p. 224). The American historian, Bruce Catton, famous for his books on the Civil War, commented on Tocqueville's observation: "A society whose lusty tradition of individualism and firm belief in the equality of all men were both based on that frontier ability [of producing of himself the commonest necessaries of life] is likely to flounder when conditions change" (Catton, 1976, p.194). Our individualism and proud independence were never designed to deal with the vast division of labor, degree of specialization, complex coordination, and levels of mutual trust required to effectively operate an interdependent high technology society such as we have become. Consequently, we are indeed floundering. One indication is our inability to solve so many of our society's problems that continue to bedevil us year after year. These include persistent dysfunctional economic inequalities, repetitive boom-glut-bust cycles, inability to provide adequate medical care, food, housing, and employment for all, unresolved immigration problems, exploitive business practices, crime and corruption, interest groups blocking and distorting governmental procedures and declining group engagement. This inability to solve major problems is generally considered evidence a society, a culture, has run its course beyond what it is capable of handling and is in decline.

Tocqueville knew what the solution had to be. He warned: "Amongst the laws which rule human societies there is one which seems to be more precise and clear than all others. If men are to remain civilized, or to become so, the art of associating together must grow and improve" (Tocqueville, 1840, p. 228).

What was Tocqueville thinking of when he said that? We know he disapproved of our individualism and saw our voluntary associations— our individualistic mutual aid—as a necessary crutch for an inadequate self-centered approach to life. His vision was certainly toward something beyond individualism and voluntary associations. I imagine he had a more community based form of cooperation in mind. Catton expresses the urgency of this quest:

> For the modern world is one in which all stakes are raised to infinity; win it all or lose it all, in this or the next generation. Man's [Americans'] problem is that he has ... arranged things so that he has no one but himself to rely upon.... he is obliged to look into his own heart.... he may find there the thing he needs most of all—the secret of the art of associating together (Catton, 1976, p. 196).

Relying only upon ourselves alone, despite the wonderfully romantic aura individualism paints around the heroic self, may lead—may already be leading—to the loss of it all.

Tocqueville saw our time, if only mistily, and prophesized clear back in the 1840s that our great challenge as a society would be to really learn "the art of associating together" if we want to remain civilized and progress. We must advance beyond the individualistic mutual-aid, voluntary associations collaborations that emerged in response to our individualism. We must learn the art of true cooperation. Fortunately, we not only have our hearts to look deeply into, but also our social sciences that have advanced far beyond what was known in Tocqueville's time.

We are also growing in our experience with complex organizations and their extensive divisions of labor that characterize our high technology and information based society. The history of intrepid Americans who experimented with communal cooperation during and after Tocqueville's time is rich in insights into what works and what doesn't. We stand on the threshold of a social era where it is clear we can easily lose it all for reasons mostly of our own making or we can learn to truly cooperate as a cultural community whose members relish working together as one. We have the capacity to master the art of associating together at the highest level.

The prominent psychotherapist Rollo May, in his book, *The Cry for Myth* (New York: W. W. Norton, 1991, pp. 108-109) said:

> Americans cling to the myth of individualism as though it were the only normal way to live, unaware that it was unknown in the Middle Ages ... and would have been considered psychotic in classical Greece. We feel as Americans that every person must be ready to stand alone, each of us following the powerful myth of the lone cabin on the prairie. Each individual must learn to take care of himself or herself and thus be beholden to no one else.

Called "rugged individualism" in political circles and "fierce individualism" by some historians, this myth has obviously great advantages for a democracy. But it exhibits the basic flaw of leaving us no solid community to call our own. May feels America is mythless in the sense of not having effective myths that help hold us together as communities. He said (p. 45):

> Surely Nietzsche is right: our powerful hunger for myth is a hunger for community.

Chapter 7. Individualism Run Riot

Tocqueville warned us about individualism. He knew it was going to cause America trouble. So what is the problem with individualism? Simply stated, you cannot build a viable, stable, adaptive society or community with self-centered individualists who pursue their own goals without regard for the consequences of their actions for others. You predictably get a variety of persistent conflicts, failures, disruptions and tensions if you try.

You get perennial tension between the individualists and the community. The individualists want to be autonomous from the community, leaving the community to fend for itself while the individualists do their own thing. But the community produced and raised these individualists and needs them to contribute to the work of the community. You can't have a large proportion, perhaps the majority, of a population lingering aloofly on the fringes of society while feeding off its products, services, and energy. It is going to produce resentment and conflict and seriously undermine the community's adaptive success.

As individualism infests a society it dissolves the social fabric of the groups and organizations within it, reducing group engagement until the groups disband or become ineffective. At the absolute extreme, society and social organization as we know them disappear.

When you do get American individualists together to try to get our government to do what they want, to give them their "rights," you get shrill confrontations and battles between the multitudes with different and incompatible goals and demands. You get the creation of "interest groups" prepared to engage in sustained political battle indefinitely. And you get a mountain of unresolved problems, unmet survival needs, and the blocking and deflecting of each other's initiatives. Individualism is totally unfit to serve as the basis for effective government.

Individualists' focus on themselves, their self-centeredness, can get to the point that they are unable to engage in deep and wholesome interpersonal relationships. They create an industry of counseling, therapy, and self-help for the lonely, isolated individualist.

This chapter examines each of these problems. When I stand back and imagine trying to get things done with nothing but individualists, I can't help thinking of the exasperated exclamation, "It's like herding cats!" No one who loves people would ever impose on them the burden of an individualistic society.

Individualism and competition both produce serious problems for the humans who engage in them. There are self-destructive elements in both. Cooperation, as I've defined it, may or may not be "perfect" but it does not come with built in self-destructive social patterns. It is depressing that we have saddled ourselves with two inherently socially and personally damaging and maladaptive sociocultural operating systems. Perversely, we Americans steadfastly refuse to see our own roles in producing these damaging conditions. We seem to be in a state of denial when it comes to our beloved individualism and its values of individual freedom, equality between individuals, and democracy. We refuse to connect the dots that show the same individualism we are so enamored with is also the cause of many of our persistent problems. We examine some of the worst of these in this chapter. If we can't or refuse to see it, we can't fix it. To recall the oft-repeated line from the wonderful old comic-strip character Pogo: "We have seen the enemy and it is us!"

The history of individualism in America is the story of the constant battle between the self-centered individual and the group-centered community; the "eternal" tension between the individual versus society with which we are all familiar. This tension, this dualism, is human made; it is not the "nature of things." It is what happens when you try to build a society around individualism. Cooperative societies have no such tension. Part 2 of this book shows what it would be like for individuals to cooperate: it is wonderful and fulfilling for the *individual*. Much more so than is possible in the midst of our individual versus society conflicts.

Looking at the common forms of individualism in America, you will see that they can be placed on a continuum from raw individualism to individualism enmeshed in some more group-centered sociocultural constraints. Robert Bellah and his colleagues, in what is one of the classical studies of American individualism, *Habits of the Heart* (Bellah et al., 1985)—the title a phrase taken from Tocqueville's book—identify four forms of individualism that permeate our history and our culture. To understand this continuum, we need to see what raw individualism is like to provide a reference point. For this there is no better example than the Ik, an unfortunate African tribe.

Many American individualists live in a fantasy that portrays extreme or "pure" individualism as the ultimate and most desirable state of human existence. They imagine it as a world of total freedom where each individual fully expresses his or her true self without constraint or intrusions from others. They generally blame society for the bad things in life. It is the "autonomous human" dream, the "noble savage" being noble, standing tall, proud and free. This is a myth, and a dangerous one. There is no such thing as an "autonomous human" that comes out of the box knowing what is best for them and how to effectively cope with life, and there is no noble savage. The end of the individualistic "rainbow" or continuum is not a Garden of Eden of human beauty, creativity, self-actualization, happiness and freedom, as the myth insists. The extreme end of individualism is a world without shared culture, where every person pursues their own survival at all others' expense. The people who come closest to this that have been studied by anthropologists are the Ik. While they still have a common language, some simple farming, house building, and hunting and gathering practices they use, they are as close to "pure" individualism, relieved of culture, with "freedom to do as they please," as we are likely to get.

The Ik, the Extreme End of Individualism

There is great danger in the direction American individualism is going because it leads to the abandonment of culture. As we approach the end of the continuum of individualism we shed culture, producing a steadily shrinking culture until at the extreme end there is virtually none. The loss of culture means the loss of adaptive capacity both as a community and as individual people. Colin Turnbull (1972) shows us in his book *The Mountain People*, about the Ik, what happens to a society that loses its culture, that loses every vestige of social organization, that becomes merely a collection of raw, extreme, individualists with little more than language and a few simple survival patterns in common.

The Ik are one of the all too numerous tragedies of human history. The Ik were once a vital tribe of African hunter/gatherers who annually migrated over a vast area within Uganda, Kenya, and Sudan. Just before World War II they were settled—in a process like our putting Native-Americans on reservations—in Kipedo Valley and the surrounding mountains, located in northeastern Uganda on the border with Kenya to the east and Sudan to the north. This small, isolated, marginal, barren land had been nothing more than a temporary resting site during the Ik's traditional migrations (Turnbull, 1972, p. 20). The barrenness of the land and the unusual difficulties of their situation, including being trapped in it and without resources, eventually stripped the Ik of their culture and revealed raw individualism for what it is.

A few examples of Icien life will suffice. Turnbull (1972) cautions, while circumstances that produced the Ik's condition were extreme, "they are circumstances into which we could all conceivably fall, and the potential for what we might care to call the inhumanity that we see in the Ik is within us all" (p. 133).

The Icien experience shows that the family is not an irreducible social unit, and "in the crisis of survival facing the Ik, the family was one of the first institutions to go," Turnbull relates (p. 133). He continues: "There is one common value, apart from language, to which all Ik hold tenaciously. It is *ngag*, 'food'." "It is the one standard by which they measure right and wrong, goodness and badness." In fact the Icien word for goodness means "individual possession of food" (p. 135). This fixation on food for one's self, alone, produces most of the behavior patterns observed among the Ik.

In the Icien world, children are a burden, are cared for perfunctorily, with ill humor, and feelings of imposition. Parents drop their babies on the ground and act as if they hope a predator will take it. Turnbull reports that happened once while he was observing "and the mother was delighted," she was rid of the child (p. 136). "So, we should not be surprised when the mother throws her child out at three years old" (p. 135). "Family" members distrust each other in direct proportion to their physical closeness and rarely share food, hunting for it and eating it alone. Turnbull tells us, "Love" the Ik "dismiss as idiotic and highly dangerous" (p. 134). Compassion is also dispensed with, as is reciprocity except in a few rare cases.

The children around the age of three go into an age cohort composed of other cast-off offspring that they form for themselves—individualistic and competitive mutual-aid—all trying desperately to fend for themselves in an environment that is indifferent to them and often hostile. There are usually two age cohorts, but there can be more or less depending upon the number of children around. "The junior band consists of children between the ages of three and seven, the senior band caters for the eight- to twelve-year-olds," Turnbull relates (p. 136). One is the youngest when entering each of these bands and must ally with another youngster near in age for protection against the older children. The younger ones gang up on the oldest and biggest when it is time and drive them out of the age band. If an Icien child survives to thirteen he moves—is driven—into the adult band. If child survive that long, the Iciens believe they will be of some value to the band. In these childhood cohorts, the children soon learn their "friend" will turn on them in time. Turnbull (1972) calls these repetitive destructions of the fragile bond that can barely be called friendship the *rite de passage* because, "When this has happened to you three or four times you are ready for the world, knowing friendship for the joke it is" (p. 137).

Each morning "the village reveals itself for what it is, a conglomeration of individuals of all ages, each going his own way in search of food and water, like a plague of locusts spreading over the land." The age bands move together for protection and lay claim to the territory they occupy at the moment, unless an older band or the adults take it away from them. The foods they seek mostly are figs they compete for with the baboons, berries, honey, certain edible barks that nonetheless make them feel sick sometimes, and if there is nothing else they will eat dirt and pebbles. The adults sometimes desultorily plant fields, of pumpkins perhaps. The entire village struggles to defend their fields from baboons, birds, grubs, and caterpillars that are as voraciously hungry as the Ik. This example of desperate individualistic/competitive mutual aid is as close as they ever come to cooperation. (Individualistic mutual aid in finding or producing the food and protection each requires; competitive mutual aid in dealing with other age cohorts or adults or animals, such as baboons, all competing for the same food sources.) The villagers plant widely scattered fields in hopes of getting rain. Three in four years they get enough rain to nurture the crops, but conditions are such the Ik can never be sure of a harvest. The only herds of wild animals they can hunt for food are in a neighboring wildlife protection park. Still, in desperate times, the Ik will chance getting caught and hunt individually. If an Ik hunter is fortunate enough to kill an animal, he will consume as much meat as he can on the spot, then bring it back to the area of the village secretively, then take the rest to sell at the Police Post "without as much as a bite for a wife or child," Turnbull (1972) observed (p. 141). The same happens if an Ik finds honey.

Turnbull (1972) said, "One of the major needs in Icien technology was vine from which cord and twine could be made" and which was used to bind many things such as roof frames and to make baskets. Obtaining it "was an activity that really required only one person, but in this, as in other such activities, the Ik sometimes went in company, though not a word might be exchanged" (p. 240). At first Turnbull thought this might turn out to be some mild form of cooperation—mutual aid in my terms—but no, it turned out to be a competition based event where all came in the hopes of seeing others fail or have difficulties and to laugh at them. (The "harm-joy" de Waal described among chimpanzees, see Chapter 5.) It was a form of competitive entertainment. Each Ik would select a sapling and make cuts in the bark and then give "a strong jerk that ripped the strip of bark clean away from the three as high as the branches had been cut. It was in the upward ripping that disaster was likely to occur, and it was then that other Ik would stop their own work and look, with hope and anticipation. If the rip was clean, work was resumed, but if the bark tore at a knot or where a branch had been cut too close or not close enough, there were howls of laughter" (p. 240).

Turnbull said, "There seemed to be increasingly little among the Ik that could by any stretch of the imagination be called social life, let alone social organization" (p. 155). Turnbull offers the contrast of the Mbuti Pygmies, whom he had also studied in the field, as an example of the kind of social organization he found common among these "primitive" tribes. The Pygmies are apparently much more cooperative, in my terms. They have no council of elders and "anyone who has influence today may be without it tomorrow" (p. 156). They have a vital family concept that extends to the whole band or even larger units. "They have an economy that demands cooperation, cutting across differences of age and sex, involving the whole band" (p. 156). And they have a "communal spirit" "centered on a love for and devotion to

their forest world," that "results in their wholehearted, unquestioning identification with it. And what more powerful force toward social unity and
cohesion can there be than such a deep-rooted sense of identity? All this, the
Ik lack, and more besides" (p. 156).

Sociologists have known since Emile Durkheim that there were two
contrasting sources of social cohesion. On the one hand is the cohesion of
the Pygmies that derives from their deeply shared set of beliefs, customs,
and knowledge concerning the nature of the world and how to relate to it.
On the other is the kind of cohesion predominant in America based upon
the organization of social roles into a division of labor, a functional inter-
dependency that must be reinforced by social sanctions—rewards such
as pay. True cooperation, especially at the large organization and national
level, blends both. The Iciens have neither. Turnbull reported,

> It is certainly difficult, through a study of Icien behavior, to establish
> any rules of conduct that could be called social, the prime maxim of
> all Ik being *that each man should do what he wants to do*, that he should do
> anything else only if he is forced to (p. 183, emphasis mine).

A clearer statement of pure, raw, individualism cannot be made. As a
consequence, as Turnbull observed, the Ik have "eradicated what we know
as 'humanity'" and have "turned the world into a chilly void where man does
not even seem to care for himself, but survives" (p. 233). And, "the excessive
individualism of the Ik, coupled with the solitude and boredom of daily life,
did not make for many significant relationships of any kind." "They were,
each one, simply alone, and seemingly content to be alone" (p. 238). This
is the true end of individualism, complete with isolation in the solitude of
one's own heart.

How close is America to this extreme end of individualism? In raw individualism such as the Ik practice, the pursuit of personal goals without
regard for others is all there is. American individualism has traditionally
been enmeshed in other cultural elements, such as religion and civic engagement that have tempered it and channeled its energy in productive channels
while muting its excesses (elaborated in the following section). The key
indicator of how close we are to the Ik is the degree to which our current
forms of individualism slip the embrace of more group-centered cultural
constraints, such as religion and civic duty, and approach raw, unfettered,
me-first, self-centered, individualism with little regard for others and the
consequences of our actions upon them. You don't have to look far to see an
increasing amount of self-centered, selfish, behavior.

As this chapter points out, our group participation of all kinds including religion and civic activities is in steady decline. Our rich multistranded connections with others, such as associating with the same people in our community, church, occupation, softball league, perhaps extended family and so forth, typical of earlier periods of our history, are being reduced to more sterile single stranded ties serving individualist's needs and goals. And with those declines comes and increase in raw individualistic behaviors. These include offensive behavior such as sex in public places including school auditoriums, loud and disruptive behavior, use of cell phones and other devices in inappropriate settings such as concerts, impatient rudeness instead of graciousness, and more, all resulting from the totally self-centered focus of extreme individualists. Their behavior makes it clear they do not even notice, let alone care about, those around them. Sometimes the rest of us are just objects occupying space like a tree. This extreme individualistic behavior is even acquiring labels such as "social autism" offered by the columnist George Will (2005, p. 7A).

A large number of social problems result, as this and following chapters detail, including high divorce and crime rates,, decline in personal integrity and responsibility, increase in interpersonal conflicts, inadequate care and socialization of children, loss of loyalty in interpersonal and group relations, disrespect for "authority," and dissolution of standards of morality that serve the common good. At the root of all this is individualists doing their own thing without regard for how their behavior affects others. The more we stop being concerned about the consequences of our behavior for others, the further we are over the hump and on the downward slide to Ik-land.

Social scientists have found four major forms of individualism in America that characterize our historical periods and our particular sociocultural mix. There are no doubt others, perhaps minor ones, we have yet to clearly identify.

THE ROOTS AND EXPRESSIONS OF OUR MODERN INDIVIDUALISM

JOHN WINTHROP, THOMAS JEFFERSON, BENJAMIN FRANKLIN, WALT WHITMAN, AND THE FORMS OF AMERICAN INDIVIDUALISM

Robert Bellah and his colleagues reported in *Habits of the Heart* (Bellah et al., 1985) that their research discovered four forms of individualism that permeate our American history and our culture: biblical, civic or republican, utilitarian, and expressive. As they point out, "Individualism lies at the very core of American culture" and is "basic to American identity." "We believe in the dignity, indeed the sacredness, of the individual. Anything that would violate our right to think for ourselves, judge for ourselves, make our own decisions, live our own lives as we see fit, is not only morally wrong, it is sacrilegious" (Bellah et al., 1985, p. 142). We are, practically all of us, caught up in one or more of these types of individualism, practicing them daily. They are the habits of our hearts, and many of us love them.

According to Bellah, our modern individualism emerged "out of the struggle against monarchical and aristocratic authority that seemed arbitrary and oppressive to citizens prepared to assert the right to govern themselves" (Bellah et al., 1985, p. 142). The land-based aristocracy form of civilization that had dominated Europe for so many centuries had reached its limit and was in the process of collapsing, helped along by the emergence of new technologies, capitalist manufacturing businesses, and the emergence of a wealthy and politically potent new middle-class. Our individualism, with its accompanying emphasis on democracy and political equality, was a new paradigm, an important cultural shift, and a response to historical challenge. That profound shift—from aristocracy to individualistic democracy—has allowed Americans to make tremendous progress and growth—though not without high costs. And now individualism, in its turn, must step aside to allow our society's continued growth.

European biblical religions, especially Reformed Christianity, and classical political philosophies contributed to this cultural transformation, and provided the basis for two of the manifestations of our individualism: Biblical and Republican or Civic. These two are at the opposite end of the community—individual continuum from the Ik. Here the more group-centered sociocultural patterns of the religious and civil communities provided constraint on the individualism and channeled self-centered individualistic expressions into those social frameworks.

John Winthrop and Biblical Individualism

Biblical individualism was exemplified by John Winthrop, one of the first Puritans to land in New England and the first governor of the Massachusetts Bay Colony. This form of individualism did not condone an unfettered freedom from community responsibility nor from judgment. One was given a "moral" freedom to choose what is "good, just and honest." God gave us free agency to choose good or evil, and to reap the results of our choices as salvation or damnation. Salvation was an individual quest, with each person succeeding or failing on their own merits, not due to success or faults of their forebears or associates. Biblical individualism encouraged Christian church members to work together to help one another and to create a community in which an ethical and spiritual life could be led (Bellah et al., 1985, pp. 28-9). This form of individualism continues to be practiced in our Christian churches. These churches and religions continue to be an important source of community based morality, concern for the whole community, responsibility for the consequences of our actions on others, and identification with community—"I am a Christian." These churches provide a meaning for life and a cultural program for continued improvement that is missing at the other extreme of the community—individual continuum.

THOMAS JEFFERSON AND REPUBLICAN INDIVIDUALISM

Thomas Jefferson exemplifies civic or republican individualism. His stirring phrase from the Declaration of Independence, "All men are created equal," gave expression to a passionately embraced element of our individualism; one that remains plastic in definition and untamed in practice from Tocqueville's time to our own. Jefferson had in mind political equality, in which "no man ... is born with a saddle on his back for another man to ride," rather than equality of condition. (In my terms, this is a rejection of dominance hierarchies, of tyrannies, such as aristocracies, as the chosen form of government.) The phrasing of this idea caused considerable debate and some dismay among our colonial forefathers. For example, when John Adams wrote Massachusetts' constitution, he borrowed from George Mason's words in Virginia's Declaration of Rights that men are "born equally free and independent" (McCullough, 2001, p. 221). Adams used these words in Massachusetts' own Declaration of Rights. Massachusetts' constitutional convention, however, rewrote the phrase, "born equally free and independent," to read that all men were "born free and equal." This was a change Adams did not like, "and would like even less as time went on" according to McCullough (2001, p. 224). Both Jefferson and Adams had in mind equal rights, especially before the law, but that is not how equality has come to be viewed in America. The common American image of equality is more nearly expressed by these words from a song in the musical *Oklahoma*: "I don't say I'm no better than anybody else, but I'll be danged if I ain't just as good!"

Jefferson was very much aware of the dangers of individualism running riot, with unfettered "freedom" to do whatever one liked. He believed that individualism and equality could *only* work politically in a republic where people accepted the responsibilities of citizenship and actively participated. For Jefferson, individual "freedom took on its real meaning in a certain kind of society with a certain form of life," requiring being involved in the republic. "Without that, Jefferson saw freedom as quickly destroying itself and eventuating in tyranny" (Bellah et al., 1985, p. 30-31). Democracy requires a level of education and understanding among participants so they know "how the game is played" and play by the "rules." They are committed to the civic community and participate in and organize civic activities, perhaps seeking and holding office. They identify themselves with their town and/or nation with pride, "I'm a Bostonian; I'm an American." Too often we try to create democratic governments in societies whose members do not have that education, or experience with those social patterns, with the results Jefferson foretold.

For both Winthrop and Jefferson, in both biblical and republican forms, individualism was not allowed unrestrained expression or freedom without responsibility. Individualism was placed in the context of more group-centered civic and religious obligations to serve the community and others that maintained a balance between the individualist and the community. Individuals were constrained by requirements for obedience and compliance to laws and values. They were given social arenas in which to enact their individualism while contributing to the public good through their church and as active citizens (Bellah et al., 1985, p. 143). The good that has resulted from the accomplishments of these forms of individualism must be credited more to the group-centered cultural patterns than to individualistic cultural patterns.

The next two forms of individualism are in between biblical and civic individualism on the one hand, and the Ik on the other, along the community—individual continuum. They do not have the group-centered cultural constraints that biblical and civic individualism do. They more completely express the values of individualism and are more focused on self-centeredness. They are utilitarian and expressive individualism. Both utilitarian and expressive individualism derive from John Locke and the 17th century defense of individual rights. Locke saw the individual as taking precedence over society. Society was the result of agreements and voluntary social contracts between individuals seeking to maximize their own self-interests.

Benjamin Franklin and Utilitarian Individualism

Benjamin Franklin best expressed utilitarian individualism. His *Autobiography* set the model for one of individualism's enduring myths: the poor boy who through cleverness and hard work makes good. Franklin's *Poor Richard's Almanack* spoke to our passion for practical self-improvement with aphorisms that are now part of our American "common sense." "Early to bed and early to rise, makes a man healthy, wealthy, and wise." "God helps those that help themselves." "Lost time is never found again." "A penny saved is a penny earned." All are expressions of our pragmatic individualism and thirst for achievement. America has long been identified with this utilitarian individualism as the "land of opportunity" wherein the individual can get ahead on his or her own initiative, and not be held back by others (Bellah et al., 1985, p. 32-3). The emphasis was on the calculated pursuit of one's own wealth and material interests, on advancement, on achievement, on success. The good American "makes something of himself."

This form of individualism has focused energy that has produced many fine accomplishments and high quality people who have contributed much to our society. Benjamin Franklin is, indeed, a good example. We still marvel at what he achieved in his life time. However, we also see in Franklin elements of civic individualism in his long service to our country in its critical formative years.

Utilitarian individualism can also create a cultural atmosphere wherein ranking people by achievements and wealth and the intense pursuit thereof can become oppressive. Mix competition into this one and you can have ruthless competition for status, wealth, and control with excessive self-aggrandizement up the ladder. You get a competitive ranking from "best" to "worst". You also get some unhappy damage and defeats in the battles. This can produce insatiable greed at extremes, and fixation on the defeat of competitors. Utilitarian individualism and competition can make for a volatile and dangerous mix.

WALT WHITMAN AND EXPRESSIVE INDIVIDUALISM

Utilitarian individualism spread rapidly in the fertile soil of late 18th and early 19th century America. By the middle of the 19th century it was so dominant it set off a reaction that produced expressive individualism. Utilitarian individualism's exuberant and at times ruthless pursuit of money and material possessions, often to be taken as evidence of superiority—in the case of some Protestants, evidence of God's favor—offended many Americans, including some clergymen, women, poets, and writers. The "American Renaissance" in literature was a reaction to utilitarian individualism. Among its leaders were Emerson, Thoreau, Hawthorne, and Melville. Melville's *Israel Potter* was a novel that subjected Franklin to "bitter" satire. Bellah selected one of them as the representative of expressive individualism: Walt Whitman (Bellah et al., 1985, p. 33-34).

Walt Whitman's poetry, primarily *Leaves of Grass*, portrays not a world of success and material wealth, but "a life rich in experience, open to all kinds of people, luxuriating in the sensual as well as the intellectual, above all a life of strong feeling," where the self is experienced as at-one with other people, places, nature, even the whole universe (Bellah et al., 1985, p. 33-34). Expressive individualism prefers "being," fully experiencing life and one's self, rejecting utilitarian individualists' pursuit of achievement. "Song of Myself," a poem in the *Leaves of Grass* volume, is a classic of expressive individualism. Here are a few lines (Whitman, 1950, pp. 22-23, 48, 49):

> I celebrate myself, and sing myself,
> And what I assume you shall assume,
> For every atom belonging to me as good belongs to you.
> I loafe and invite my soul,
> I lean and loafe at my ease observing a spear of summer grass.

> I believe a leaf of grass is no less than the
>   journey-work of the stars,
> And the pismire is equally perfect, and a grain
>   of sand, and the egg of a wren.
> And the tree-toad is a chef-d'oeuvre of the highest,
> And the running blackberry would adorn the parlors of heaven,
> And the narrowest hinge in my hand puts to scorn all machinery,

> And the cow crunching with depress'd head surpasses any statue,
> And a mouse is miracle enough to stagger sextillions of infidels.

Speaking of animals "so placid and self-contained," Whitman takes some jabs at the other forms of individualism:

> They do not sweat and whine about their condition,
> They do not lie awake in the dark and weep for their sins,
> They do not make me sick discussing their duty to God,
> Not one is dissatisfied, not one is demented
>   with the mania of owning things,
> Not one kneels to another, nor to his kind that
>   lived thousands of years ago,
> Not one is respectable or unhappy over the whole earth.

In expressive individualism people decide what is useful, beautiful, or desirable by consulting their own desires, sentiments, and feelings. Each person "knows" what is best for him or her. As with utilitarian individualism, the individual takes precedence over society.

Expressive individualism experienced a heyday during the counterculture and New Age movements of the 60s, 70s and later. It is still a popular form of individualism that has been incorporated to one degree or another into a number of current American lifestyles. It tends toward simplicity, making do with enough rather than accumulating wealth and stuff, sometimes a back-to-nature approach, experiencing strong feeling and social relations, sometimes music, drug, and stimulant augmented, and sometimes rejecting existing authorities, preferring their own social world.

One of the dangers of this sometimes romantic, poetic, artistic, and "spiritual" lifestyle is it can come close to, even go over the edge into forms of individualism that are self-destructive or self-deluding. For example, some expressive individualists place human subjectivity at the center of the universe. Everything has to be understood and judged by each individual from their subjective viewpoint, according to their "feelings". There can be no shared culture since everything and every act must be, is, the product of each person's subjective interpretation of the situation. (That the shared belief that this is so constitutes culture is utterly lost on these extreme expressive individualists.) The source of this internal "wisdom" and guiding emotion is often metaphysical, even global spirituality. Here we have the mythologizing of the individual into something sacred and self-contained.

Locked in the solitude of their own hearts, heads, sympathetic-adrenal physiology (the source of many "feelings"), spiritual "power", and imagination, they may live in a fantasy world only tenuously connected to reality. Not a lot of rapid adaptation to changes in the environment as a community going on here.

The individualistic trends in America are toward Ik-land. Society is dissolving before our very eyes and with it such adaptive effectiveness as America now has.

INDIVIDUALISM AND THE FORBIDDEN COMMUNITY

INDIVIDUALS VERSUS COMMUNITY

Bellah and his colleagues found that American individualists harbor a deep ambivalence concerning community. Community is viewed as a seductive world tempting us to enter but we cannot; we must be forever on the edge, isolated, wary, looking for ways to use our talents without, heaven forbid, conforming. Our individualistic myths express this ambivalence again and again. These myths display "the fear that society may overwhelm the individual and destroy any chance of autonomy unless he stands against it, but also recognition that it is only in relation to society that the individual can fulfill himself and that if the break with society is too radical, life has no meaning at all," Bellah et al. recount (1985, p. 144).

To glamorize and justify to themselves this bittersweet—and pointless—stance, American individualists have invented individualistic, autonomous, heroes. Two of the most enduring and quintessential—as Bellah and his colleagues observed—are the cowboy and the detective.

Individualists invented that marvelous mythic hero the cowboy, "who again and again saves a society he can never completely fit into" (Bellah et al., 1985, p. 145). Examples given include Shane, the Lone Ranger, and Will Kane the hero of *High Noon*. The cowboy has special talents and qualities that are valuable to society—he has his own superior sense of justice, great courage, and can shoot straighter and faster than other men. He is also irresistibly attractive; the society's fairest females usually love, and sadly lose, our romantic loner. Our mythic cowboy is just too "unique," too special, to belong to a society generally portrayed as weak and cowardly, needing the cowboy hero to rescue them. "It is as if the myth says you can be a truly good person, worthy of admiration and love, only if you resist fully joining the group" (p. 145).

Bellah finds the "connection of moral courage and lonely individualism is even tighter" in the case of our other great mythic hero, the hard-boiled detective (Bellah et al., 1985, p. 145). Sam Spade, Philip Marlowe, Lew Archer, and Serpico are examples. The detective often works "out of a shabby office where the phone never rings. Wily, tough, smart, he is nonetheless unappreciated. But his marginality is his strength, because when a crime comes his way it almost always leads to discovery of corruption in society, especially in high places." A society, particularly "high society," that is corrupt to the core, is a recurrent message in detective stories. Frequently, this heinous society tries to buy our honorable detective off with money, power, fantastic sex, expensive cars, and other goodies, even belonging— "There's a place for a man like you in my organization." But no, even at great cost to himself, our hero pursues the case to a "just" end. The moral is that one can have integrity only outside of this corrupt society.

The cowboy and detective are valuable to society only because they are autonomous; they "stand alone, need no others, do not depend on others for their judgments, and do not submit to their wishes," echoing Toqueville's observations of individualists (Bellah et al., 1985, p. 146). This heroic individualism is not portrayed as selfishness, but as heroic selflessness; one must remain alone to serve society. There is loneliness and fragility of purpose in this heroic quest that can easily slip over into madness, nihilism, and despair. Perhaps this is why whiskey is so often our hero's best friend.

This madness is vividly dramatized, according to Bellah et al. (1985), in Ahab's obsessive pursuit of the great white whale in Melville's classic *Moby Dick*. When we seek the "good," not through community or society but through flight from it, the fine line between ethical heroism and madness can easily vanish, "and the destructive potentiality of a completely asocial individualism is revealed" (p. 145). Remember the Ik. The growing threat of our increasingly asocial individualism to the survival and vitality of our American society must not be taken lightly or ignored; it is already dissolving our social fabric and can destroy us in the long run.

THE COLLAPSE OF AMERICAN COMMUNITY

There is evidence that this dissolution of our society is well underway.

Robert Putnam (2000) in his *Bowling Alone: The Collapse and Revival of American Community* does a convincing job of showing us in detail the collapse of community, civic involvement, church attendance, club and organization membership and participation, of voluntary and mutual-aid associations in general in America since the 1960s. This is a steady decline with no end in sight. The title is unfortunate because the book does not demonstrate that any revival is occurring—only that there is a thread or two of hope—nor is one likely given the problems and social trends in the United States with individualism running riot. Indeed, speaking of the steady decline in club meeting attendance over the last quarter of the twentieth century, Putnam (2000) said, "If the current rate of decline were to continue, clubs would become extinct in America within less than twenty years" (pp. 62-63). It is a book well worth reading to see in thoroughly documented detail the disintegration of our competitive individualistic society along lines we would expect as a consequence of our increasingly unfettered individualism.

Tocqueville anticipated this collapse when he said that our "Individualism is a mature and calm feeling, which disposes each member of the community to sever himself from the mass of his fellow-creatures, and to draw apart with his family and friends; so that, after he has thus formed a little circle of his own, he willingly leaves society at large to itself" (Tocqueville, 1840, pp. 202-203). Social changes and trends since Tocqueville wrote that have increased Americans' disposition to sever themselves from community and society dramatically, especially since around 1960, as Putnam demonstrates.

Putnam's statistics show a watershed peak occurring roughly around the 1960s, with increases in participation in various civic, fraternal, social, political, religious, and special interest organizations occurring from around the turn of the century until that time, followed by steady, dramatic declines in most cases, with a few cases of flattening or slow declines. The nature of our voluntary organizations has changed dramatically too. Our organizations tended earlier in the twentieth century to be grass roots organizations that served local clubs or chapters, such as the Boy Scouts and the Grange. In the later part of the century, our organizations changed to advocacy and lobbying groups mostly headquartered in Washington D. C., such as AARP and some of the environmental groups. Though there may be some local chapter participation, most members simply send money to the organization and get a newsletter or magazine; they have little or no contact at the local level with other members of the group. Putnam notes that before the 1960s Americans were tied together by many social threads to a variety of individuals and groups—a rich social web—but now many of our social ties are single stranded, just one tie to this person and another to that person. "More of our social connectedness is one shot, special purpose, and self oriented," Putnam (2000, pp. 183-185) found.

Of our individualism Putnam said, "community has warred incessantly with individualism for preeminence in our political hagiology. Liberation from ossified community bonds is a recurrent and honored theme in our culture, from the Pilgrims' storied escape from religious convention in the seventeenth century to the lyric nineteenth-century paeans to individualism by Emerson ("Self-Reliance"), Thoreau ("Civil Disobedience"), and Whitman ("Song of Myself") to Sherwood Anderson's twentieth-century celebration of the struggle against conformism by ordinary citizens in *Winesburg, Ohio* to the latest Clint Eastwood film" (Putnam, 2000, p. 24). Moreover, Putnam (2000) continued, "our national myths often exaggerate the role of individual heroes and understate the importance of collective effort." If we go back and look at some of our heroes, such as Paul Revere, we see that it was really the local communities that made history. "Towns without well-organized local militia, no matter how patriotic their inhabitants, were AWOL from Lexington and Concord" (p. 24).

Putnam summarizes:

> Civic disengagement appears to be an equal opportunity affliction. The sharp, steady declines in club meetings, visits with friends, committee service, church attendance, philanthropic generosity, card games, and electoral turnout have hit virtually all sectors of American society over the last several decades and in roughly equal measure. The trends are down among women and down among men, down on the two coasts and down in the heart-land, down among renters and down among homeowners, down in black ghettos and down in white suburbs, down in small towns and down in metropolitan areas, down among Protestants and down among Catholics, down among the affluent and down among the impoverished, down among singles and down among married couples, down among unskilled laborers and down among small-business people and down among top managers, down among Republicans and down among Democrats and down among independents, down among parents and down among the childless, down among full-time workers and down among homemakers (Putnam, 2000, pp. 183-185).

Putnam (2000) found that, "In 1992, three-quarters of the U.S. workforce said that 'the breakdown of community' and 'selfishness' were 'serious' or 'extremely serious' problems in America" (p. 25). Self-centeredness is the hallmark of individualism.

INDIVIDUALISM AND THE BEFOULING OF THE DEMOCRATIC POLITICAL PROCESS

In yet another depressing incongruity, the practice of individualism befouls the workings of the very democratic government individualists produced for themselves. In this government, individual freedom and liberty, equality among individuals, individual voices expressed and heard, and a vote in matters of concern to each individual were enshrined. Unfortunately, however, our democratic government has produced a set of processes that too often frustrates, blocks, deflects or diffuses to vapor individual political initiatives. This is surely not what American individualists were hoping for, yet it is the consequence of trying to translate a cacophony of conflicting individual voices and demands into laws and governmental actions. Our government is an incredibly unwieldy tool for getting work done and problems solved, especially quickly. And it rarely produces a consensus.

How well our founding fathers knew us. Our government was formulated by men who could see what kind of people we were, and are. The checks, balances, and procedures characteristic of our American democracy were constructed with our multi-opinioned individualism and adversarial, often aggressive, competitive social nature in mind. It is a governmental form designed to try to create reasonable order from what could otherwise be clamoring chaos; it is not designed to be an efficient engine to get things done quickly and effectively. Madison and the Federalists who formed our constitution created a system that requires involvement, often intense involvement, in government processes in competition with other interested parties and groups to advance or protect one's values, goals and agendas. This leads inevitably to the formation of competitive and individualistic mutual-aid associations—interest groups—whose purpose is to more successfully do battle in our democratic political arena.

Madison was reputed to welcome diversity and conflicting groups and interests, the more the merrier. Then no one group, certainly not some majority group, could ever dominate and tyrannize the rest. It was the fear of dominance and tyranny by any given selfish, competitive group—the memory of centuries of aristocratic tyranny, state religions and our revolutionary war still very fresh—that motivated Madison. The Federalists conveniently espoused a philosophy similar to Adam Smith's invisible hand in market economics to explain how our democratic government would serve the common good. As Daniel Kemmis, the former mayor of Missoula, Montana and author of the widely read book, *Community and the Politics of Place* (1990) described this philosophy: "Individuals would pursue their private ends, and the structure of government would balance those pursuits so cleverly that the highest good would emerge without anyone having bothered to will its existence" (p. 15). The conservative pundit George Will wittily refers to this as the "Cuisinart theory of justice." This sees society as "a lumpy stew of individuals and groups, each with its own inherent 'principle of motion.' This stew stirs itself, and in the fullness of time, out comes a creamy puree called 'the public interest" (cited in Kemmis, 1990 pp. 53-54). Tastes of that nearly mythical puree are rare and far between.

As Daniel Kemmis (1990) perceptively puts it, among our founding fathers, "The option which was chosen, then, was to place between the individuals in conflict, not a substantive choosing of a common good, but a *process* for weighing, balancing, and upholding rights" (p. 56, emphasis as per original). Obeying our individualism, we have chosen to be "unencumbered selves," with the pursuit of our separate expressions of "happiness" and our various imaginings of our "rights" bringing us to a standstill as our several paths intersect and block each other, leaving us impotently screaming at one another. As Kemmis (1990) concludes:

> This shrillness and indignation, which is so familiar to all of us, is a symptom that something is profoundly wrong with the way we make "public" decisions. The successive blocking of one another's initiatives is another symptom. A third is the ever more frequent withdrawal of people from all public involvement—either because they are frustrated with the pattern of blocked initiative or because they don't like shrillness and indignation, in themselves or in others (p. 62).

Those that remain in the political fracas for the long run are either highly motivated, such as ideological fanatics and extremists; greedy self-aggrandizement seekers; those well financed and representing powerful economic interests; or mutual-aid associations representing the particular interests of large groups of individuals from which money can be endlessly collected and activists recruited. These special interest groups have the resources and tenacity needed to outlast competitors and triumph despite the clever maze of processes Madison and the Federalists and their political progeny have created.

Since Americans political actions are focused on pursuing their own individualistic goals without regard to others or the welfare of society as whole, coming to a consensus on some issue and acting together as one is rare and problematic. As the economist Lester Thurow (1997) observed, "Without a crisis galvanizing public attention, democracies almost never act" (p. 311). Kemmis lamented how Missoulians could not seem to grasp the consensus, the common goal that lurked just beyond their awareness, because their awareness was focused on doing battle with those of opposing opinions. Competitive individualism hides our common goals and degree of our consensus from us and prevents us from acting on it, unless shocked into it by a crisis.

There is a fatigue and disillusionment growing among Americans, a lack of faith in our government, that is both worrisome and a signal. It is time for a new political system, one that can keep track of the common good, as Jefferson had hoped our new government would. As we see, competition and individualism can't do it. That leaves true cooperation as the only candidate. Democracy is a difficult, expensive and time consuming way to govern; cooperation operating from a consensus is easy, clean, fair and far cheaper. And it focuses on the common good every day.

NARCISSISM AND DEPRESSION, AN INDIVIDUALISTIC LEGACY

The prominent psychotherapist Rollo May (1991) in his book, *The Cry for Myth* sees us as functionally "mythless." May (1991) believes Americans are suffering an "endemic feeling of loneliness, a prodding of restlessness ... that imprisons our souls." He also states that "our clinging to cults and our narcotic passion to make money is a flight from our anxiety, which comes in part from our mythlessness" (p. 48). He calls attention to two serious problems resulting from our extreme individualism and mythlessness, record levels of depression and the narcissistic personality.

According to May, the narcissistic personality has become "the dominant type of patient in the decades since the 1960s," the same time our communities began their disintegration according to Putnam's research, described above. The narcissistic personality is self-absorbed, lonely, and isolated. "This person has few if any deep relationships and lacks the capacity for satisfaction or pleasure in the contacts he does have" (May, 1991, p. 112). Narcissistic people demand immediate gratification, gain no lasting pleasure from their sexual relations, have limitless cravings for acquisitions, and live in a "state of restless, perpetually unsatisfied desire" (p. 112). May says this restless, insatiable quality in American individualists has been recorded by many observers and scientists including Tocqueville, who noted even in the 1830s our restless moving from place to place and constant discontent "because they never stop thinking of the good things they have not got" (cited in May, 1991, p. 108).

And in yet another of the ironies of individualism, according to May, "Narcissism destroys individuality, contradictory though that seems" (1991, p. 113). For example, the narcissistic personality has a tendency to become unhealthily dependent in therapeutic relationships for advice and guidance while never developing the deep relationship with the therapist good therapy requires. May, like Bellah, criticizes American therapists for defining love and meaning not in terms of caring relationships but simply as the fulfillment of the patient's emotional requirements. "Therapy, for a number of reasons ... moves toward narcissism and excessive individualism, each empowering the other" (May, 1991, p. 114). Our cold, empty, lonely, narcissistic personality with the superficial happy smile on his or her face "can be considered in America as a further development of American individualism" (p. 114).

Ours has been called the "Age of Melancholy", May (1991) notes, because of our widespread depression despite the "gleeful noises" of our lotteries and shopping sprees (p. 120). The rates of depression in America are skyrocketing, having increased by more than tenfold since before World War II. This can be attributed, according to May, to the break down in the family, the community, and to the loss of meaningful, community oriented, myths—the consequence of our increasingly unrestrained self-centered individualism. May believes that commitment to the common good—a corner stone of cooperation—would do much to lower depression and make life more meaningful. "It is imperative that we rediscover myths which can give us the psychological structure necessary to confront this widespread depression," May (1991) insists (pp. 121-123). True cooperation can provide the foundation for such healing myths. (See the end of Chapter 18 for more on our need for new myths and the content our new myths require, including commitment to the common good.)

Looking out over our society and the abundant literature demonstrating both our love affair with individualism and the problems it causes us we can conclude with Bellah,

> *We thus face a profound impasse. Modern individualism seems to be producing a way of life that is neither individually nor socially viable,...* The question, then, is whether the older civic and biblical traditions have the capacity to reformulate themselves while simultaneously remaining faithful to their own deepest insights (Bellah et al., 1985, p. 143, emphasis mine).

Rather than attempt to return to the more group-centered civic and biblical individualistic traditions, it is time for us to move on, to go through the portal of a paradigm shift, to the new purely group-centered world of cooperation. It's time to leave individualism in any and all of its forms behind. It is time to abandon at last the destructive made-up separation and pointless struggle between the individual and the community. It is time to bring the lonely and struggling people caught in our individualistic nightmare home at last to the safe, warm haven of cooperative community.

If anything, the other principle component of our current American culture, competition, is even worse than individualism. The next two chapters show why.

Chapter 8. Competition, Economic Stratification and Boom–Bust Cycles

Most of us would choose peace and harmony over conflict, human kind-ness and compassion over meanness and efforts to exploit or dominate us, and a safe and civil world instead of a rude one that requires constant vigi-lance to protect ourselves, if given the choice. (Having to be constantly vigi-lant is a source of social stress.) And yet we have set up our society to give us what we don't want and to block the good things we long for. We choose competition.

Perhaps it is not obvious how much negative baggage we opt for when we embrace competition as one of our basic social operating systems. Some of us have learned to love competition, to thrive on it, and protect it by keeping one eye closed and denying its destructive consequences. Alfie Kohn (1986) exploded many of the myths of competition in his book *No Contest: The Case Against Competition.* "Why we lose in our race to win" is the perceptive phrase on the cover. Competition does not reliably produce the best, is not the most productive, does not build high character and whole-some people, is not necessary to have fun, and is not inevitable. We don't need people who relish defeating and humiliating others.

Fortunately, we are not stuck with a life of internal—within group—competition. People who have thoroughly internalized the competition of our society as they have grown up will find themselves defending competition as they read this. But, the contrast with cooperation makes competition's flaws much clearer and vivid.

Competition is an adversarial social "game." That is its nature. To try to generate peace, mutual understanding, and cooperative harmony with a game designed to create conflict and adversarial battles is madness and mocks our intelligence. Amazingly, Americans living competitively repeatedly lament, "Why can't people get along with one another?" The answer is we practice competition that automatically sets us at adversarial odds with one another. Toss selfish individualism into the pot and you wonder how we get anything useful and praiseworthy done at all. If the good things listed above are what you desire, competition, even for "fun," has to be rooted out and discarded. But don't panic. The transformation from a competitive individualistic society to a cooperative one will proceed gradually over time. Those Americans who love their competition have several generations to enjoy it before it finally fades away, obsolete , unloved and discarded. Those who want their cooperation now can take the lessons from this book and get started.

In this chapter we focus on some of the most damaging problems inherent in competition: extreme economic inequalities, insatiable greed, boom-bust cycles, and positive feedback loop feeding frenzies. All of these are automatically generated when a society adopts competition as one of its basic sociocultural operating systems.

Economic Inequalities

Competition Generates Economic Inequalities and Rankings

One of the persistent tensions in our Western culture has been over the extreme inequalities in our economic stratifications, whether it was with royalty in our agrarian era or the "robber barons" of our modern capitalist industrial societies. Capitalism, private ownership of property, has traditionally been the presumed culprit in our history. Consequently, a common strategy among communities seeking a more cooperative and equitable lifestyle has been communal living. In communal living property is held by the community in common and shared equally. Most of these communities have been ascetic and egalitarian. Everyone has the same quality of clothing, food, living conditions and live simply with just enough and no individual accumulations of property. This discontent over economic inequalities and the conviction that private property and capitalism were at fault generated socialism and communism as political ideologies; let the people own the means of production and common public facilities, and let there be more economic equality.

Competitive Capitalism Is the Problem

But private ownership and capitalism *per se* are not the problem; they are not the cause of economic inequalities. Competition is. Look at all of the socialist and communist countries and you will find that every one of them has the same economic inequalities as capitalist countries, maybe even worse. Socialist and communist countries are famous for their internal competitions for control, power, and yes, relative wealth. It is *competitive* capitalism that is the problem. I can imagine a more cooperative capitalism such as the joint stock operations practiced by some of our isolated pioneer communities.

Some of the great economists and thinkers knew it was competition that produced the battles for economic supremacy that generate our gross inequalities of wealth. The classical economist Keynes believed that our basic or absolute wants—those derived without comparison with others—were not insatiable, but our relative wants—those based on comparison with and desire to be superior to others—were, indeed, insatiable. John Stuart Mill also grasped this characteristic of competitive societies and stated it succinctly: "Men do not desire to be rich, but to be richer than other men" (Daly, 1996 p. 36). Toqueville saw that insatiability was deeply ingrained in our culture right from the start. He realized that our "competition of all" produced a sadness and "restlessness in the midst of prosperity" because Americans "never stop thinking of the good things they have not got" (quoted in Bellah et al., 1985, p. 117). Adam Smith knew this was a problem and in the *Theory of Moral Sentiments* said "most of the world's troubles come from somebody not knowing when to stop and be content" (Phillips, 2002, p. 347).

Competitive Winning is Relative

A major source of this insatiability in competition, as Robert Frank and Phillip Cook (1996) pointed out, is the ranking of people by comparisons between competitors on a sliding, relative scale. Who is on top and winning is determined by who has the most of whatever they are competing for at the moment. There is no set amount of either accomplishments or consumption that is declared the "enough" point where competition ceases; instead there is a sliding scale of what constitutes "winning" that goes up as accumulations grow. In most competitions, to become and remain a winner means unceasing pursuit of more and more of whatever the competition is over, such as money and material wealth in America. Since there is no end, there can never be contentment or surcease of competition, consequently, dedicated competitors become insatiable and greedy in their pursuits. Dysfunctional economic stratification polarizations result, with a dramatic disconnect between what those on top of the wealth ranking have, and their realistic contribution to the adaptive success of American society. It is easy to see why many Americans are furious with excesses of wealth accumulated at the top at the expense of the welfare of those in the middle and lower economic levels. The culprit is the culture of competition; its elimination from our American society can permanently correct this festering problem.

This focus on relative rankings characterizes just about everything Americans do. We rank everything. Athletes and teams, products of all kinds, communities, people on a wide variety of qualities, subcultures, companies and their services, and on and on. All of us have been ranked multiple times in our lives on many scales, popularity among them. We are constantly comparing and competitively ranking the "winners" and "losers," the "best" and the "worst," in every sphere of our lives. One of the unnecessary sources of social stress competition generates is the low self-esteem of the "losers," "the rejects," "the worst," millions of them. Competition produces losers, who too frequently become discouraged and disengage, everywhere, everyday, where a cooperative society would see only potentially productive members of an adaptive community and embrace them. Competition's penchant for rejection of competitive losers is costly in human terms and lost contributions to our collective quality of life.

AMERICA'S HISTORY OF ECONOMIC INEQUALITIES

Economic inequalities have been a persistent characteristic of America from our founding to the present. Our competitive capitalistic economy and individualistic democratic government create a dualism in our society that is in constant tension, similar to the individual versus the community tension. This dualism has had a direct influence on the degree of economic inequalities throughout our history. Kevin Phillips (2002) understands that our government and economy are profoundly different, often incompatible, sociocultural systems. In his political and economic history of America, *Wealth and Democracy*, Phillips said: "We can begin with a simple premise: *Democracy and market economics are not the same thing*" (p. 417, emphasis as per original). He notes that while there are interactions, essentially the market economy favors concentration of wealth while democracy promotes more equitable distribution (p. 418). He quotes Supreme Court justice, Louis Brandeis, who said: "We can have a democratic society, or we can have great concentrated wealth in the hands of a few. We cannot have both" (Phillips, 2002, p. 418). The prominent economist Lester Thurow, who also understands that our democracy and economy are culturally different, in *The Future of Capitalism* (1997, p. 245) elaborates:

> Capitalistic economies are essentially like Alice in Wonderland where one must run very fast to stand still—just stopping inequality from growing requires constant effort. Historically, since market economies haven't produced enough economic equality to be compatible with democracy, all democracies have found it necessary to 'interfere' in the market with a wide variety of programs that are designed to promote equality and stop inequality from rising.

Phillips (2002) said, "The 'Invisible hand' [which should make things work out to everyone's benefit] beloved of market theologians periodically sprains its theoretical wrist in speculative collapses, gluts of oversupply, or private monopolistic distortions" (p. 418). From my perspective, since our capitalistic market economy is based on competition, this is just what we should expect. Phillip's book is rich in historical and statistical details revealing the travails of our economy—government battles. At times the wealthy have so much control of our government, it looks like a plutocracy.

One measure of the fluctuations in our extreme economic stratification looks at the difference between the wealth of the richest American in a period compared with the median household income at the time. This data is from Phillips book *Wealth and Democracy* (2002, p.38). I selected four examples. It is clear that extreme economic stratification has always been with us.

In 1790 Elias Derby was the wealthiest American, worth $1 million dollars, with median household wealth at $250, for a ratio of wealthiest to the median of 4,000/1. Derby was a privateer during the revolutionary war who made his fortune selling captured British vessels and cargoes (Phillips, 2002, p. 9).

In 1848, John Jacob Astor was worth $20 million, the median household wealth was $400, and the ratio was up to 50,000/1. Astor made his fortune with his American Fur Company, trading animal furs obtained from Indians and mountain men trappers on the American frontier from 1808, later moving in to the China trade and New York City real estate (Phillips, 2002, p. 21, 26).

John D. Rockefeller made his fortune in oil, founding the Standard Oil Company, and was the wealthiest man in America from around 1912 to around 1940, with his wealth growing from $1 billion to $1.5 billion. However, since median household wealth grew from $800 to $1,750 during that time, the ratio was 1,250,000/1 in 1912, but down to 850,000/1 in 1940, still a huge disparity.

In 1999, Bill Gates, the founder of Microsoft, was worth a whopping $85 billion, the median household income was $60,000, and the ratio was an all time high of 1,416,000/1 (Phillips, 2002, pp. 38).

Another measure of inequality is the concentration of wealth in the top one percent of the population that has cornered the lion's share of wealth pretty much routinely in American history. Looking at the period from 1922 to 1997, Phillips (2002, p. 123) shows the top one percent's share of household wealth fluctuated between 44 percent and 20 percent but was mostly in the 30s. In 1997 it was at 40 percent.

According to Phillips, there have been three periods when our competitive capitalism got away from us, forming peaks of economic inequality: the Gilded Age (1870-1900), the 1920s, and the last two decades of the 20th century. These were "zeniths of corruption and excess... when the rich in the United States slipped their usual political constraints" (p. xii). These peaks of economic stratification and wealth accumulation by aggressive competitive capitalists occurred during periods when Americans' wariness and vigilance over them flagged. "Deviations from such wariness mostly have come during optimal periods of broad based prosperity in which economic opportunities far outweighed these qualms"(p. xi).

Each of these "zeniths of corruption and excess" were followed by economic crashes, with progressive and reform movements reasserting democratic restraints upon our economy through government legislation and regulation. There was the "progressive" period from 1900 to about 1912, the period of reform following the 1929 crash that included greater government financial involvement in job creation and entitlements, and we witnessed the vigorous government investigation, criminal charges, and new legislation and regulations in the aftermath of the disastrous crash of 2001 that lingered until 2004-2005, and to some extent beyond. This was followed by the subprime mortgage market and derivatives collapse in the latter part of the first decade of the 21st century. And so the cycle continues.

According to Phillips (2002), there have been only two periods "in which wealth and opportunity clearly nurtured democracy" (p. xii). The first was in the early 19th century when "the frontier settlement decades humming with bargain-priced government land sales empowered millions of new small landowners" (Phillips, 2002, pp. xi-xii). It drew poor immigrants from Europe, many of whom became wealthy, such as Stephen Girard and John Jacob Astor. In that period of history, with capitalism still growing in power, landownership—primarily for agriculture—was still one of the principle bases for wealth and power in the world and the availability of cheap, sometimes free, land in America was like a real pot of gold at the end of the rainbow.

The second period was the quarter century following World War II (1945-1970) "when the middle class pushed its share of national wealth and income to record levels" (p. xii). It was a time when "skepticism of the rich imprinted by the Great Depression guided politics and public policy through the 1960s" (p. xii). It was also a time when our competitive capitalism that "imploded" during the Great Depression was weak and being rebuilt by our government, according to Lester Thurow (1997, p. 208). It was during this period that the American middle class, as we know and value it, flourished. As Thurow (1997, p. 246) also said, it is democracy, not competitive capitalism, which is responsible for the middle class in market economies. Even so, the richest Americans still managed to control a disproportionate amount of the wealth during these two periods.

The ever-prescient Alexis de Tocqueville in 1840 "hedged his praise for democracy in America with concern that the new industrial elite, 'one of the harshest that ever existed,' would bring about the 'permanent inequality of conditions and aristocracy'" according to Phillips (2002, p. 3).

THE BITCH GODDESS OF SUCCESS

Our American individualistic and competitive cultures are not always at odds with each other; sometimes they reinforce each other. The competitive capitalistic free market economy coupled with utilitarian individualism produces a consequence network, a reward structure that generates our often ruthless competition and pursuit of "success" as defined by our current culture. Robert Bellah et al. (1985, pp. 32-33) described the drive for individual "success" generated by our utilitarian form of individualism, which includes the American dream of the poor boy who works hard to make something of himself and succeeds. It includes the drive for "achievement" and pride in goals reached. This couples powerfully with competition generated greed to produce the compulsive behavior Rollo May (1991, p. 115), William James, and others have decried as the pursuit of the "Bitch Goddess of Success" and of winning. I believe this social dynamic is one of the sources of the Type A coping pattern, which includes hard-driving efforts to do more and more in less and less time while attempting to overcoming any obstacles encountered (see Preface). A few hundred million Type As with free-floating hostility anyone? As dysfunctional as it is, this is just what the goddess of competitive capitalism ordered. The economist Lester Thurow, in *The Future of Capitalism* (1997, p. 11) described greed's fundamental place in competitive capitalism:

> In the Middle Ages avarice was the worst of all sins and the merchant could never be pleasing to God. Capitalism needed a world where avarice was a virtue and the merchant could be most pleasing to God. The individual needed to believe that he or she had not just the right, but the duty, to make as much money as possible. The idea that maximizing personal consumption is central to individual welfare is less than two hundred years old. Without this belief the incentive structure of capitalism has no meaning and economic growth has no purpose.

Competitive merchants work diligently to get us to maximize our personal consumption and maximize their sales and profits. Seeking to maximize our personal consumption and wealth puts us in competition with others pursuing the same goal and on the ultimately unwinnable treadmill of relative comparisons with our competitors. The competitive capitalistic market economy is most emphatically not the system of choice to provide people reliably with all of their adaptive needs and economic and material security.

COMPETITION AND SOCIAL STRESS: THE UNNECESSARY WAR OF ALL
AGAINST ALL

Our internal American competition generates more social stress with
unhappy and unhealthy consequences than any other cause. Abandoning
competition in all of its forms will do more to relieve our stress and discon-
tents than any other one thing we could do. I could write a book just on
the social stress generated by adversarial competition in our homes, work-
places, political arenas, communities, schools, over ideologies and beliefs,
in our recreations, and even our arts (see for example Blair Tindall, *Mozart
in the Jungle*, 2005). It is omnipresent and pernicious. It creates a world of
uncertainty and danger. We have to be constantly vigilant for competitive
attacks, cunning efforts to deceive and demean us, exploitive tactics, and
plots to defeat us; all of which can make us losers. Competitors block our
efforts, put down our successes, and steal our prizes. We are caught up in
a constant war of all against all. As this chapter demonstrates, all of this
internal competition does not benefit our society or most of us. Even the
"winners" are never secure, can never rest, but are caught up in an eternal
struggle surrounded by enemies plotting their failure. For many there is no
freedom in a competitive world, but rather a feeling of being trapped in a
dangerous and unkind social game.

Anger, free-floating hostility, generated by our competitive culture is a
major trigger for physiological responses (sympathetic adrenal) that produce or increase the risk for many diseases, including coronary heart disease (see for example Williams, 1989; Chesney and Rosenman, 1985). The
hopelessness and helplessness of those trapped in competitive situations,
especially on the losing end, can produce many psychological problems
such as depression and burn-out. Free-floating hostility easily triggered by
almost anything contributes to many of our social problems such as road
rage, rudeness and incivility, abuse of family members, pointless violence,
obsession with vengeance and more.

Pull the culture of competition out of our society and you strip out these
maladaptive, wasteful, and stressful stratifications, motivations, and struggles with it. Throw it all away. You'll never miss them. Indeed, the absence
of the clamor of adversarial competition allows us to hear the sweet beck-
oning sounds of harmony cooperation offers us.

Cooperation is a completely different kind of culture with community
group goals that benefit all. Cooperation is organized so differently that

there is little need or benefit in ranking people or things within the society and little reason to produce stratifications along any lines except perhaps competence—including cooperative skills—and vigor of engagement in the pursuit of cooperative group goals. Cooperative people use material goods and services and other social sanctions in ways that motivate members, provide them with positive and secure self-images, give them a place to belong as part of something much bigger than themselves, and nurtures them by providing their survival needs. Chapter 18 explores one possible way a cooperative America may be constructed and shows how cooperation distributes everything of value without stratification.

Positive Feedback Loops And Boom-Bust Cycles

Positive and Negative Feedback Loops

Competition has a number of inherent problems that make it a burden not worth carrying culturally. Here is another major one: positive feedback loops. Competition sets up the rewards, the positive sanctioning framework, to produce routinely positive feedback loops in virtually all arenas of our lives. These positive feedback loops generate our feeding frenzies, many of our gross excesses, our speculative stampedes, the glutting of markets, and our repetitive and damaging boom-bust cycles. Positive feedback loops are wild competitive races to grab as much of something as you can before others do or the supply runs out. You don't want to miss or be left out of a "good thing," a chance to make a big "killing" financially or in other ways. "Everybody is doing it!" is often used as justification.

It's easier to understand positive feedback loops if we first describe their more benevolent opposite: negative feedback loops. Negative feedback loops are fundamental to the functioning and internal control of any living system whether an organism, ecological system or social system and are equally fundamental to our technology. Negative feedback loops are the "that's enough" switches that turn off certain forms of constructive behavior when they have done their job. They could also be thought of as the "change directions" switches.

Negative feedback loops regulate our house's temperature through a thermostat, our body's temperature by turning off and on heating or cooling biological processes, make our car's cruise control work, and keep our body processes in balance by controlling levels of blood water, sugar, hormones, nutrients, white and red blood cells, and other components. If you keep giving a monkey bananas there will come a point where he won't eat any more, but if you then offer him peanuts, which have different nutrients from the bananas, he eagerly starts eating the peanuts. In some European countries there is a negative feedback loop that keeps litigation from running wild. The losers in the litigation have to personally pay the expenses and fees of the winning legal team. Frivolous litigation is negatively sanctioned by economic losses, turning them off.

Positive feedback loops unrelentingly encourage behavior that is getting the desired response without regard for excesses or the accumulation of negative consequences. As Holldobler and Wilson (1990) describe it, positive feedback loops occur when each successful product of an action leads to an increase in the frequency of that action, and consequently in the products of that action, escalating and increasing until "supervenient negative loops" activate or else "the materials needed to create the product are exhausted" (p. 362). Positive feedback loops are comparatively rare in biology, and for good reason, they are generally running out of control loops. Nothing will stop them until the organism, ecology, or society is glutted with the loop's products, exhausted by the increasing energy demands of the positive feedback loop, or the environmental resources used in the loop are totally consumed. In America the primary "supervenient negative loop" is supposed to be the government. The government is supposed to watch the economy and keep it from doing unfair or destructive things to the society. Unfortunately, our government is more likely to come up with laws to prevent a particular boom-bust cycle from occurring again after the bust rather than nip the next one in the bud.

Positive Feedback Loops in America

These positive feedback loops have characterized American history. Our rapacious consumption of natural resources including lumber, grazing grasses, wild fish and game for food, mining products, water, oil, land for "development," and the like have left scars and emptiness where conservation and care could have supplied us with many of these for a long time, even indefinitely. We are still consuming oil, water, and land as fast as we can go. Threats to the biodiversity of our ecology, necessary for your own survival, are serious. Efforts at alternative energy sources and conservation are encouraging but they will have to battle the excesses of competitive feedback loops to succeed. The movement may generate its own positive feedback loops as well.

The dot com stock frenzy at the end of the last century, the subprime mortgage debacle and the financial meltdown from derivatives and the like we are currently suffering through (2008-10) are just the latest in a long string of economic boom-busts. They will go on forever as long as we have a competitive economy. The daily news is filled with descriptions of companies in competitive frenzy in one arena or another. These include the auto industries' constant competitive shifting to the "latest" thing in cars such as SUVs, huge pickups, hybrid energy efficient small cars, and more gadgets for the user, all in order to stay ahead or keep up with other auto companies while producing an overabundance of similar models. What's next? The upscale coffee market is glutted and even Starbucks has had to scale back a bit.

As a golfer I'm always watching for good deals on greens fees, and those deals are going to get better. "Golf courses find the rough; Glut of layouts forces creative marketing" reads a January 1999 newspaper headline (Hiestand, 1999, p. 1C). While the number of golf rounds played had stayed steady at about 500 million over the previous decade, the number of golf courses expanded rapidly, over shooting the demand in many markets. Owners were forced to bizarre lengths to promote their courses: dressing staffers as bananas to hand out free bananas, free car washes, discounts to customers wearing Halloween costumes, and women's "Bad Fast Golf League" where players don't keep score if they don't want to and can kick the ball or pick it up and throw it. "There are far too many golf courses out there now," said one owner, and "Every course is fighting for dollars," said another. The same seems about to happen to ski resorts. The number of skiers has remained, as with golf, fairly constant, while numerous new ski resorts are being built and old ones expanded. Fancy new megaplex theaters may also have reached the glut stage (Eisenberg, 1999, p. 40).

The beer industry is another example of the desperation this positive feedback loop generates in many business and industries. An insider, Philip Van Munching (1997) revealed, "big brewers, desperately afraid of what the other guy might do next, have advertised, promoted and generally spent themselves into the frenzied overkill that is today's beer business" (p. 6).

Jack Welch, then CEO of General Electric, commented on the effects of these competitive positive feedback loops for business and market share on business leaders. He said that being named CEO years ago was the culmination of a career; now "it's the beginning of a career. You cannot be a moderate, balanced, thoughtful, careful articulator of policy. You've got to be on the lunatic fringe" (Samuelson, 1997).

There are all kinds of positive feedback loops operating on the internet threatening to overwhelm our technology to handle them. Litigation in America seems to be in an endless positive feedback loop. Personal communication devices and capacities are also in development frenzy. More of our entrepreneurs are joining competitive positive feedback loop competitions than are looking for unmet needs.

Economic Growth Is a Positive Feedback Loop

And then there is the grand daddy of all positive feedback loops: eternal economic growth. The only way competitive capitalism can con democratic governments and their individualistic citizens into believing that the competitive capitalistic market economy is a humane and beneficial economy for all is to keep the economic pie constantly expanding and thus providing money for new jobs, "improved" living conditions, and a middle class. It is this expanding economic pie that makes possible the social services democratic peoples want to balance out the harsh natural consequences of competition. (See Thurow, 1997, pp. 242-278.) Consequently, since competitive capitalism is based on consumption of material goods and services, consumption must be forever expanding and accelerating, with no end in sight except the exhaustion of natural resources necessary to produce the products and services and/or the absolute glutting of the population with stuff and services.

Never have I heard or read of any free market economist suggesting there will be a plateau of "enough" when economic growth will no longer be required or desired. It appears, then, that within the fabulous mythology of competitive capitalistic free-enterprise market economics there is no limit on the size and number of homes, cars, televisions, phones, sports equipment, toys, clothes, increasingly elaborate tools, personal computers and accessories, beauty and hygiene products, products to clean our homes, furniture and decorations, and so forth we are expected to consume. Realistically, how much can we consume before we are overwhelmed and simply unable to use more, to even find any place to store it? Then, of course, there is the planned obsolescence especially in things like software and some technologies that encourage us—sometimes require us—to wastefully abandon still useful products and buy new ones.

We have swallowed the basic cultural mantras of competitive capitalism hook, line, and sinker: the idea that maximizing personal consumption is central to individual welfare and that our social status and worth are determined by whom we have more than. The use of the maximization of individual wants as the motivator for human behavior in our competitive capitalistic free market, I believe, is approaching the burnout, glutted level that precedes collapse of positive feedback loop systems. Run up those credit card bills! Borrow on your home equity! The consequence is a voracious positive feedback loop we hide from ourselves by labeling it benignly: "economic growth."

In his book *Beyond Growth* the economist Herman Daly (1996) provides a model for sustainable development within a steady-state economy that does not require constant expansion and growth; one that is more in harmony with the environment and our natural resource pool, and is much better integrated into our civilization as a whole and its adaptive requirements. He suggests that in rich countries like America we may be getting to the point where economic growth may contribute more to the relative wealth differences than to the aggregate increase in wealth (Daly, 1996, p.36). He points out that not only is the positive feedback loop of endless economic growth not necessary, it is not even based on sound economic theory. Daly (1996, p. 27) observed that economic growth, generally meaning an ever-growing Gross National Product, "is the only magnitude in all of economics that is expected to grow forever—never to reach an economic limit at which the marginal costs of further growth become greater than the marginal benefits." He notes the theoretical anomaly that in microeconomics every enterprise has an optimal scale beyond which it should not grow, yet when all microeconomic units are aggregated into macroeconomics, the concept of an optimal scale mysteriously—without theoretical foundation or justification—disappears.

Competition is not working for our collective adaptive benefit and never will. It offers us a future of continued carnage and hurt. It's time to advance to the next level of social evolution: cooperation.

American's might have produced cooperative organizations many times over if our competitive individualism had not undermined the efforts. The next chapter offers an example of how competition can destroy cooperative efforts.

> Benjamin R. Barber, in "The Lost Art of Cooperation: Americans often forget that cooperation and collective effort are the foundation of freedom," *The Wilson Quarterly*, 31.4, Autumn, 2007, pp. 56-62, said:
>
> > Whatever we make of it, today competition dominates our ideology, shapes our cultural attitudes, and sanctifies our market economy as never before. We are living in an age that prizes competition and demeans cooperation, an era more narcissistic than the Gilded Age, more hubristic than the age of Jackson. Competition rules (p. 56).

Chapter 9. Saturn and What Might Have Been

The formative years of the Saturn automobile corporation—the first ten—are an example of what happens too often when Americans try to create a cooperative company or organization within a competitive company, rather than isolating it physically and/or organizationally as successful cooperative efforts in America have had to do. Jack O'Toole (1996) was there and appropriately characterized that whole arena as the "land of the adversaries." His book, *Forming the Future: Lessons from the Saturn Corporation*, is the story of good people on the right track towards cooperation, if only...

A Noble Effort Doomed from Inception

What is frustrating about the Saturn story is that the original planners and organizers, drawn from management and union and working together, came up with ideas, plans, and practices as the company gestated and grew that incorporated many of the elements of cooperation. This is both amazing and encouraging. It shows that there are Americans who can discern many of the elements of cooperation and are ready to try to construct organizations based upon them. But, unhappily, in Saturn's case these cooperative initiatives were doomed from the beginning.

The established competitive dominance hierarchies of that social arena were General Motors (GM), the controlling parent of Saturn on the one hand, and the International United Auto Workers Union (UAW) on the other. There was no indication that these two competitive juggernauts had any intention of transforming themselves to more cooperative systems despite the tentative collaborative explorations by a selected group of their people with Saturn.

This effort to discover ways for management and labor to work together more collaboratively sounds noble. But it ignored the fact that keeping the competition generated adversarial management/labor power split in Saturn's organization locked Saturn into the old competitive culture with little real maneuvering room to develop fresh, fluid, cooperative-style task-related work groups. They did, however, try to bridge and minimize this gap. The founders of Saturn frequently had to use competitive/adversarial techniques—bargaining, for example—as well as common individualistic practices—such as democratic voting—to negotiate more cooperative work patterns and role prescriptions.

We have seen in earlier chapters how important it is for an organization or group that wants to develop cooperation in the United States to establish independence from our competitive individualistic society. This Saturn did not do. To do it right, they would have had to start from scratch with fresh, competent, people willing to try a cooperative approach to car building, completely independent of both General Motors and the UAW and other competitive individualistic influences. Predictably, GM and the UAW created a vise that eventually squashed the more cooperative Saturn initiatives and eliminated the elements of cooperation that had been put in place with so much struggle. I tip my hat to those people—such as Jack O'Toole, whom you are about to meet—who fought the "good" (but futile) fight and glimpsed for a time what might have been.

Jack O'Toole's (1996) book is a powerful personal and detailed historical account by a union man of the blow-by-blow struggle to found what he and his co-creators hoped would be a new and fresh car company. One that would be run without many of the problems and flaws constraining General Motors and the UAW. He was there from the beginning, through the exciting years and successes, to that sad and bitter end: the crushing of the cooperative efforts. Those who want to follow the historical sequence and details will find them in his book. I will focus on the cooperative elements they were working to implement and how the competitive adversarial relations from without and within Saturn crushed them.

In 1983 General Motors was feeling the pressure from foreign competition, especially the Japanese. It was losing market share and consequently sharply reducing the number of employees. The challenge was to compete with the Japanese in producing small cars. General Motors had "an engineering study under way to design a new product to compete in this market as well as a new plant in which to build such a car." The United Auto Workers Union was asked "if the union would be interested in studying how to manage such a facility as well as the people systems" using a "clean sheet of paper" approach. The union enthusiastically responded, "Yes!" O'Toole recalls (1996, p. vii).

Don Ephlin, vice president of the UAW, however, expressed the Union's goals this way, "We are here to prove that we can build an automobile with UAW workers and GM managers that is competitive in quality, cost, and customer satisfaction and do it without lowering our standard of living" (p.71). These were the goals of a workers' mutual-aid association—both individualistic and competitive—rather than of a cooperative enterprise.

O'Toole (1996) caught the crucial insight:

> Saturn Corporation's roots come from the premise that we can't keep doing what we've always done and get different results—for that is called insanity. So the quest began to explore ways to do things differently in building a world-class quality, competitively priced small car. We knew we had the technology needed, but we also, finally, realized that technology wasn't enough. The union and management had to work together if we really wanted to compete successfully over a sustained period of time (p. 3).

O'Toole (1996) expressed the frustration many employees were feeling with the status quo and their hopes for Saturn. Employees

> would enter and exit the machine [General Motors] every day; but slowly, gradually, they changed from caring human beings to either cynical critics of everything, or nonverbal automatons seemingly devoid of life. We had a glimmer of hope now. The opportunity of breaking this brutal pattern was within our grasp (p. 24).

On February 5, 1984, on a bitterly cold Detroit night, "100 strangers from a cross section of GM and UAW came together to undertake the most revolutionary study in the history of the auto industry," O'Toole recalled

(1996, p. 3). One of the hundred didn't like it, left, leaving 99. This became the Committee of 99 that would "ultimately present its radical 'breakaway' recommendations to" GM and the UAW. They were organized into seven teams of 6 to 15 members, matching the engineering systems of an auto, each composed of people from labor and management. Each team had a "process consultant," a skilled facilitator to help. Among the ground rules: there would be no voting, instead consensus was required on all decisions; no "designated leader"; they would operate from a "clean sheet of paper"; and they could go wherever they wanted to see whomever they wanted (O'Toole, 1996, p. 7). The facilitators took them through team building exercises; then they set about visiting a wide variety of auto plants in America and Europe, including Sweden and Germany, and studying the Japanese approach in depth.

O'Toole was especially impressed with the differences between Volvo's and Volkswagen's (VW) approaches to automation. O'Toole observed (1996, p. 15),

> Volvo spent untold hours in an attempt to make the assembly of an automobile as easy as it could make it for those who were building its product. VW chose to put its hours and dollars on repetitive tasks, seemingly ignoring all the data that give this method very low quality ratings, especially in mass production,

In May of 1984, the committee of 99 made their report. Some of the committee returned to "the land of the adversaries"—GM/UAW—because they were on the fast track or for other career reasons. Some were invited back to participate in the next phase of gestation of Saturn, forming the UAW/GM Saturn Resource Center to begin to apply what the committee had produced in planning a new company and plant. We see some of the insights of cooperation emerging at this point. For example, "We had to insulate ourselves, somehow, some way, from GM and the International Union," O'Toole said (1996, p. 32). This crucial insight was never fully realized, unfortunately. And, "The importance of how we went about attracting the 'right' people was a point vividly driven into us during the study by every world-class organization we had the good fortune to borrow from" (p. 30). Competence in participants is crucial for successful cooperation.

At the same time, while examining the most recent GM/UAW National Agreement—it was 600 pages long—they were stunned to realize

> the stark reality of the depth of animosity between the adversaries shone as it never had in the past before.... The distrust and disdain

for each other, having never been addressed over the last five decades, had taken form in voluminous verbiage....

O'Toole (1996) warns:

> When engrossed in a world of collaboration and mesmerized by the charms of synergy, don't ever forget that the world as a whole is not where you are. The daily reenactment of the first battle of the adversaries repeated for decades and honed to Oscar nomination form, will go on. For no matter if, esoterically, each adversary was desirous of a different approach, all their respective herds [constituencies] hold them unwaveringly accountable to defend their win-lose golden calves of the past (p. 51-52, insert mine).

O'Toole decries our competitive idea someone else has to lose for us to win, and the way it interferes with creating more cooperative organizations. "When creating 'a new order of things' in which no one losing is the ruling norm, remember that we all came from a zero sum-based world" (p. 52).

O'Toole and his team, charged with coming up with a fresh Memorandum of Agreement for Saturn—a draft of a potential contract between labor and management—found the lack of commitment individually and mutually in the existing GM/UAW contract disturbing. "The brilliance of picking out the lack of mutual or individual commitments in the traditional agreement, and making respective commitments the cornerstones of the [Saturn] memo," O'Toole (1996) said, was "the 'breakwith' thinking that allowed Saturn to crest every monstrous wave of resistance it faced in those crucial forming years" (p. 51). True cooperation requires focus on, and commitment to, the group's goals; this provides a basis for group cohesion, for organizing daily work, and for decision making. As O'Toole observed, "Reach agreement on principles and all the details will be easy" (p. 91).

Among the problems they faced at this stage was getting agreement for the innovations in the new memo, which were eventually forthcoming after plenty of good old adversarial political negotiations and persuasion. However, a bigger problem was getting money—either from General Motors or various government sources—in order to train the employees coming into Saturn in the more cooperative working relations necessary for success. They felt the importance of this training, and lifelong education of the work force in general, were not appreciated in the upper echelons of GM (O'Toole, 1996, pp. 60-63.) O'Toole (1996) said, "Here is where we must truly leapfrog our competition. Through competency based training. . . " (p. 119). This appreciation of the importance of training in cooperative relations and continued training of participants to keep competence and understanding high is another important insight. Too often would-be cooperative organizers assume competitive individualistic Americans already know how to do this adequately, an assumption that generally spells doom for the project.

ELEMENTS OF TRUE COOPERATION PERCEIVED AND ATTEMPTED

O'Toole (1996) expresses his enthusiasm for the new social relations they were visualizing for Saturn:

> A whole new people system awaited birth. With the fragile partnership between union and management having been agreed to in principle, it now awaited the operationalization of the details relative to this bold move. Just the thought of creating a human resource organization that would really care about people ran shivers up our spines. We talked about all the elements of our organization, but this was, beyond a doubt, the topic that meant the most to those of us who were represented by the union. Imagine, we could design out the labor relations department; we could eliminate the segregation of salaried and hourly personnel; and we could relegate the role of committeeman to the Land of the Adversaries and *put decision making where it belonged, in the hands of those who must implement the decisions.* We could unite human resources and organization development into one focused group, seeking only the development of our most valuable asset, our people, rather than have two groups competing for the most notoriety in achieving the organizations goals (p. 70, emphasis mine).

This quote is full of appreciation for what a more cooperative work environment would look like, but most striking is the realization that decision making should be done by those "on the line," the ones who are going to implement them. This is a cooperative practice. In cooperation these people would be the most competent available to both make the decisions and do the implementing.

A number of more cooperative insights and elements emerged during the development of the Saturn company. This list is taken from different points in O'Toole's (1996) book.

The organizers wanted "what you do, not what you are to determine your worth" (p. 73). They wanted to replace seniority, classifications of labor or management, and the like with competence.

"We were very aware that one of our strengths lay in our ability to accept change and grow from it" (p. 75). Adapting rapidly and easily to changes in the environment is a fundamental quality of true cooperation.

"Our critical success factor would always be taking the time to get the buy-in up front; we could make anything work that we believed in" (p. 75). Cooperative organizations hire and retain only those who have "bought into" the organization's shared group goals and to cooperation as their operating culture; it is critical to everything else that follows.

The Saturn organizers saw that in the changing business world, "the future indicates the emerging structure of the 'New Capitalism' or 'New Management' is expected to have fewer levels of traditional decision-making layers and significantly fewer managers itself" (p. 96). Cooperative organizations have a minimum of hierarchy, and that is focused on coordination rather than control.

"The new structure of the union had greatly enhanced our ability to get real time data on the entire organization, thereby enabling the partnership to grow less encumbered by many isolated decisions being made that, when discovered, adversely affected a different part of the organization than the one in which they were made" (p. 124). This kind of information flow and coordinated decision making is a hallmark of cooperation. This is an impressive selection of the elements of true cooperation.

Unfortunately, group-centeredness was never achieved for the Saturn Corporation as a whole, though they seemed to be flirting with it at times, nor would we have expected or hoped for it given the labor/management split-power structure of the company and the overbearing and intrusive presence of the parent competitive dominance hierarchies of GM and the International UAW. Add the competitive individualistic cultural habits of the employees and I doubt that anyone grasped what group centeredness looked like or its centrality to cooperation. Individual commitment was a step in the right direction, however. Group centeredness is critical to cooperation. Just as strikingly absent was cooperation level consensus. The Saturn employees as a whole never came close to achieving it. Consequently, even with all of these cooperative elements, true cooperation could never have emerged or survived in Saturn.

Enough of these cooperative efforts were in effect in the first few years to contribute to making the new company surprisingly productive and successful. For example, at the end of only their second year of production, the J.D. Power quality survey of new car owners found Saturn was "sixth [in quality] among all makes, up from 16th in 1991, first among all domestic makes, problems per 100 vehicles improved 27 points to 108, down from

137 in 1991, fourth in sales satisfaction," and "third in customer satisfaction, behind Lexus and Infiniti" (p. 174). This is an amazing accomplishment for a brand new, start up car company.

SPRING HILL, TENNESSEE: NEW COLLABORATIONS AND CONTINUING AD-VERSARIAL STRUGGLES

In April of 1986, ground was broken for the new Saturn plant in Spring Hill, Tennessee. Spring Hill would be home to the manufacturing plants, but almost all of the advanced manufacturing engineers stayed in Michigan, working with technicians at the preproduction facility in Madison Heights. This geographical split would cause continual problems including a great deal of commuting and too many decisions made on computer screens. For example, there was a problem with a new model station wagon's door late in production because of this, and the engineers had to be dragged down to Spring Hill to actually work on the assembly line before they could see the problem and go back to Michigan and redesign the door (O'Toole, 1996, p. 131).

About the time of the ground breaking and move to Spring Hill, O'Toole (1996) realized there was another problem, "I'm not sure exactly when it dawned on us, but two distinct cultures were being created that at a point in time would battle for control of Saturn" (p. 79). On the one hand were O'Toole and those with him who had put so much time and energy into the "clean sheet of paper" planning of a brand new kind of car company along a more cooperative model who were the new culture, on the other hand were those who favored the traditional auto culture. He was concerned that "The SAC [Saturn Automobile Corporation], left to itself, now earth had been turned, would put pedal to the metal at building little [competi- tive] fiefdoms and putting line after line on our clean sheet of paper" (p. 79). This would override all of the careful planning and dash the hopeful dreams it had aroused. O'Toole and his compatriots battled successfully to keep these turfs to a functional minimum. For example, management meeting separately created 12 business units—turfs, which O'Toole and the union were eventually able to reduce to 3 (O'Toole, 1996, pp. 93-94). This struggle between cultures would continue until the traditional auto culture eventu- ally triumphed.

The "collaboration" between management and labor found its funda- mental daily expression in two person teams, one management and one union, who together directed each work unit (O'Toole, 1996, p. 116). The "module advisor" was a company man, such as a manager or engineer, and the "Charter Team Member (CTM)" was a union man. These were important teams with real responsibility over how the company operated. For example, the first team O'Toole worked on was directing the people systems, which included seven areas of responsibility: "recruitment, application, screening and selection, training, reward systems development, human environment group, operations, systems and planning, and Saturn information systems (EDS)" (p. 130). Each team partner had equal authority and responsibility for the socio-technical development of the work unit. Thus, the management/union team pair had to develop a working relationship, forcing them to learn each other's point of view or mentality, and develop honesty in their communications. A cooperative organization would have a consensus, operate in a culture of cooperation, and have clear common group goals so that having to learn each other's points of view and mentality would be unnecessary. When new problems arise, cooperative organizations are designed to focus on those problems as an organization and solve them, including trial and error testing of solutions. This shows how far from a cooperative culture Saturn was even at this stage.

O'Toole worked in four partnerships over his career at Saturn; in addition to people systems they were materials and management, facilities, and manufacturing and engineering (pp. 129-132). O'Toole (1996) said "one key reason all our partnerships worked was we took the time up front to form a contract with each other on our respective expectations" (p. 133). They did seem to work rather well, though energetic debate frequently preceded a decision or action by the pair. O'Toole commented upon the frequent debates with his various partners and how they "always ended up doing the right thing, but not without a fight" (p. 145). While this collaboration was an advance in labor/management relationships, especially in power sharing, these are not cooperative roles in a cooperative social system. They institutionalize the management/labor power split rather than eliminate it, as a cooperative system would.

Among the adversarial problems O'Toole's (1996) collaborative culture group experienced over time were: the UAW appointing local union leaders for Saturn who did not understand the culture being developed, and this before the locals were even organized and without adequate input from the union people affected (p. 76); management meeting separately on the business plan without the UAW representatives (p. 93-94); continual competitive infighting among union, management, and engineering at Saturn (p. 124); the Union threatening to throw in the towel, to strike, when management tried to revert to practices as usual (p. 134); other divisions of GM, jealous of what was happening at Saturn, battling them (such as for resources and their own small cars); many personal, self-seeking, power struggles; battles with the GM dominance hierarchy (p. 59 and throughout the book); and, one of the worst, Saturn began to get adversarial union members from closed plants as a result of Union contracted rules for placing workers from closed facilities (p. 135). Some of those plants closed because these very union members would not accept less adversarial relations with the local management. These extremely competitive and inflexible union workers played crucial roles later in the power struggles within the Union that led to the demise of the more cooperative social patterns and the loss of the more cooperative employees at Saturn, and a return to the adversarial union/management approach of the traditional automobile culture. This reinforces my emphasis that true cooperative social systems must limit membership to only those who believe in, and are committed to practicing, cooperation; internal competition will always destroy cooperation.

Many people know the story of how Saturn's first model design was rejected when exposed to the public for preproduction evaluation, and the extreme time pressure the company faced to get an acceptable car designed and produced by the announced debut date (O'Toole, 1996, p. 107). They started shipping cars on July 30th, 1990 (p. 145). Despite these challenges, the quality of the Saturn cars in these early years was high, with many positive assessments and awards from various publications and organizations (e.g. pp. 169-170). However, this did not occur without constant "down and dirty" conflicts over quality. O'Toole (1996) said, "The union side of the partnership was firmly committed to quality not quantity. Our non-rep [management] partners were committed to quality, too, but they would always lean toward 'Let's build them and put them in the back lot until we can fix' whatever the [quality] issue of the day was" (p. 145). In addition to quality, the early attractions of the Saturn cars for buyers included the care given to customers (pp. 155, 164), the promptness, and honesty of dealing with recall repairs (pp. 154, 158), and the lack of price haggling due to fixed prices. Sales were good, reaching, for example, a record of 31,814 cars for the month of August in 1995 (p. 196). Saturn turned ten years old on January 7th,

1995 (p. 201). These five years, from 1990 through most of 1995, when Saturn was producing cars were the golden years of the Saturn success story, especially from O'Toole's perspective.

THE END OF THE COLLABORATIVE EXPERIMENT

Right when everything seemed to be going so well, disaster struck. The International UAW, goaded and facilitated by actions taken by those adversarial UAW workers from closed plants, came to an agreement with Saturn on changes to the "memo" or union contract that would effectively return Saturn to the traditional automotive culture. In November of 1995 the changes were put to a vote and were resoundingly rejected 75 percent to 25 percent by the workers; they liked things the way they were. "The International Union was shocked", O'Toole recalled (1996, p. 197). Nevertheless, the International Union persevered, requiring additional votes, the last one taken after the beginning of the Christmas holidays when many of the workers had left the area. Thus, the International UAW's manipulations finally triumphed and the contract was changed. It was the end of the collaborative culture in Saturn.

In the new contract or "memo," the UAW locals 1810 and 1853 for the Spring Hill plants "could no longer issue a letter of intent to modify the memo. That would be the exclusive domain of the International Union," O'Toole said (1996, p. 197). The International Union, the competitive dominance hierarchy astraddle the auto industry labor arena, wanted all of its power back and got it. The kind of rapid response to new conditions by those "on the line" that had characterized Saturn and the collaborative relationships and culture had now been seriously undermined, with the old set of traditional auto cultural values reestablished.

Among the critical changes, seniority and political democratic elections replaced selection and appoint to positions by competence. For example: "teams would no longer hire their own members; all transfers in manufacturing would no longer be based on skills, experience, and ability but strictly by Saturn start date (seniority); the crew coordinators, three in Powertrain and Body Systems, six in Vehicle Systems, and two more in the trades area would no longer be jointly selected but now elected; our three crew/two shift/six day operation would changed to three eight-hour shifts five days a week," O'Toole (1996) recounted (p. 197). "Those whose mindsets were adversarial" predominantly won the later elections for various positions such as crew coordinator (p. 202). Elections are the democratic solution Americans are familiar with and comfortable accepting. But it is not the cooperative way, which emphasizes competence. O'Toole and his group had it right. Cooperation lost big to adversarial competition on that day. A day that was inevitable from the beginning of the Saturn adventure.

After that gloomy denouement, O'Toole (1996) reflected and wondered,

> What is behind the International Union's unending assault on our progressive new model for a labor relations agreement that is flexible and vague or nonspecific enough to allow us to meet the constant force of change and not be overwhelmed with specific rules and guidelines that would stifle our ability to meet the challenges of the 1990s and beyond? (pp. 205-206).

And,

> We stand less than four years from the dawn of a new century, which should be primed and ready for this new labor/management model of codetermination, win-win abundance perspective, and collaboration (not confrontation) as the keys to survival in an ever-increasing competitive global economy. Yet, we are not prepared for it. America is not prepared for it (p. 207).

This is, sadly, too true.

What O'Toole never fully understood is that the near-cooperative dream he helped nurture briefly to life cannot live in an organizational environment based upon a competitive, adversarial, sociocultural operating system, such as General Motors and the International Auto Workers Union. That was what was behind the International Union's unending assault. The collaborative social patterns emerging in Saturn were a direct threat to the basic values, social practices, and survival of the highly competitive International Union. Unions are a product of adversarial competition and will not exist in cooperative civilizations. There will be no place for competitive management—the union's adversarial counterpart—either. First, competition as a basic operating system has to go, and then the cooperation can begin.

After the triumph of the International UAW and the adversarial local union members ended the cooperative experiment at Saturn, O'Toole moved to Saturn Outside Services full time. Ironically, he worked there full time as a consultant, trainer, teacher, and speaker working with the many companies wanting to learn about what Saturn had just given up, including the personal touch. Representatives from as many as twelve to fourteen companies came each week (O'Toole, 1996, p. 203). O'Toole (1996) expresses his loss philosophically, quoting William Hazlett, "Man is the only animal that both laughs and weeps. For man is the only animal that is struck with the difference between the way things are and the way they might have been" (p. 201).

The Saturn experiment reinforces the fundamentals of cooperation and the cautions that must be observed when trying to form cooperative groups in competitive individualistic America described in this book. I personally believe there are millions of Americans ready to learn and live cooperation. People like Jack O'Toole and those who helped design the "clean sheet of paper" culture for Saturn and made it work for several years are examples. I am amazed at how many of the cooperative elements they came up with on their own. If we can awaken such cooperation ready Americans and get them talking and working together, we have the makings of a cooperative social movement.

Margaret Wheatley (1994) in her widely read book, *Leadership and the New Science: Learning about Organization from an Orderly Universe.* (San Francisco: Berrett-Koehler, 1994, p. 5) said:

> I believe that we have only just begun the process of discovering and inventing the new organizational forms that will inhabit the twenty-first century. To be responsible inventors and discoverers, though, we need the courage to let go of the old world, to relinquish most of what we have cherished, to abandon our interpretations about what does and doesn't work. As Einstein is often quoted as saying: No problem can be solved from the same consciousness that created it. We must learn to see the world anew. (p. 5)

It's very difficult to solve problems using the culture that persistently creates and perpetuates them.

Part 2. The Tools of Cooperation: Creating the Self-Renewing Society

Introduction to Part 2

When scientists and engineers set out to build the first rockets and su-
personic air planes and when they contemplate new ideas such as 30 story
indoor urban farms for our cities (Dickson Despommier, "The Rise of Verti-
cal Farms," *Scientific American*, November, 2009, pp. 80-87) they expect to go
through a period of trial and error experimentation. Even with extensive
research, calculations, and preliminary scientific work, they know there is
much they need to learn that can only be discovered by giving it a try and
seeing what happens. Then trying again until they figure it all out and it
finally works. The search for true cooperative organizations and societies
is at that stage

Eventually we will be able to produce a working manual showing how
to build cooperative organizations. It will show us what to expect and how
to solve common problems. Creating and operating our first generation of
cooperative social systems requires us to use our sociological tool kit in
fresh ways. This is the topic of Part 2.

John W. Gardner, *Self-Renewal: The individual and the Innovative Society*, New York: Harper & Row, 1963, said:

> When organizations and societies are young, they are flexible, fluid, not yet paralyzed by rigid specialization and willing to try anything once. As the organization or society ages, vitality diminishes, flexibility gives way to rigidity, creativity fades and there is a loss of capacity to meet challenges from unexpected directions (p.3).

> Does this mean that there is no alternative to eventual stagnation? It does not. Every individual, organization or society must mature, but much depends on how this maturing takes place. . . *In the ever-renewing society what matures is a system or framework within which continuous innovation, renewal and rebirth can occur* (emphasis Gardner's, p. 5).

> This brings us to the modern emphasis on process, an emphasis suggested, in its broadest implications, by Arnold Toynbee when he said, "Civilization is a movement ... and not a condition, a voyage and not a harbor" (p. 7).

Chapter 10. The Age of Culture

Human Culture: The Newest "Big Thing" in Evolution

Donald Johanson and Blake Edgar (1996), authors of *From Lucy to Language*, examined the fossil and archeological evidence of human evolution and concluded, "the most distinguishing feature of our species is our dependence on culture for survival" (p. 41). Culture is our species' primary adaptive tool. This evolutionary development makes humans forever interdependent for their survival. We have yet to optimize the effectiveness of our cultures for our mutual benefit. For that we must *all* understand what culture is and how to use it, maintain it, and change it. Then we can master cooperation—the "art of associating together"—by incorporating it into our cultures.

Historians far into the future may well call our times the "Age of Culture." Humans using culture dominate the earth as few species ever have. But we are infants in our use of it. We are only now coming to understand what culture is and how to use it. We have much to learn and unlearn. We have many maladaptive cultural habits. We are in the midst of a massive social transformation, which provides an ideal time to construct a new cooperative culture. In this chapter I spell out in simple terms what culture is. In the following chapters we go into some of the essential techniques for shaping it and enacting it.

What Is Culture?

Culture is the key. It is the key to everything that matters to humans and to our adaptive survival. Culture contains everything we collectively know, our beliefs and myths, our skills and technologies, and the structures of our social systems and institutions. The quality of our culture definitively determines the quality of our lives. Thus, culture is the most critical possession humans have. But we are doing a poor job of taking care of it and using it adaptively.

Creating a cooperative human social group of any size, from a dyad to a civilization, involves shaping culture. It is something we are already doing continually, if clumsily. We are just not shaping cooperative cultures. Instead we are maintaining our competitive and individualistic ones, among many others.

Culture is both simple and profound. The mechanisms for creating, maintaining and changing culture are very simple and straight-forward as you will see. We routinely use them every day, but usually without understanding what we are doing. We just need to be more aware of the consequences of our actions, take responsibility for them, and agree that we want to cooperate, and it will be so.

Defining "Culture"

In this book I'm defining "culture" sociologically as learned information and behavioral patterns that two or more people share. Culture is built upon consensus. If there is no agreement, there is no culture. If two or more people agree on something, such as what they consider "good" or "bad" or the "best" way to do something, they have culture. If, for a variety of reasons, people in agreement change their minds and decide together that something else is "better," they have changed their culture. Cultures of any size contain shared values, and norms that put these values into action, giving us shared social patterns we can understand and anticipate. Culture spells out the "way," of "this is the way we do things here." Social roles and counter-roles—such as husband and wife—are described and their places in social systems spelled out—as in a family. All of this exists because those participating in the culture maintain it. It can evaporate at any time if the participants abandon it or if the consensus is lost.

While we don't usually think of it this way, we have produced cultures—some of them minicultures—we share with our friends, family, neighbors, and coworkers, as well as our special interest groups, our occupations, and then on to the larger groups such as our religions. The several cultures we each practice get mixed together to produce our personal behavior, values and beliefs. Our personal unique mix of cultural memberships distinguishes us from one another and makes us both like many others who share one or more of our cultures, and unlike any other because of our unique combination. We may, for example, share our religion with one cultural community of people; our occupational culture with a different group of people, some of whom may also share our religion; our participation in a softball league with still a different group of people, a few of whom might share our religion and occupation, and so on. Sometimes the cultures in our personal culture set are compatible and sometimes in conflict. Conflicting cultures in our personal set are an important source of social stress, such as the conflicting demands on time and energy of being a hospital nurse and being a mother and wife at the same time.

Among larger groups such as tribes, ethnic groups, religions, societies, and civilizations, the culture is the store-house of everything that cultural community has learned and uses, accumulated over generations. It is everything they know and the skills and technologies they have developed. It includes their language, arts, religions, family and marriage customs, culinary style, architecture, technology and gadgets, government, economy, how they treat "deviants" (those who violate their norms such as criminals), their fashions ... everything. For all of those cultural elements to exist, be applied, and "happen" daily, a consensus on the culture and how to enact it is required. Despite our cantankerous competitiveness and insistent individualistic independence that make consensus hard to achieve and maintain, we have managed enough agreement to produce some impressive cultures such as science and engineering. It is easy to see how culture distinguishes our species and is the source of our preeminence.

WHERE IS CULTURE?

Culture is wonderful, but many people are confused about where it is located. We can observe it in action when people enact it. But it is recorded in our heads. That is the only place it exists. It's written on our brain cells. No people, no culture. When a people die out, such as old tribes and civilizations, their culture dies with them. We have only their artifacts left to study. When we use and enact culture as we live our daily lives, we turn culture into social systems and social behavior. We also produce artifacts, such as our houses, cars, TVs, books, tools, and the like. Culture is our script for social interaction. We learn it from our parents and teachers and others in our cultural communities and teach it in turn. It is easy to see how critical successful socialization of participants to the culture is; the shared culture must get cleanly and correctly into everyone's head for it to produce well-coordinated and effective social systems. We also develop new cultural patterns that we adopt together. We bring culture to life when we enact it.

The societies and complex organizations we produce when we collectively enact our cultures easily elude our individual conceptual grasp. It is easy for people to think of culture existing somewhere else and hovering over us, both constraining and enlightening us, often without our permission. But it's just us carrying our culture in our heads, enacting it skillfully or incompetently, and reinforcing it or undermining it in our behavior and responses to others' behavior.

While books, computers, and other devices help us keep track of all the information in our cultures, they are artifacts and not culture itself. Culture is a living, changing, and dynamic phenomenon in our living brains. Artifacts, including pottery, architecture, records and the like, are expressions and snapshots of cultural content. To observe culture you have to observe humans using it and talking about it.

Obviously, modern-day society and civilization-wide cultures require millions of heads to carry it all—each head with its comparatively tiny but important piece of the whole—producing the huge divisions of labor and specializations that characterize our societies. The more we collectively know, the bigger the culture, the more elaborate the division of labor and specializations, the more we need each other to enact our culture. If ever there was anything that absolutely required people to work together, it is preserving, using, and adaptively evolving our huge, complex, living culture.

Far from being an evil monster enslaving us, culture is the source of every-thing that matters. It gives us everything from something as profound as meaning to something as simple as our daily bread. If we are unhappy with our lives and our social condition it is our own fault because we persist in living a culture that produces discontent.

Sadly, years of experience teaching sociology as a university professor made me acutely aware of how little Americans comprehend culture. Evo-lution's greatest recent breakthrough is—astoundingly—unappreciated by its beneficiaries. Culture's content, dynamics, power, and centrality to the human experience are rarely considered. That it is the engine of our survival is a vague notion, overshadowed by our individualistic focus on our daily lives. Blaming the "System" and mocking what "They(or some authority) say we should do" are common manifestations of ignorance of the fact that culture is created by all of the members of the community that use it and is maintained by their daily enactment of it. They are blaming themselves along with others without realizing it. Our culture belongs to all of us, all of the time. We are all responsible for its current shape, all of the time. It is in our heads culture resides. Cultures are the sum of a given civilization or social system or group at that moment. If you take culture away there is not much left. The quality of our lives directly expresses the quality of our cultures. Poor quality cultures produce poor quality societies. "Perfect" cul-tures are as possible as our willingness to create them together.

What an astounding gift evolution has handed us. What an astounding amount of control over our condition and destiny we have inherited. No other species has achieved more than a rudimentary culture, nothing ap-proximating the complexity of our cultures and the richness of information they embody. We humans have ushered in the Age of Culture. Culture is currently the premier adaptive tool on earth.

OUR ETERNAL CULTURAL PROGRESSION

The heart of our human history is the accumulating knowledge, techni-cal advances and skills that we keep adding to our culture, our living re-pository, era upon era. Many of our sociocultural transformations were the product of major technological breakthroughs and advances. Things like bronze, steel, plows, gun powder and guns and explosives, ships that could sail into the wind, steam and internal combustion engines, electricity and all of the electrical wonders of our times, and computers mark our progress. What a wonderful story they all tell. Our species' eternal struggle in a challenging natural environment to make our lives safer, more predictable, comfortable, disease free, abundant, and rich in understanding characterizes our journey on Earth. In the process, our collective culture of understanding has grown huge and is growing ever more rapidly. We are an amazing species, defined by the culture written and carried collectively in our heads.

But we didn't get here overnight. First came human intelligence and then came human culture. While there were rudimentary forms of culture among our ancestors and other *Homo* species, it took some time for *Homo sapiens* to develop the elements we generally associate with modern cultures. Scientists make a distinction between "anatomically modern humans" that emerged around a 100,000 years ago, and "behaviorally modern humans" with more developed culture and language that emerged roughly 50,000 years ago (Johanson and Edgar, 1996, p. 51; scientific estimates vary). It could be considered our first "cultural explosion" and it occurred between 60,000 and 30,000 years ago when the first art, religion, and comparatively complex technology appeared. These included clothing, shelters, boats, the working of bones—for fish harpoons for example—finely worked stone blades, beads, necklaces, carved figures and paintings on stone walls. By comparison, common stone tools often remained unchanged for millions of years among other *Homo* species.

The second cultural explosion was triggered by the development of agriculture and animal domestication 10,000 years ago, especially in the fertile crescent of the Middle East, producing much larger, more stable, more complex societies and richer cultures. A steady stream of advancements followed: for example, the use of ceramics for pots about 8,000 years ago, the wheel 6,000 years ago, writing 5,000 years ago, and metal smelting 4,000 years ago (Mithen, 1996, pp. 9-31; Johanson and Edgar, 1996, pp. 49-52). Our culture was evolving nicely and our adaptive success accordingly.

We are in a cultural explosion right now that began with the industrial revolution in the 19th century and the emergence of modern science. Inventions, innovations, and scientific discoveries continue at an accelerating pace. We are now in the middle of a massive transformation of human culture resulting from our adoption of electricity, computers, the Internet, television, cell and landline phones, and rapid transportation.

We are in an astounding period. For one thing, our evolutionary gift of intelligence is really expressing itself, dazzling us with daily advances and marvels. At the same time, we are unevenly sloughing off the obsolete remnants of our millennia long agricultural era and much shorter industrial period and moving at varying paces into uncharted sociocultural territory. This causes incompatibilities that bedevil our daily work as well as our efforts to advance. Many of our current social problems and conflicts arise because elements of the entrenched political systems, religions, ideologies and cultural patterns traditional to our agricultural period—especially worldwide—and of our industrial period are incompatible with the emerging requirements of our new era. Understandably, people carrying these "traditional" and old habitual cultures in their heads feel threatened and many resist the changes. This is "cultural lag" and accompanies all major social changes. When new technology is the trigger, the technology always leads and develops first, and then the rest of society haltingly catches up. It is always a painful and confusing time.

How many of our old and current cultural patterns can be adapted to our new plateau of human development and social evolution is an open question. One that will be answered with accompanying pain and nostalgia.

Since our collective culture is becoming huge and evolving qualitatively, it creates a gargantuan coordination task for all of this information, technology, and skills to be productively utilized. Millions, billions of humans with essential portions of the culture in their heads must work together harmoniously and effectively. This is a task utterly beyond adversarial competition and self-centered individualism-based social systems. We need a group-centered society that routinely pays attention to the whole cultural community and generates a community wide consensus. We need cooperation, which is designed to use culture and all of its products as a tool to adapt to our changing environment. Cooperation is the sociocultural system for the new era emerging in our midst. It is the only sociocultural system that we know anything about that can do it.

As the technologies of our new era develop and spread, the direction of our cultural transformation becomes clearer. Bits and pieces of the new culture are taking form from the amorphous fog surrounding the changes. For one thing, we humans love the "gadgets" and technology of our new era and are embracing them with gusto. There is no going back. We are committed. The new technologies tie us continually together with instant communications and rapid transportation while requiring us to use the resources and human power—especially competent human power—of the whole earth to build this emerging new technological era.

While we are becoming a huge functional community we are also facing acute challenges. We are already running into limitations of energy, materials, water, and land to accommodate this new way of life. It has been questioned whether there is enough steel in the world to provide washing machines and other consumer appliances for all the people on our planet. The demands on oil and other resources are going uphill fast as countries like China and India and other developing countries implement our modern high technology civilization.

We are enthusiastically entering a new high science and technology era that is expanding our accumulated culture dramatically. It is also transforming our society, as major technological advances have done repeatedly in our history. We're headed for a new plateau of human development. It is extremely fortunate that what will likely be the greatest, most profound, social and technological transformation in human history is accompanied by our awakened understanding of culture, societies, and human behavior. We know enough scientifically to pay attention to what is happening and guide the birth of our new era effectively for the benefit of all. We can shape it to be in continual harmony with the Earth's environment and to provide a home for everyone. We can avoid mistakes, wrong turns, fruitless dead ends, what Ronald Wright (2006) calls "progress traps," and escape the dominance hierarchies we've suffered under all the years of our existence as a species. With cooperation we will be entering a bright new world of harmony.

CULTURE AS A TOOL IN COOPERATION

Cooperative cultures are designed and planned. They do not just happen as the product of wishful thinking and are not negotiated between participating individuals with a variety of values and goals. They are not voted on, with the majority deciding what the rules will be. They are designed using the guidelines provided in this book to produce particular cooperative social systems serving particular purposes. The first step is to be sure of the content of the cooperative social system you plan to construct. If you are transforming an existing culture, you need to examine that culture for what you can use in the cooperative one and what must be discarded. If you are starting from scratch it is easier, you can go right to the cooperative design. The list of the basic elements of cooperation in Chapter One serves as a guide and checklist. The details provided in Part Two fill out the picture of what we are trying to do.

Most Americans are not used to thinking about and articulating verbally the full contents of their cultures. They are not used to looking at a culture as a coherent whole and recognizing where it works well and where there are problems or built-in incompatibilities. That will change in cooperative societies. The culture and how it is working will be a continual subject of conversation and analysis, something like the endless and multilayered discussions of sports and political activities in our current society. What problems and goals did we pursue today, what worked and what didn't, and where are we going tomorrow? This articulate familiarity with the cooperative culture is a must for all participants for the cooperative social system to reach its full potential and power. That is because the cooperative culture provides the reference point and guide book for everything the participants do while they enact the culture into a social system. The cooperative culture is the dynamic, evolving blueprint for the social system and all must know it, accept it, and embrace it until it becomes internalized, among the habits of our hearts.

THE CHALLENGE OF ETHNOCENTRICITY

Using culture as an adaptive tool requires us to keep an honest on-going appraisal of our cultures and not be seduced by ethnocentricity. By definition, ethnocentric people believe their culture is the best way to live, the right way, perhaps even God's way and the way everyone should live. Ethnocentricity contributes to cohesion, pride in one's community and identification with it. (See Chapter 14 for more details.) A group must have some ethnocentricity, a reasonably strong cultural consensus and commitment to the group to exist at all.

But getting the level of ethnocentricity just right is a tough challenge; one we seldom consider or act upon. Ethnocentricity is the fire in the lodge of culture, so to speak. Too little and the lodge is cold and lifeless, too much and it can burn the lodge down, just right and it warms the lodge and cooks the food. Too little ethnocentricity and no-one is particularly committed to the community and it has little cohesion; too much and there will be intense cohesion and cultural rigidity producing constant combat between the various cultural communities with none willing to give or compromise; just right and cohesion is moderate, there is mutual tolerance between cultural communities, and willingness to see flaws in one's own culture and make changes (Moss, 1979). Many of our wars and political, racial, ethnic, and religious conflicts are the result of excessively ethnocentric cultural communities' rejection of each other's values, norms and beliefs and rigid commitment to preserve their own culture as it is. Excessive ethnocentricity is burning us unnecessarily; moderating it can help us resolve many problems. In these times, being ethnocentrically stubborn benefits no-one.

Since culture is really all we humans have to guide us, explain and portray the world, and give life meaning, it is understandable we will be touchy about challenges to it. That is where the common group goal of adaptation to the environment and changes in it comes in. If we have an external, empirical reference point—is this information or behavior pattern adaptive or not—it becomes much easier to evaluate cultures and accept or reject elements, while moving toward an ever more accurate and effective shared culture.

This is a tough one. Making the transition from competitive individualism to cooperation requires us to see our existing cultures as they are, not as we imagine them with the glorified and idealized packaging we have ethnocentrically wrapped them in. We must be wary of "tradition." There is a place for traditions in cooperation but cultural patterns should not be preserved solely because they are traditional. They must have some adaptive value, if nothing else to celebrate our history and remind us that we are a community. Cooperative societies will be ethnocentric too. But it will be an aware and moderated ethnocentricity that does not insist that some cultural patterns are sacred and not to be questioned, tested or changed, but to be ritualistically performed even if no one can remember for what useful purpose.

MASTERING THE CULTURE OF COOPERATION

The cultural content is the substance of the group consensus and must be clear and coherent, understood in enough detail by everyone to operate as a unit. All of the key elements are embedded in the culture, including the common group goals, the division of labor, the competencies required, the communication channels and patterns, how rewards including compensation are handled, the criteria for terminating employment or membership, and so forth. The rules of the game must be clear and work. In the beginning there will be gaps in the cooperative culture to be filled by trial and error. For the most part you'll know where these unclear areas are and be consciously prepared to explore alternatives by trying them out. When the cooperative group is up and running, its culture becomes a living element of daily life. Enacting it, enhancing it, sharing it and enjoying their common well-functioning social world are what participants do. The cooperative culture flows cleanly through the participants and all they do.

To become a cooperative society, to create cooperative organizations and communities, we must learn as a people the skills of using culture and all of its components and applications. This is a new, group-centered way of looking at the world that understands we are all one, going the same places together in harmony. We must all become competent amateur sociologists, behavioral scientists, understanding thoroughly our culture and society and how they work. We must all know how to create culture and modify it on the run as we adapt. We must learn the fundamental mechanisms for shaping our behavior because all take part in doing it, whether we currently are aware of that or not. We must be constantly alert to the consequences of our personal social behavior for our cooperative community. This is part of the necessary minimal competence required of all participants for cooperation to take off. This may sound like a big hurdle, but drawing on my experience as a sociology professor again, most people catch on pretty quickly and enjoy the insights into their lives that come at the same time. One reason I, and many of my colleagues, enjoyed teaching introductory sociology was watching the students get "aha!" experiences, the sudden insights that opened vistas of new understanding as they learned about human social behavior and the nature of culture and social systems.

In this chapter we looked at culture. In the next chapter we look at social processes, the social "structure" such as roles and organizations that we produce when we enact our culture. Chapter 13 looks at the concrete social mechanisms we use to shape, maintain, and change our culture. When we understand all of this, we will be prepared to begin the process of creating our new cooperative groups, organizations, societies and civilizations.

Chapter 11. Social Systems As Games and Mastering the Process of Social Performance

SOCIETIES AND SOCIAL SYSTEMS ARE PROCESSES

Human behavior is a process. Whether we are interacting with others or performing tasks with the environment, we produce a process. Whether we successfully accomplish what we are attempting depends on how well these processes fit the task. If a company is trying to produce a profitable product, it will pay attention in detail to how it goes about manufacturing the product, constantly looking for ways to improve the process of production. If you are a fly fisherman or a golfer, you spend hours studying and practicing the processes of fly casting in different situations and the golf shot in various conditions. Perfection and mastery of the process produces the desired results: catching fat trout or par rounds.

When things don't go right and we don't get the desired results, we should be looking at our social processes, our social interaction and our task performance patterns. The golfer may ask, "Why do I keep getting a slice when I hit my drive?" The answer will be found in the process of the golf swing. So the golfer starts studying his swing, perhaps talking to a pro for suggestions. He then fixes the process. That is how adaptation takes place.

One of the primary ways social systems adapt is by discovering problems with their social processes and fixing them so they work. Then they incorporate the new pattern into their culture. Anything that prevents this fixing of the process blocks adaptation and undermines that social system's vitality, effectiveness, and perhaps its survival. Frequently, people operating social systems have a variety of ways to avoid fixing processes that aren't working so they won't have to admit their culture is in error. They deny anything is wrong, blame others, charge the people reporting the problem with not doing it right, and so forth. A recent example that received a great deal of publicity was claims by Toyota car owners that they experienced sudden, uncontrolled acceleration that often caused accidents. Toyota's public responses included initial denials—that couldn't happen to a Toyota car for a number of reasons, blaming the drivers, then making minor mechanical repairs and floor mat replacements, and finally conducting an in-depth search for possible electrical system flaws. (These kinds of problems and the ways they are mishandled are one of the sources of social stress.) A cooperative society uses these problems as cues that something is wrong with their culture and its performance, and that adaptive changes need to be made; then it makes them. In doing so, the social stress associated with the problem is also eliminated (See Moss, 1973).

One of the mistakes people make about societies is they sometimes treat them as if they were material things. "The System," "bureaucracies," "the economy." We say that these are things that we can't do anything about; as if they were somehow separate from human beings and constraining people against their will. There are no *things* in social behavior, only *processes*; processes of people behaving. We have to watch our noun oriented language, which quite often gets us into trouble by labeling processes as nouns. "Society" is a noun in English, and so are the words for most of its components. Don't be misled; they are all processes, interwoven with one another. These processes are nothing more than people behaving and interacting. If we were to freeze all of the people, there would be no social systems and no society.

Constantly Monitoring and Improving the Social Processes

Cooperative societies and social systems are environmental tracking devices, constantly testing for the accuracy of the current culture and social practices and making adaptive changes as required. In Chapter 5 we learned from Wilson that one of the goals of cooperative ant colonies is the maximization of the adaptive fit between their social structure and the environment. This requires adaptive changes to the social structures as changes in the environment indicate and constant effort to improve the fit between the social structure—its division of labor, for example—and the environment when it is stable. The ants handled this in part by evolving new morphological specializations among the ants of the colonies to fit ever more refined tasks and niches. The efforts to improve and refine the culture and social systems in human cooperative societies are continual. These efforts include refinements and changes in the divisions of labor and production of new specialties, competencies, and technologies. This process includes continually correcting the culture and adding new information. This dynamic process occurs in the daily social interactions of those enacting the cooperative organizations and societies. It is all happening in plain sight of everyone, and each of us participates.

The Japanese companies in America have taught American workers some practices from their more group-centered society that show a deep understanding of the power and value of paying attention to our social actions and interactions (Rehfeld, 1996; see Chapter 16 for more details). The Japanese pay careful attention to the process of performing a task. They focus on completing the task in the most effective manner, letting the social interactions unfold at their own pace. The Japanese are not clock driven as we Americans are to complete a task by a certain time, with all of the short cuts and haste that often produces. The job is done when it's done, effectively and thoroughly. How much time it takes is irrelevant. What by-ways and unexpected paths this effort may take are pursued without impatience. That is the cooperative way.

They also practice "kaizen." Americanized, kaizen produces the kind of constant attention to the processes of social interaction that is necessary for the high quality enactment of our cooperative cultures into social systems, the successful pursuit of the common group goals, and effective adaptation to changes. The Japanese, famously, "fix the problem, not the blame." They look at mistakes and problems as spurs to group problem solving and innovation. In cooperation, when something doesn't work, it produces a check on the society's culture. Did it fail because our information is incorrect, our techniques or technology inadequate, our skills inappropriate, our training inadequate? Correcting the problem is the essence of ongoing adaptation and contributes to the constant improvement of the match between culture, the social system processes, and the ever-changing environment. This is a component of the fundamental cooperative common group goal. Kaizen also focuses on the constant assessment and improvement of the process of group task performance even when there are no problems, encouraging participants to make suggestions. In cooperation, as task performers discover improvements and advances, they make the necessary changes in how they do things and thus modify the culture and communicate this to the rest of the social system. The improvements are made on the run in the arena where they occur by the competent specialists operating there. There is no need for extensive review and decision making by various authorities in a dominance hierarchy or in committees. This produces improvements much in the same way the ants' constant response to more refined matches to the environment does. But we do it consciously with culture while the ants must wait for natural selection to do the job. All this, too, is the cooperative way.

Learning to Live as One, as a Dynamic Whole

When we put all of this cooperative social interaction together we have a social system operated by and for its membership. In Chapter 5 the colonial ants showed us a key organizational piece we need in order to create cooperative social systems. They do not use the top down style of organization with those on top telling those below how to perform—the competitive dominance hierarchy predominant in human societies. The ants flip organization over, so to speak. Holldobler and Wilson (1990) told us "the highest level of the ant colony is the totality of its membership rather than a particular set of superordinate individuals who direct the activity of members at lower levels" (p. 355). Cooperation is the work of the "totality of the membership."

Among cooperative humans the totality of the membership can work as a coordinated whole without hierarchical control and supervision because they have a consensus on what they are doing. They have a refined division of labor enacted by the most competent specialists available responsible for task areas. Open communication keeps all aware of what is going on so they can do what is required in their task area as the daily efforts unfold. They have the ability to see the big picture and the local picture, macro and micro, at the same time. Some coordination of efforts facilitates the work—

the coordination hierarchy. Our modern electronic communications make the kind of communications required easy; we could not build a cooperative society the size of America without them. This kind of social system, especially at the level of a society, requires highly trained and dedicated participants paying attention to what is happening and who understand the power of their everyday social interactions, the social processes, and the high level of personal responsibility required.

The scientists working on the proximity fuse in Section T of OSRD described in Chapter 2 are an example of the totality of the membership being the unit of action. While Tuve provided some hierarchical management and coordination, he found the dynamics of the social interactions among scientists as they operated as a cooperative adaptive unit pursuing a common goal frequently outstripped his ability to keep up with them. The constant shifting of the locus of "the action" to different areas of competence as work progressed with the responsibility and coordination shifting accordingly is typical of cooperative social systems. The social structure is never fixed, but constantly changes to match the needs of the task pursuit process at that moment.

Understanding the Significance of Cooperative Social Interactions

I doubt that many Americans comprehend how much power they exercise in their daily social interactions. They exert considerable influence on their social systems and culture by how they enact their roles and the norms of their various groups and of society. Unfortunately, they frequently see themselves as acting alone in the individualistic manner, not paying appropriate attention to those playing roles and enacting norms interdependent with our own. We have to be able to take the others' roles to effectively enact our own. Instead, we just go about our self-centered pursuit of our personal goals and compete crankily with one another with nary a thought for what we are creating. When you put all of our daily social interactions together you have society, you have our various subcultures and social systems, including our families, work organizations, educational institutions, governments and so forth. If we don't like the social systems we produce day in and day out, we have only ourselves to blame. That should be obvious. If we want to change our social world to a more cooperative one, the place to start and the location of the power is in our own daily social interactions.

It is in our daily social interactions that culture is created, enacted, tested, taught, and modified. It is in our daily social interactions that we engage our environment to understand it and for our survival needs. It is in our daily social interactions that we create many things from technology to artistic works. It is in our daily social interactions that we produce one another's self-images and self-esteem. It is in our daily social interactions that we produce the social cohesion that energizes our social systems including engaging us. In cooperative societies we are constantly aware as individuals of all of this. Our perspective of our life is much bigger, more inclusive, we understand how all the parts, the many social role performances and cultural enactments, fit together to form a whole and keep track of how they are doing. A cooperative social system will make that information constantly available, perhaps using modern electronic devices and "news" updates. In cooperation we pay attention to how our personal social actions and interactions contribute positively to these critical social processes and developments.

Cooperative people would be appalled, for example, with the damage we competitive individualistic Americans do to one another's self-images and self-esteem and the ways we undermine, like social termites, the social cohesion of our groups and organizations. Cooperative people would look in stunned shock at the thoughtless manner in which we relate to one another, not seeing the hurt we are doing or the lost opportunities. The requirements of participation in cooperative social systems, especially at the society level, include that we be aware of all of this and that we take personal responsibility for the consequences of our actions.

As you can see, living in a cooperative society or social system is not a matter of being a zombie cog in a rigidly controlled piece of machinery. We will have to operate at high levels of competence, personal responsibility, and have the capacity to evaluate situations and take action on our own to successfully advance the cooperative society's well being and common group goals. This is a lifestyle that utilizes our talents, energies, and intelligence, and explores our potentials and rewards us generously. It is a lifestyle that gives us all the challenges and responsibilities we want and can handle. This is an engaged lifestyle in every sense of the word, for everyone and in every social interaction. Indeed, every social interaction is an act of power.

SOCIAL SYSTEMS ARE FRAGILE GAMES

RECREATING AMERICA EVERYDAY

We recreate America everyday collectively. Americans generally imagine the primary goal of our daily social interactions is to take care of ourselves and our families and do our job, finding our own way through life as best as we can. However, from the point of view of society, the most important consequence is the perpetual recreation of the social organizations and institutions that compose society, keeping society alive. Each of us everyday contributes to or interferes with the continuation of our society and its many component cultures and social structures. Each of us everyday helps, or refuses to help, maintain the social systems we live in, including our families, occupations, communities, churches, and special interest groups. We contribute constructively by enacting our roles, performing the norms of our cultural communities, and reinforcing other's performances. If we didn't do it reasonably reliably day after day, there would be no culture, no social systems, and no America.

That we accomplish this despite our chronic complaining, internal competitive squabbling, and individualistic rebellious resistance is something of a daily miracle. That we tend to focus on ourselves and our situation, unaware or uncaring of the collective consequences of our actions is irresponsible and often damaging. If we can keep America running while our internal competition produces useless battles and our self-serving and greed create costly deficiencies, it is mind-boggling to imagine what we could do if we cleaned up our stumbling-bumbling act and cooperated.

If there is a huge snow storm, schools, government, and businesses in that area are closed because nobody can get to their places of work or education to enact them. That part of society doesn't exist on that day. The culture to create the schools, governments, and businesses is in our heads, but we can't perform it. Social systems are processes of cultural enactment. Our society exists only when we enact it.

If you want to see a social system, you have to be there when it is being performed. Think of a symphony orchestra, for example, we know it will be performing a program for us only for a few scheduled hours on several weekend evenings. Then the performers will move on to enact other roles in addition to the practice and meetings required by the symphony, such as spouse, parent, church deacon, or even cabdriver. During those periods, the symphony orchestra we listened to does not exist as a social system, only as a cultural idea in people's heads.

If you visit a university campus at different times of the day and different times of the year, you will encounter different social systems. The people present and the roles they are enacting are different on those occasions. Different faculty, students, and staff will be doing different things. That's why you often need an appointment, to be sure that the people you need to interact with will be present and performing their roles, such as professor or admissions officer. Thus, when people interact, enacting the norms and roles contained in their culture, they repeatedly bring all of the social systems, institutions, and groups composing that society temporarily to life. If we could see it all at once and if the social systems were colored lights, we would see a constantly changing kaleidoscope of colors winking on, getting brighter, fading, and being replaced by others and then repeating all over again. That is a society.

TAKING CARE OF OUR SOCIETY

Society is actually a very delicate creature. It is easily modified but it is also easily disrupted and can dissipate like a gusting breeze through a sand painting if we're not careful. The perception that societies are hard to change comes from the difficulties and conflict those seeking change experience when the rest of the participants don't want to change. The obstacle is other participants, not the nature of societies and cultures, which are comparatively easy to change.

In America, society is pretty much on its own, as are many social systems from families to large businesses. Few people are paying attention and taking care of them as social systems. Our individualism teaches us to do our own thing while resisting, even rebelling against, those in authority in our social systems. It encourages us to criticize our society, government, and other social systems and to have our own opinion to express and press. With competition it encourages us to form power bases, protect our "turf," and undermine competitors' efforts. What emerges from our social interaction everyday includes an amalgamation of all of our self-serving and adversarial competitive efforts. Unfortunately, there is no "magic hand" here that will mysteriously and reliably coordinate all of this into something benefiting us individually and society as a social system despite the wishful thinking of many economists. Yes, it is indeed a miracle that we recreate everyday in America a society that produces anything much of value. However, the huge and discouraging amount of waste, misdirection, incompetence, exploitation of people and resources, cheating, blocking of one another's initiatives, and so forth, generated by our self-centeredness and competition are disheartening.

In contrast, for more group-centered people, especially if they are cooperative, the society and its social systems are the primary focus of action and energy. Recreating them, using them adaptively, and keeping them well organized and running effectively are what they do every day. There are a few people in our society that have some group centeredness in their daily social interactions. Some are practicing what Robert Bellah et al. (1985) described in their classic study of community and individualism, *Habits of the Heart*, as biblical individualism (this includes most of our churches) that teaches the Golden Rule and creating a moral community, and republican individualism, which harks back to the proud patriotism of our early years as country. These are the people who still devote themselves or a portion of their time to service to church and community and are the backbone of what effective social systems and society we have. These are the people who still think of the Golden Rule in their interactions instead of only what's-in-it-for-me. They are the people who "support" the activities of the organizations they belong to, even if on occasion they would rather be doing something else. Unfortunately for America, these very valuable people are steadily declining in numbers with each passing age cohort (Putnam, 2000), which spells eventual doom for the integrity of our social systems and effectiveness of our society. Americans are becoming less and less interested in recreating all of America every day. Where might that take us eventually? Remember the Ik from Chapter 7.

If America is to have a bright and long future, it is critical that we learn to cooperate and start taking care of our society and its component social systems. Learning to recreate an effective society everyday with our social interactions is a must, and is a step every one of us can take now. Paying attention to the good of the social system while pursuing group goals as we enact our roles, perform the norms, and consciously refine those roles and norms, starts here with daily social interaction. It is in our daily social interaction that we will gradually introduce cooperation into our society. It is in this process that we transform our social systems into cooperative ones. This is where the power is.

I have often found that looking at games helps students understand a bit better the importance of maintaining our groups and social systems and what, exactly, we are maintaining.

The Rules ARE the Game

While we American individualists too often equate society's rules with infringement on our freedom and personal dignity, we relish games that are nothing but a set of rules for behavior. Basketball, football, Monopoly, bridge, charades ... there are thousands of card, board, behavioral, and sports games we Americans play. Some people are professional game players; we are willing to pay to watch experts perform according to the rules of the game in competition. We also have norms in some cases for what is okay rule-breaking or cheating.

If you take away all of the rules for Monopoly, and that would include the board, cards, dice, and tokens, there is no Monopoly game to play. The rules and constraints, such as rolling dice and moving a token accordingly along a board and obeying directions for the spots landed on, buying property with an allotted supply of paper money, and so forth, ARE the game. The rules for football and basketball are completely different. You cannot have some people trying to play basketball at the same time and place as others are trying to play football. That is obvious, though in our daily social interactions we frequently attempt such nonsense. If we do not delineate a field and erect goal posts of a certain size and distance from each other, and do not specify how many players on each team can be on the field at one time, and do not spell out what you can and can't do with the ball during a "play" and what constitutes a "score" and for how many points, and so forth, there would be no football game to play. We even have officials—authorities—running around the field calling fouls when the rules are broken. When we set out to play a game, the first thing everyone wants to know is, "What are the rules?" One of the first things we should all ask when we create a social system is, "What are the rules?" What are the norms and roles we will play? There is no difference been societies and games; society is a great big complex game and collection of component games.

For a game to be played there must be agreement, consensus, on the rules of the game. That includes the equipment, the physical artifacts to be used. If one player declares a change in the rules and the other players refuse, there is no change. If all agree to change some of the rules when they play Monopoly or whatever, then those changes become the rules and social structure of the game for those players. Societies are the same. Players and members of society can change the rules of the game anyway they like as long as they agree, have a consensus. In society, the first place those changes take place is generally among those playing the social game. Changes are proposed and take effect in our daily social interactions, negotiated among the players. One can challenge those not playing by the rules by asking, "What game are you playing?" From this perspective, it makes perfect sense to toss people out of the game who refuse to play the game by the rules, disrupting the whole game performance. This is especially true of cooperation where a fine tuned, competent, interwoven "team" performance as a unit is crucial.

Looking at your social groups as sociocultural games you are playing can be revealing. In our cultural couples and family games, for example, you may find you are playing internally competitive games when you really want to cooperate; but you don't have any rules for a cooperative game. You may find you are blaming each other for being selfish and hard to get along with, when the problem is really not with you but with the competitive culture you are playing. All couples and families have their own cultures, their own rules of the game.

A fact of life is that all cultures, all societies, are essentially games composed of rules. Our American constitution is the set of rules we use to operate our democratic republic. We are right to be proud of our founding fathers for producing it and the quality of life it gives us. It is a good example of what I am talking about in this chapter. However, the "constitution" of a mature true cooperative society will be completely different.

Sometimes transforming social systems and cultures can seem like a daunting task. Suggesting we switch from competition to cooperation easily triggers the "You cain't get the'ah from he'ah" resigned response in many

Americans. In the classic research study in the next chapter, we see how easy it actually can be to create more cooperative groups where competition once reigned.

Chapter 12. The Robber's Cave Experiment: Turning Competition Into Cooperation

The Robber's Cave study illustrates how quickly we can produce competitive or cooperative groups by changing the "rules of the game," the culture, goals and social processes/structures.

The Robber's Cave Experiment is a classic in the cooperation literature. Muzafer Sherif and his colleagues did a series of social psychological experiments on boys 11 to 12 years old in summer camp in 1949, 1953, and 1954, researching conflict and cooperation between groups. The 1954 study was conducted in Oklahoma at a camp near Robber's Cave, a famous hideaway of Jesse James (Sherif, 1956, pp. 54-58; Sherif et al. 1961; Sherif and Sherif, 1969, pp. 221-266).

These studies were an attempt to deal with a pressing social problem in America: our cultural diversity and the conflicts that too often result. Sherif (1956, p. 58) observed: "Much attention has been given to bringing members of hostile groups together socially, to communicating accurate and favorable information about one group to the other, and to bringing the leaders of groups together to enlist their influence," but these have not been particularly successful in reducing conflict and hostility between groups and replacing them with harmony and willingness to work together.

This study illustrates how changing goals can produce improved relations between groups. The researchers tested two hypotheses. The first one was "when two groups have conflicting aims" and their ends can only be achieved at the expense of the other group, "even though the groups are composed of normal well-adjusted individuals," the members of the two groups will become hostile toward each other (Sherif, 1956, p. 57). The second hypothesis was:

> When groups in a state of friction are brought into contact under conditions embodying superordinate goals, the attainment of which is compelling but which cannot be achieved by the efforts of one group alone, they will tend to cooperate toward the common goal (1961, p. 159).

TESTING HYPOTHESIS ONE

The boys were brought to the camp in two separate buses and then kept separated until they developed some group cohesion, leadership, and divisions of labor. Then the researchers tested the first of their hypotheses. The investigators/camp counselors planned to introduce conflict by organizing a tournament between the two groups using a variety of competitive games, such as baseball, touch football, a tug-of-war, a treasure hunt, and so forth. However, some of the boys in the two groups spontaneously expressed interest in such contests (Sherif et al. 1961, pp. 96, 97).

> The tournament started in a spirit of good sportsmanship. But as it progressed good feelings soon evaporated. The members of each group began to call their rivals "stinkers," and "sneaks" and "cheaters." They refused to have anything more to do with individuals in the opposing group (Sherif, 1956, p. 57).

The groups displayed a variety of aggressive and hostile acts against each other. The groups had taken on the names of Rattlers and Eagles. They made threatening posters, collected secret hoards of green apples for their nearly daily raids, captured and burned each others' banners, frequently engaged in name calling and scuffles and similar behavior. As generally happens when people have to unite to defend themselves against a common enemy the two groups' internal cohesion, morale, democratic behavior, and "cooperativeness" strengthened.

It is amazing how quickly people who are getting along just fine can be turned into competitive adversaries actively attacking each other and engaging in hostile behavior when they are divided into groups that must compete with one another; where the rules of the game are now competitive.

TESTING HYPOTHESIS TWO

Sherif and his colleagues then turned to their second hypothesis and the other half of their research agenda, exploring: "How can two groups in conflict be brought into harmony" (Sherif, 1956, p. 57). Sherif (1956) said, "We first undertook to test the theory that pleasant social contacts between members of conflicting groups will reduce friction between them" (p. 57). The activities they tried were going to movies together and eating in the same dining room. But the competition persisted, such as squabbling to be the first group in line for food, name calling, and bickering.

> The researchers didn't really expect these simple social activities to make much of a difference in the competitive hostility they had generated, and soon moved to their primary concern, reducing intergroup conflict by creating a compelling common goal for both groups.

> The first goal the experimenters/camp counselors came up with was a manufactured problem with the water supply. The camp's water supply came from a tank about a mile away. The counselors turned off the valve on the tank to the pipe and covered the valve with boulders. There was a faucet at the other side of the tank that they stuffed with sacking. The researchers made sure the boys were good and thirsty when they finally approached the solution to the lack of water to add urgency to the effort (Sherif et al., 1961, p. 160).

The counselors then told the boys there seemed to be a problem with the water supply, which happened from time to time, sometimes due to vandals, and that it was being investigated. The boys were told to fill their canteens just in case. Then, out of sight of the boys, the researchers drained the pipe dry. Later in the day when the boy's canteens were getting low, the counselors showed them that there was no water coming through at all. The boys were told the problem had not been found and that it could be anywhere on the pipe, at the tank, or at the pump at the reservoir from which the water came. They were told it would take about 25 people do a thorough search and all of the boys in both groups volunteered.

Four groups were formed, two each from the Rattlers and the Eagles. Two groups divided up the area from the reservoir to the tank, and the other two from the end of the pipe in camp to the tank. After about an hour or so the teams that had found no problems in their area converged on the tank. By this time the boys' canteens were empty and their thirst contributed to the sense of compelling urgency to solve the problem.

Since the boys were thirsty, the blocked faucet gained their immediate attention. The boys worked enthusiastically on the project of clearing the faucet, giving advice, checking the water level in the tank, and exploring the faucet to find the problem without regard to group membership. Eventually they found the sacking blocking the faucet and took turns trying to remove it and sharing such tools as they had, such as knives. Eventually they turned to the staff for help and using wrenches removed the sacking. There was then no group related animosity in gaining access to the water by the boys.

In the spirit of common effort that followed the boys relaxed and good-naturedly mingled in a variety of spontaneous activities such as catching lizards and making wooden whistles from willow. However, when the valve blockage on the other side of the tank was discovered and cleared some of the old competitive tensions appeared over who discovered the problem, and reemerged during dinner in the common dining hall. It was, however, toned down and some common friendly conversation and exchanges occurred. Clearly, the competition-generated hostility and conflict had not yet been replaced by the formation of a common group and more cooperative sentiments, so it was time for the next common goal experiment.

For the next superordinate goal the researchers created that would capture the attention and engagement of the 11 and 12 year-old boys was obtaining a movie the boys wanted to see: Treasure Island. The boys were told the rental was $15 and the camp could not pay the whole fee. The boys shouted out several alternatives including one group suggesting the group pay the whole $15. But gradually the suggestions became more equitable until one boy suggested each group pay $3.50 of the shortfall. All of the boys agreed to that. Then each group had to figure out how much each boy would pay. Since the groups were not of equal size, the Rattlers settled on 31 cents each and the Eagles on 39 cents each and both groups insisted their counselors contribute since they got to watch the show too. At dinner that night there was less scuffling and contesting that usual, but seating at the film was still almost entirely along group lines. Progress was being made but the conflict between the boys had still not been replaced by camaraderie.

Both of these activities are of the individualistic mutual-aid form. The water was something each boy needed for himself; it was not a group goal for the good of a cooperative social system. The movie was the same, an event each boy wanted to enjoy himself, and working together they obtained the film. The researchers were not seeking to construct one true cooperative social system from the boys, but rather, in my terms, attempting to use individualistic mutual-aid as a means of resolving and replacing competition generated inter-group conflict and hostility.

The third experiment involved relieving hunger as the compelling superordinate goal. The boys were taken to a lake thirty miles distant for a camp out. Again a staged problem confronted them. This time the truck that was to go for the food wouldn't start. The boys first offered to push the truck and then realized they could use the tug-of-war rope, tied to the front bumper in the middle of the rope so that there were two ropes to pull on. On the first try, which failed, the Eagles and Rattlers each took a rope by group. On the next try, the boys were intermixed and this time the truck started. Later, when the food arrived the boys were still debating whether to eat as separate groups or to take turns preparing meals to be eaten in common. As it happened, they just spontaneously prepared the food together.

There were a number of other related incidents orchestrated by the investigators including the boys having to work together to sort out purposely mixed up camping equipment before they could pitch camp. These several efforts of working together for temporary common or superordinate goals gradually reduced the friction and conflict between the Rattlers and Eagles until they became friendly and, "In the end the groups were actively seeking opportunities to mingle, to entertain and 'treat' each other," Sherif reported (1956, p. 58).

SOME CONCLUSIONS

Sherif's (1956, p. 58) Robbers Cave experiment and similar research projects that he and his colleagues did, in his opinion, demonstrate that "the possibilities of achieving harmony are greatly enhanced when groups are brought together to work toward common ends and "hostility gives way when groups pull together to achieve overriding goals, which are real and compelling to all concerned." This study confirms the importance of a common goal as the basis for cooperation, whether it is a form of mutual aid or the group goal of a cooperatively structured social system.

This study also shows in elementary form how easily sociocultural patterns—the current rules of the game—and our ongoing social interaction influence behavior. The researchers were able to produce competitive hostility between the two groups of boys easily in a matter of days by setting up competitive contests between them. They were able to turn that around and generate a single group of boys "cooperating"—individualistic mutual aid—and enjoying one another's companionship also in a matter of days by giving them compelling common goals to pursue and—with some gentle guidance—letting their social interactions produce a resolution. The common group goal of creating and operating a rapidly adapting information-processing social system that maximizes our success in our environment for the benefit of all, eliminating a great deal of conflict, uncertainty, and suffering and providing us all a place and harmony is such a compelling goal. It can appeal to all humans. The Robber's Cave Experiment is an example of how easy it is to use our social interactions and cultural patterns—including our goals—to produce cooperative relations and communities and to move from our competitive hostility to cooperative harmony.

We still need to understand how to use what I call "social sanctions", the rewards and punishments we all give for performances, to shape and maintain our cooperative social systems. The next few chapters explore this critical topic.

Chapter 13. Powering Up Cooperative Societies

If I told you I had a magic device that at no cost could be given to people so they could instruct, train, and motivate everyone in the society, shape their behavior for the good of all and give them high self-esteem into the bargain, I expect you would close instantly on the deal. What if I told you that every member of our society already has this magic device, they are just not using it properly? I expect you'd want to know what it is and how to use it properly. That is the subject of this chapter.

Our approval of others' behavior, and of them as valuable people, is the magic device. We woefully underestimate the social power of approval, especially when applied collectively at the group level. At the same time, we enthusiastically use approval in its many forms to get people to do what we self-centeredly want them to. We are too often failing to raise our children properly so that our approval can inspire and guide them and uplift them to its full capacity. We fail because we don't appreciate the central power of approval in running high quality social systems or how to treat our little ones so they are social psychologically prepared to respond to approval from many sources. When people do not respond to approval from members of society, such as teachers, employers, family, co-workers, and counselors, we have a serious problem incorporating them constructively into any society, but especially a cooperative one. Our cultures of competition and individualism seriously contaminate and disrupt efforts to fully develop and utilize the power of approval at the societal level.

In a cooperative society the members build a social "sanction" (defined below) network that embraces the whole society. Its application is guided by the cultural consensus and group goals. This network creates a "consequence" network so that every behavioral action has consequence of approval, neutral or disapproval that informs the actor of how social things are and how they are doing personally. This is analogous to nature's consequence network.

CONSEQUENCES ARE EVERYWHERE

Everything we do, every action we take, has a consequence. If we like the consequence, it is a reward. If we dislike it, it is a punishment. If we don't much care, it has little influence on our future behavior.

The natural world surrounds us with constraints and conditions. Hot and cold. Winter ice and desert heat. Each environment provides its own unique pattern of conditions and consequences for human actions. Learning what these consequences are in the environment we are living in is critical for our survival. The name of the game in animal survival is adapting to the environment and any changes that occur. If there were no consequences in our natural world, such as we wouldn't get burned no matter what we did, and nothing we ate was nutritious, and you couldn't fall down or up, there would be no world and no adaptive evolution going on. We wouldn't exist. The natural electromagnetic and other "forces" that make our world produce these consequences. It is the constraints of these consequences that shape the genetics and biology of living things. It also shapes animal behavior including our own.

Here again, humans with culture are unique. We have two distinct, if overlapping, behavioral consequence systems. We have the natural one all living things live in and where we pursue our survival as a species. We humans also have the consequence network we generate when we create and use our culture. We humans have comparatively little control over the natural consequence systems except as we intrude with our science and technologies. Mostly, we use technology to protect ourselves from punishing consequences, such as asbestos gloves for touching hot things, clothing and furnaces for cold climates, and air conditioning for hot ones.

The sociocultural consequence network, on the other hand, is all ours. We made it and we can change it any way and any time we like. The overlap with the natural system is where we produce cultural patterns that help us adapt and survive as species in a given environment. That is actually a big chunk of our culture. Because of our individualism, many Americans have a hard time grasping the fundamental, inherent connection between cultural values, norms and beliefs that make up our societies, and the rewards, such as approval, and punishments, the consequences that shape and maintain those values, norms and beliefs. Many of us just don't see the connection between culture and the rewards and punishments we give each other. We tend to use the rewards and punishments unthinkingly for our personal or competitive reasons, as if that were the only reason they existed.

If we are to use our cultural as our adaptive tool, we must grasp the necessity of also creating what I'm calling a "positive social consequence network," using primarily the giving and with holding of approval, to teach and maintain our cooperative culture. While we can change what we reward and punish and how much of each, there *must* be rewards and punishments, consequences, attached to all of our norms or they will not exist.

Science has shown that rewards are by far the most powerful and effective tools for teaching and reinforcing social patterns and skills, and approval is by far the most valuable reward. A cooperative society with a cultural consensus will also use positive consequences—rewards—applied by all of the participants upon each other in the same manner. Any child behaving anywhere in a cooperative society will be taught the same things the same way with the same reward by any and all. This can quickly lead to the "internalization" (defined below) of the cooperative culture and a continuing refinement of skills and understanding. A cooperative society creates a living social reward system that is focused on the adaptation of the community and the wellbeing of all. Getting lots of rewards—especially approval—can have amazing results. The opposite is the unpredictable, wildly variable and generally negative consequence patterns imposed upon America now by competition and individualism and our multiple incompatible interest groups.

Remember, when you use the rewards and punishments you have to give you are shaping, or misshaping, our whole society.

SOCIAL SANCTIONS: THE REWARDS AND PUNISHMENTS

Rewards and punishments have been called many things depending upon how they are being used. I'm going to call them "social sanctions" when they are used to let people know what the culture's norms are and if the norms are being performed properly and skillfully. A *"social sanction,"* as I'm using the term, *is any social action that communicates to the performer and/ or observers that another social action is acceptable or unacceptable.* Sanctions can be anything that is perceived as a reward or punishment or the withholding of a reward or punishment.

All social sanctions express approval or disapproval of a given behavior. Among the positive sanctions we give is money in various ways to show we approve of the social action performed. We give goods and services. Goods are anything we value including food—a double-decker ice cream cone or a pile of prime rib eye steaks, clothing, electronics, cars, house items, sports equipment, flowers, music, and books. Services include providing skilled performance of a needed service such as repairs or construction; it may be a back rub, a haircut, a make-over. It could be fixing a special dinner, a trip to an entertainment or sports event, and so forth. We give valuable information, ranging from a special recipe for bread pudding to how to fish a particular trout stream, to insider gossip, to knowledge needed in some profession, to tips on how to be more skillful in some endeavor, to important new discoveries not yet public. We express disapproval by withholding these positive sanctions.

The use of force to get people to obey is a special case. Force should not be used unless absolutely necessary and then only by those authorized to do so by the society. Competitive people and others that favor using punishments—negative sanctions—to get things done, may threaten the use of force. "Do what I tell ya or I'll mash your face." You obey and your reward is the withholding of the punishment. While punishments are sometimes required, in cooperative societies they are kept to a minimum with the emphasis on the use of positive sanctions.

By far the most important and powerful social sanction is our personal approval. When we give others compliments, high fives, detailed praise for their performance, hugs and kisses to our spouse for doing well, recognition including awards such as trophies, we reinforce the norms they are performing and their skill in their roles. Behavioral scientists have demonstrated that high levels of skill can be caught only by using approval to re-fine and advance the person's success. In cooperative societies, approval is used continually, and those performing well can expect a flow of approval throughout their day from their fellow participants. As we will see, this also contributes to our self-esteem and the group's social cohesion. The power of approval is especially amazing. It is free and we all have it to give in prac-tically unlimited supply. The only "catch" is that the person receiving the approval must value our approval; they must care what we personally think about him or her. People will work very hard for the approval of others, especially significant others.

Mark Twain, in an essay, "Corn-Pone Opinions" (Oates and Atwan, 2000, pp. 1-5), written in 1901 and published after his death made a serious effort to understand sociologically why people engaged in desperate confor-mity, sometimes to what he judged to be silly social patterns. While he was mocking such conformity and the lengths people went to dress and behave according to the fashion with seemingly no will of their own, he actually grasped the reality of the matter. He concluded it was to get approval from others so we could approve of ourselves. He said: "But as a rule our self-approval has its source in but one place and not elsewhere—the approval of other people" (p. 2). Twain grasped one of the basic and most powerful facts of human life: we will work very hard for a positive self-image, for self-respect and self-esteem. We all want to like ourselves and who we are. And the *only* source of that self-esteem is the approval of other people.

Charles Horton Cooley (1864-1929), a classical sociological theorist, also working around the turn of the 20th century, as was Twain, expressed the same insight scientifically. Cooley was among the first scientists to real-ize the significance of this insight. He labeled it the "looking-glass self". We see ourselves in the "mirror" of others' responses to us, in the qualities they pay attention to, in the judgments they make. Our self-image grows and changes through our social interactions in our society. It is extremely im-portant that the image we see mirrored back to us is a positive one, showing our good qualities and skills, using approval and other positive sanctions. And it is important that we mirror to others in our responses to them the fine qualities they have and are developing, using positive sanctions to re-ward, guide, refine and teach them. To do this we all have to pay attention. Attention to others and ourselves in a cooperative context.

Social sanctions are so valuable that we are willing to put out enormous energy to acquire them. Their competitive pursuit in our society leads to the stratification of people according to how much money they have, their material wealth, their social prestige and popularity, the special knowledge they have and their access to the use of force on others (dictators for example). Those who have acquired large amounts of these sanctions can use them as rewards or punishments to shape the behavior of others. A capitalist may use his money to start a company for example, paying people to do as he wishes.

To appreciate the centrality of social sanctions in operating our society, imagine a social world where no one gets paid for work, no one is loved by family, no one is punished for stealing or hurting others, no one responds to you whether you are dirty or clean, refined or crude, kind or mean, no one is "popular," there are no prizes or trophies or recognition or honors, no gifts for fine accomplishments or jobs well done. In such a world your actions are initiated by you and no one but you will pay attention to them (unless you annoy someone). It is the land of the Ik, described in Chapter 7. You dress up and cook a great meal for a friend and all they do is gobble up the food and go. No attention or admiration or praise. Why would you ever do that again? What's in it for you? Some thoughtless individualists seem to want a world like that with their demands to be left alone to do their own thing. Believe me such a world is cold, lonely and joyless with no admirers.

What people want is positive sanctions, the approval of others. Getting a strong and reliable positive self-image for contributing constructively to society from competitive individualistic Americans is problematic. We Americans are constant—if often witless—sanctioners, constantly judging one another, things, and whatever is going on at the moment. A major component of our daily conversations is exchanging judgments, opinions, and rankings. This is mostly the result of our competitive culture that encourages rankings with winners at the top and the losers at the bottom, a continuum from best to worst. (Elaborated in Chapter 8) From the point of view of cooperation, the problem here is that we sanction behaviors for selfish individualistic and adversarial competitive reasons. One way our competitive individualism makes a hash of our adaptive social efforts is to make a hash of our society-wide social sanctioning patterns.

A cooperative society would sanction behavior to further cooperative group goals. What would be sanctioned, how much and the overall sanctioning pattern would be very different in a cooperative society from our current one; it would be based on consensus and on giving rewards. There will be few, if any, judgmental rankings. The positive cooperative social sanctioning pattern provides the rewards for enacting the cooperative culture. These rewards are consistent and reliable. Enactment of the roles and accomplishing the tasks required for rapid adaptation to the environment is strongly positively sanctioned using direct interpersonal expressions of approval, material abundance, access to information, education, medical care, freedom from force or coercion, belonging, and a place to be somebody. It includes a positive self-image as a worthwhile member of a society that is marvelous and larger than one's self. This is the joyous and delightful payoff and incentive for cooperation.

Take a moment and review how you are using your personal social sanctions today. What are you approving, disapproving, ignoring? Are you doing it for selfish goals? Competitive goals? Constructively or destructively? Enhancing or demeaning others' self-esteem? Punishing? Generous or stingy or sneeringly withholding?

LEARNING TO CARE WHAT OTHERS THINK ABOUT YOU: VALUING APPROVAL

In the beginning, people trying to build cooperative organizations will have to be a bit choosey about who to hire or recruit. It will be necessary to select competent people who are cooperation ready. Otherwise too much time and effort will be spent on rooting out competition and individualism and getting quality performances. When cooperation is up and running, we can train people for the cooperative life.

You have to prepare people for membership in a cooperative society. You can't drop just anybody in the middle of a cooperative organization and expect it to work out. Cooperative social systems are fine tuned and organic wholes with every participant providing important skills and knowledge. Cooperative people have to be socialized and trained for cooperative living and fitted into their task area of competence. Important things have to happen in the socialization process for the person to be able to function at the high level of skill and sensitivity required in cooperative communities. When I think of "cooperation ready" people now, I am thinking of people who got this kind of socialization and training in their families, education and work experiences. Those who are not now cooperation ready who want to try living cooperatively may have to go through a resocialization process first, which is possible. It takes more than just a desire to live "cooperatively," however one may imagine such a world.

One of the crucial tasks of socialization for cooperation is learning to care what others think about you, to value their approval. Parents during the child's early years must connect with the child so that he or she cares about what their parents think of them, so they will value parents' approval and be hurt by their disapproval. This is done by giving the child love and feelings of security and being cared for from the time they are born. (There are many good books and manuals showing how to do this.) Then as the child moves through life he or she can generalize that caring about other's approval to teachers, employers, church leaders and others. Only then can the full power of approval be used to operate a cooperative society. The failure by parents or care takers to do this can permanently impair the child's ability to relate to others and to be socialized into a given culture. This is one reason some orphans, abused children and similar unfortunates have difficulty relating to others, forming close relationships in their lives and holding jobs. It also makes helping them in later life difficult.

We have to want other's approval and be willing to work for it, and dislike their disapproval and work to avoid it. People who really, truly, do not care what others think of them or their behavior are incapable of functioning effectively or "normally" within a given society or social system. They won't let the necessary communications of what to do and how to do it that are contained in the approval/disapproval patterns into their heads. They are thus incapable of becoming fully integrated into a cooperative society. They will perform or work only for things they want or need such as money, food or a car, and then with questionable skill and honesty and no concern for others or the social system.   Only people who care about what others think of them and respond to approval can be socialized into the culture and trained to perform social roles skillfully, and to happily embrace this training. They are the ones who can "internalize" the culture, an essential outcome of the socialization.

Internalizing Cooperative Culture's Norms, Values And Skills

A second critical task that must occur during the socialization of the person is the internalization of the cooperative community's culture, its norms and values. In cooperation, the socialization of young people and new recruits is done thoroughly and skillfully so that these people know what the norms, values, beliefs and skills are, they can perform competently and they prefer to do things this way. They are refined to moral, ethical and compassionate people. They become self-sanctioning so that they do not need others to constantly remind them how to behave or competently perform their roles. They "choose" to perform competently and to be moral and ethical even if no one else is watching. Some things just become habits common to the cooperative society and do not require any further reinforcement. These people are also capable of being self-correcting. Making changes in their behavior as adaptively required without outside social sanctioning in many cases. They have learned quality "habits of the heart," as Tocqueville would say.

A cooperative society will continue to reward them with positive sanctions appropriately to reinforce and maintain and when necessary change the shared dynamic culture. They will always be positively sanctioned for their ongoing performances in their specialized task areas and for other ongoing services to the community. Society then has a well-trained population of people who know and can perform the culture and understand how it all works, who can be counted on to do well what is needed without supervision or "bossing." These are people who are committed to the cooperative community and culture. They carry in their hearts and heads the cooperative culture safely, completely and with pride. Remember, culture *only* exists in our heads, no heads carrying it, no culture. This is the goal of socialization of people in true cooperation.

This level of internalization dramatically reduces the amount of "law enforcement" required. It is the first and most important line of social control. If cooperative people make a mistake or for some reason violate a norm, they feel guilt and take appropriate action. Poorly socialized people only feel shame when caught breaking the norms or nothing at all.

Fitting

One of the repetitive and staggering failures of our current competitive individualistic American society with its market economy is matching people, their talents and training with the work that needs doing, to the current task roles in our society. We are in the midst of a massive high tech driven social transformation that is expanding rapidly in some areas and shrinking in others where the technologies and skills are becoming outmoded. This requires constant adjustment to the training programs provided. But this is not happening promptly or thoroughly enough in America; often not at all. This is a major element in our cultural lag in response to these profound social changes.

There is also a personal dimension to this problem: people are not fitted to an occupation for which they are well suited. "I just never fitted in," "I don't fit in here," "I just don't feel any connection with these people;" these are common laments among Americans. I imagine most of us have felt this way at sometime, in some place. I have a friend raised on a farm in Idaho who could do the farming work well but just never felt like he fitted in. It was not his place, his world though he was born into it. After some false starts and struggles he eventually became a very effective and engaged university English professor. In a cooperative society those talents and interests would have been discovered early on and he would have been helped and trained into the place he fitted well. Too many of us never do find that fit and live lives that feel incomplete and unfulfilled. We may feel we just never found or had the opportunity to express our "true" selves. A fully mature cooperative society is a very loving and compassionate society. Taking care of its people is a top priority. Leaving us to flounder through life, trying to find a place we fit with limited knowledge of our extremely complex society, and of our selves, as we do in America is abandonment.

This fitting process in cooperative societies is part of the socialization and training process. It goes on for a life time as adaptive changes are made and one's competencies change with age. This process is elaborated in Chapter 19.

POWERING UP THE COOPERATIVE SOCIETY

Positive sanctions of all kinds are constantly flowing through a cooperative society or organization. The spirited flow of approval lights up and energizes the society. You can see it in people's eyes and on their faces and in the way they walk. This is possible because of the consensus, the coordinated work of the task areas pursuing the common group goals and the society wide positive social consequence network. All participants are playing the same game with roles that contribute to the effort, engaged in their work and delighting in their accomplishments and performances. It reinforces their positive self-image and self-esteem, and it helps produce strong social cohesion. It produces camaraderie and oneness and belonging. It produces physiological states of harmony and highs, feelings of oneness (See following chapters). Cooperative people have something to jump out of bed in the morning for, a fun, exhilarating, and literally rewarding day awaits them. The cooperative society is very alive and vibrant.

By creating a consistent sanctioning pattern throughout the cooperative society, participants are also producing a positive social consequence network that is coherent, consistent, and "fair," that people can trust, predict and anticipate. It provides a life free of a great many stressors that come from living in a society where the rules of the game and sanctioning patterns are inconsistent and unpredictable. This flow of positive sanctions energizes the whole society and keeps it operating at high levels of adaptive effectiveness indefinitely.

Now we know how to get from a consensus on a cooperative culture and an understanding of social processes to a fully operational cooperative society where we are all one, working together as a rapidly adapting information processing system. We just turn on the positive sanctioning power, the "electricity" that lights it up and keeps it all running. This power we each have in our approval and when we use it all together we bring to life our new cooperative society.

The Dalai Lama in his bestselling book *Ethics for the New Millennium* (N.Y.: Riverhead Books, 1999, pp. 23, 24, 41, 47) called for a spiritual revolution that he emphasized was not a religious revolution or otherworldly, magical, or mysterious. Rather,

> It is a call for a radical reorientation away from our habitual preoccupation with self [self-centeredness]. It is a call to turn toward the wider community of beings with whom we are connected, and for conduct which recognizes others' interests alongside our own.

Because it

> becomes apparent that our every action, our every deed, word, and thought, no matter how slight or inconsequential it may seem, has an implication not only for ourselves but for all others, too.

Of the notion of "self" The Dalai Lama observed:

> If the self had intrinsic identity, it would be possible to speak in terms of self-interest in isolation from that of others. But because this is not so, because self and others can only really be understood in terms of relationship, we see that self-interest and others' interest are closely interrelated. Indeed ... we see that there is no self-interest completely unrelated to others' interests. Due to the fundamental interconnectedness, which lies at the heart of reality, your interest is also my interest. From this, it becomes clear that "my" interest and "your" interest are intimately connected. In a deep sense, they converge.

Chapter 14. Identification, Cohesion and Community Oneness

When it all comes together in the construction of true cooperative societies and social systems we blend into a single operating whole; we become all one. While this might seem a bit scary to individualistic Americans taught to fear being absorbed by "The System," it is actually one of the big payoffs of becoming cooperative. It provides a wonderful feeling of belonging, being important and needed, of using one's talents and skills for the benefit of all, of being secure, and having an active part in the ongoing adventure of adaptation in a changing world and the social evolution of humanity.

WAYS WE ARE ONE IN COOPERATION

So far we've shown several ways that cooperative communities are "one," be they families, small companies, large organizations, or societies.

They are one in their consensus on their culture, which is built upon cooperation.

They are one in sharing and pursuing their common group goals.

They are one in constructing and operating a community wide positive social consequence network.

They function as one as they collectively operate and cooperatively co-ordinate their rapidly adapting information processing social system.

They are one in their singleness of mind, of purpose, as they each pursue their task areas of responsibility competently in their service to the community.

They are a coherent social organism that only exists as they collectively continue to create and recreate it each day as one.

In this manner they produce a living social organization in which all take part and all benefit, maximizing their adaptive survival in their environment as one.

In this and the next chapter we add two more ways participants in a cooperative community are one. In this chapter we see how our self images become one with the cooperative community; we become identified with it. When we enact our social roles we enact our self-image as well. This generates the clean and strong social cohesion necessary for any social organization to flourish and act collectively with confidence and vigor. In the next chapter we explore the group physiology and rhythms of cooperative oneness and the benefits and consequences, including the "cooperative high."

IDENTIFICATION AND GROUP COHESION

As we noted in the last chapter, sociologists have known for a long time that our self-images emerge through social interaction, mirrored in others' responses to us, they do not come preformed. They *only* emerge through social interaction. They are never fixed and final. What happens in our social interactions produces and continually shapes our self-images and our self-esteem. Some of this shaping comes as we move through the stages of life and assume different roles and responsibilities from student to professional, from parent to grandparent, and so forth. We might take pride in being successful in our occupation or feel depressed from having failed.

Whatever culture we are raised and live in gives us the content of our self-images and the criteria for assessing our self-worth, our self-esteem. These are two of the most important outcomes of our relations with one another: our self-images and self-esteem. They are among our most valuable personal possession. If we don't have self-respect, which is an ongoing *social* product, what are we? Yet we Americans rarely take any thought or responsibility for what we are doing to one another. Our competitive attacks and putdowns and our individualistic aloof ignoring of one another are very damaging to our self-images and produce negative or unclear self-esteem. This is a major source of the social stress and degradation of group cohesion inherent in our current competitive individualistic culture, and can only be resolved by adopting cooperation.

A Cultural Community and Its Members Are a Seamless Whole

In true cooperation practitioners are very aware that their selves and their society are in reality one seamless whole; we are literally one with society. It is not a metaphor or poetic vision, it is reality. It is the nature of human societies. One of the social scientific theoretical perspectives I am using here is Symbolic-Interactionism based on the work of the sociologists Charles Horton Cooley (1864-1929), George Herbert Mead (1863-1931), Herbert Blumer (1900-1987), and one of my mentors, Glenn M. Vernon (1920-1985). From the point of view of true cooperation, Symbolic-Interactionism provides some powerful insights for understanding the fluid dynamics of group behavior and makes it easier to see the oneness of participants and the social systems created by our interaction.

Charles Horton Cooley recognized clear back around the turn of the 20th century that individualism was distorting our understanding of our social systems. He said:

> So strong is the individualist tradition in America and England that we hardly permit ourselves to aspire toward an ideal society directly, but think that we must approach it by some distributive formula, like "the greatest good of the greatest number."... The ideal society must be an organic whole, capable of being conceived directly, and requiring to be so conceived if it is to lay hold upon our imaginations (qtd. from *Social Process* in Coser, 1977, p. 307).

For Cooley society was a seamless web: "Our life is all one human whole, and if we are to have any real knowledge of it we must see it as such. If we cut it up it dies in the process" (quoted in Coser, 1977, p. 307). Cooley went further and said, "'Society' and 'individuals' do not denote separable phenomena, but are simply collective and distributive aspects of the same thing . . ." (p. 305). This is a critical insight—that our social selves and society are dimensions of the same thing—that must be understood before we can fully embrace cooperation. And, "If ... we say that society is an organism, we mean ... that it is a complex of forms of processes each of which is living and growing by interaction with the others, the whole being so unified that what takes place in one part affects all the rest. It is a vast tissue of reciprocal activity" (p. 307).

The sociological theorist Lewis Coser (1977) points out, "The self, to Cooley, is not first individual and then social; it arises dialectically through communication. One's consciousness of himself is a reflection of the ideas about himself that he attributes to other [people's assessment of him]. Thus, there can be no isolated selves" (p. 305). Citing Cooley, "There is no sense of 'I' ... without its correlative sense of you, or he, or they," (p. 305) or, I might add, of us. Cooley coined the catchy concept "the looking-glass self" to illustrate the reflective quality of our self-images and self-esteem. Others' opinions of us are critical and central to our self-image and our self-esteem, positive or negative. The individualist retort, "I don't care what other people think of me," is patently false. If they really didn't care there would be no motivation for the retort. In the sad case of a competitive reject or loser in our society, this retort may be a lonely, last-straw, effort to retain some shred of self-respect and identity.

Mead also emphasized that the "self" was a process and not a structure of some kind. He, along with Cooley and others, pointed out that humans are reflexive, we can see ourselves as objects as if standing outside of ourselves and assessing our qualities and behavior (Blumer, 1969, p. 62). Both animal sociobiologists and child psychologists examine the emergence or presence of this ability. One common test is how primates and children of different ages respond to their image in a mirror, especially after something has been added such as a chalk spot on their face or a cap. When the viewer notices that there is a spot or cap that wasn't there before, and examines it and perhaps removes it while looking into the mirror, reflexiveness—self-awareness—and the capacity to build a self-image are present. (See Chapter 4.) Because of this we can attribute properties to ourselves as a person just as we can to other creatures and things in our world. Our self-esteem is how well we like or dislike these attributed properties.

A PLACE TO BE SOMEBODY

Our self-image comes to life and is expressed in our enactment of our social roles. This is where we are our selves. Thus, it is important to have social roles to perform that are well integrated into the society and positively social sanctioned routinely. If we have no social role to play, or if our social role gets lower respect from others, we may have a poor self-image and low self-esteem and feel less motivated to perform our roles or the norms of our culture. Perhaps we may have had a major social role, such as our occupation, that became obsolete and this leaves us adrift with no place to enact our self-image, to use our training and skills.

One of America's grand stories is the technological evolution that is ongoing in our history. But as innovations occur, the social roles that produced and used the old technologies disappear. Part of the sadness of social change is the disappearance of proud social roles and the nostalgic loss of self-expression of those people remaining whose roles have faded from around them. The many books and movies about the closing of the American frontier and the fading away of the mountain men, the cowboys, the proud Indians, and the pioneers are an illustration. Larry McMurtry's (1991) bestselling novel, *Buffalo Girls*, is one such example (as is the 1995 CBS television movie special of the same name based on it). The replacement of the great sailing ships, such as the clippers, by steam ships is another example.

The consequences of the fading of our romance with railroads as airplanes and automobiles replaced them in our lives and imaginations I witnessed in my hometown—a major railroad center—as I grew up. The "glory days" were gone, and many railroad related occupations disappeared or became pale, sad vestiges of the originals. For example, the highest status person in my neighborhood as I was growing up was a locomotive engineer whom we all envied. These people no longer had a place to enact their roles with pride and competence. They were left with nostalgia and memories. Of course, they could, and many did, still take pride in who they were. And this sustains their self-image and esteem, sometimes for the rest of their lives. The elderly sometimes encounter a similar problem when they retire from their work. With no place to enact their self-images, no place to be somebody, their health and enthusiasm for life may decline.

My home town was a major railroad center and I knew it in its glory days and watched the decline with the coming of airplanes and the interstate highways. The hero of my neighborhood as I grew up was a man who was an engineer for the Union Pacific railroad. What an exciting and responsible job driving those huge engines pulling those long freight trains or the elite fast passenger trains with their own names! There are no more engineers in my town—maybe a few—but the glow is gone. There are just the occasional freight and Amtrak train and local commuter trains left.

The wonderful train station is now a museum with restaurants, shops and meeting rooms. I worked my way through college in a railroad related occupation that doesn't exist anymore. A whole bustling, romantic era is gone forever, living only in memories. At the foot of the Rocky Mountains, my home town is now being reborn as an outdoor recreation and equipment manufacturing center, and, with the expansion of our home-grown college into a university, an educational center.

We must all have a place to be our selves. A good society would provide us all with a respectable place, a role or collection of roles that contribute to the life and success of the society. There we all can enact a positive self-image that is reinforced and nurtured through its changes and evolution. Then we can rejoice knowing who we are and that we will always have a place to be ourselves and belong. Only cooperation reliably does this.

ENACTING ONE'S SELF, SOCIAL ROLES, AND SOCIETY SIMULTANEOUSLY

When we enact our social roles, we are enacting our self-image as well, and also creating that social system at that moment. It may be a doctor in a hospital, a father in a family, a violinist in a symphony orchestra, or a deacon in a Christian church. We are doing our self-image enactment and social system creation simultaneously with one role performance. We can look at this performance from the standpoint of the individual actor or from that of the organization, but it is still the same performance. Just as Cooley said, they are different aspects—individual ("distributive") or collective—of that social organization in its larger society.

"Identified" people identify themselves, their self, with their social roles and the social systems wherein they enact those roles. When asked to answer the question, "Who am I?" they respond with name of their role(s) and/or the name of the organization or cultural community they belong to. "I am a doctor," "I am a Catholic," "I'm a Toyota man," "I am superintendent of the Wasatch School District," "I'm an engineer," "I'm Mary Jones, a wife and mother with 3 children." They may also mention desired qualities of those roles and social systems, such as being a hard worker, being thorough, caring about others, being spiritual and so forth. Identified people are ethnocentric members of their cultural communities. They believe their life style is good, perhaps the best, maybe even God's way of doing things. They are loyal and dedicated participants who are concerned about the wellbeing of other participants and of the survival of their organization as a social system. This produces social cohesion. They don't want their company, family, or church to disintegrate and disappear. If it did, they would lose their place to be themselves, to enact the roles that are them, their self image. If their social system prospers and is respected, the participants prosper, take pride in their roles and their self-esteem is high. The identified participant and the social system are one.

Creating and maintaining this oneness and high social cohesion is highly desirable for both individuals and the social systems. Individualism teaches participants to use the social organization for their own purposes without regard for the others trying to create a cohesive social system, and to rebel against and question the authority of the social organization. Competition divides the social organization into adversarial individuals and camps, battling for control, status, dominance, and wealth. Competitors, as a rule, have no concern for the role identification of their competitive coworkers or the effects their competitions have on the cohesion and vitality of the social system. When they engage in competitive mutual aid or as a competitive "team" to defeat other teams, there may be comrades-in-arms, all-in-this-together, type of cohesion among the competitors that dissolves as soon as threats and battles are over. Individualism and competition prevent us from creating oneness and strong, clean social cohesion. Once we experience co-operative oneness, there will be no turning back; we will wonder what we ever saw in competitive individualism.

To fully understand cohesion and the challenges to creating and maintaining it, we have to understand the relation of accurate information to both social stress and social cohesion, as well as to successful adaptation and survival as a society and species.

SOCIAL STRESS, INFORMATION INCONGRUITIES, GROUP INVOLVEMENT, AND COHESION

INFORMATION INCONGRUITIES

Any culture can be judged by the degree it matches accurately and completely the world in which it exists. This includes how adaptively those using the culture can operate using it. One of the fundamental goals of true cooperative communities is to constantly maximize this fit. The importance of this match cannot be over emphasized. The ramifications for society and its people, including their health are considerable.

Few people realize how crucial a continuing flow of accurate information about the environment and our society is. Accurate information that is constantly being checked and updated is at the core of successful human adaptation and survival. When we don't have it, all kinds of problems emerge and persist. In my search for the sources of social stress, I discovered that every social stressor was an information incongruity (Moss, 1973). These are mismatches between what we wanted and what we got, between what we expected and what we experience, discovering what we were taught to do didn't work or was incorrect or a lie causing us to fail, finding our information doesn't fit the real world—the world doesn't work that way, discovering conflicts or mismatches between the norms or values or teachings of two or more of our cultures, hurting when we learn that people we thought were our friends are not, learning that we don't know the answers to crucial questions, and more. For conceptual purposes, I labeled these mismatches "information incongruities." As you are no doubt aware, our personal, social and larger cultural lives are full of information incongruities. Often our attention on a given day is on dealing with some incongruity or another.

Over the years of research on social stress I realized that these same information incongruities damage our self-image and self-esteem and undermine the social cohesion of our organizations and communities. These information incongruities are the cause of our social stress and come right out of our current sociocultural patterns. Social cohesion goes down and stress goes up as the level of information incongruities goes up, and vice versa. Consequently, one of the primary goals of a cooperative society seeking to maximize our adaptive success and wellbeing has to be eliminating as many information incongruities as possible. Obviously, the best way to do that is to keep the society's information accurate and effective. That turns out to be a big challenge and life-time undertaking willingly shouldered by cooperative societies. Our competitive individualistic society actually generates all kinds of incongruities. Some of these incongruities are created on purpose to gain competitive advantage or further self-centered goals, such as lies, misrepresentations, conniving and withholding critical information. Worse, our cultural groups and organizations have all kinds of tricks they use to make it look like their information is accurate when it is actually full of error and incongruities. While competitive individualists see this as necessary for their success and survival, it seriously undermines group cohesion. We need to watch out for these practices when we build our cooperative organizations.

THE FOUR TYPES OF INDIVIDUAL RELATIONSHIPS WITH GROUPS: IDENTIFIED, ALIENATED, ANOMIE, AUTONOMOUS

Each of us belongs to several groups. We may belong to a church, work for an organization or company, live in a family, be active in a political or ideological group, have recreational group memberships, and all within the larger American society's cultural community. Each of these groups has its own culture and social systems. As we use those cultures we are in fact testing whether those values, norms, beliefs and descriptions of the world are correct and work. If they work fine, we pay little notice and just go happily along living those cultural patterns. When this happens we have "information congruity," which simply means there is a match between the information in our heads and what we experience. The world works as we expect and want it to.

When we experience information congruities in our group(s), we become identified with those groups. We make ourselves to home, so to speak, and enjoy enacting our roles in the group and its culture. Then we generally have a positive self image and good self-esteem. We are engaged and express ourselves through our roles. We advocate for the group and are proud of our membership. Living in groups and cultural communities where the information is congruous with reality and works is the ideal. It is a fundamental goal of true cooperative cultural communities. The sociopsychophysiological benefits to participants are at their highest and much to be desired.

However, if we experience some serious information incongruities with any of those groups, we may become alienated from them. We may reject their culture and distance ourselves from our roles. We may perform only minimally and with little enthusiasm our roles and find little joy in our membership. We may become critical of the group, finding fault and attacking it in public. If possible we may leave that group. Alienated people undermine and weaken group cohesion, sometimes actively.

Participants can also experience anomie. Immigrants, for example, may not understand the culture of their new country and be unable to participate fully or engage with it. New employees may feel lost, adrift in their new company until someone socializes them or they figure it out. This situation produces a whole set of information incongruities between what the person has in their heads and what they are seeing and being asked to do. This can be a very stressful period. They are definitely not identified with the group and don't know enough about it to be alienated from it. People in a state of anomie dilute group cohesion and may engage in practices from their old culture that disrupt the collaborative pattern of the group.

Some people may have enough experience in a variety of groups and cultural communities to be able to move comfortably from one to another, behaving appropriately in each. They are able to conform to the various cultures they move in and fulfill roles successfully. These are what I call "autonomous" people. Many individualists would like to be autonomous. They can get what they want from many sources but may be unable to ever fully identify with any social system. The danger is that being aloof from any social system may put them in a critical, fault-finding, self-contained world wherein all cultural communities are found lacking and rejected, even one's own. This can lead to the loss of meaning in life. Harry Haller in Hermann Hesse's (1969) *Steppenwolf* is an example. He has to search each day for some reason to go on living. That is a massive information incongruity. The human world is a cultural world, a world of communities, not one of isolated autonomy. From the group's point of view, the autonomous have little to contribute to cohesion given their aloof engagement with the group. They can functionally fill a role or gap for a time but do not provide the energy and total commitment of identification that is necessary for cooperative group oneness.

The accuracy and adaptive vitality of the culture is the determinant of which of these four forms of group-individual relationship a person will have with each of their groups. One can be alienated from one's job and occupation, identified with their religion, autonomous with various community and civic groups, and occasionally anomic when moving to a new town or new job. (See Moss, 1973 for more details.)

Maintaining Information Congruity or Appearances of Congruity

Organizations and societies want their members to be identified. They want the devotion and enthusiastic commitment to the group and belief in its culture. Cultural information congruity is the ideal, most stress-free, and

permanently effective source of such devotion. However, maintaining identification of the members is a challenge if there are, in fact, many information incongruities in that culture. Consequently, virtually all competitive
individualistic social systems and cultural communities use one or more of
the common social techniques to discount or cover up these incongruities
when they can't or won't correct them.

The cultural community may attempt to isolate the participants from
information that disproves the culture's, such as by discouraging association with groups that have conflicting information. They may blame someone else or some other group, such as an enemy or rival or scapegoat, claim-
ing it is their fault things are not working right. Those in control my hide
or lie about the information incongruity. They may attempt to explain away
the information incongruity, such as by rejecting the source who called attention to it—"You can't believe them, they're just . . ." They may find fault
with the participant who has experienced and is complaining about the incongruity—"You didn't do it right." Or, they may justify the presence of the
incongruity—"Such challenges to our faith are necessary for us to grow."
These are all attempts to redefine the situation so it is not experienced as an
information incongruity with the shared culture that could lead to rejection
of the group. Our social stress experiences are tangled up in all of this. The
more a cultural community relies on these efforts to hide real problems with
their culture and the organizations performances, the less adaptive that system is and the greater the risk for failure and eventual collapse. (See Moss,
1973 for elaboration.)

THE OPTIMAL CURVE OF COHESION

In my article, "Identification and the Curve of Optimal Cohesion,"
(Moss, 1979) I examined the sensitive relationship between our identification with our groups and the adaptive functioning of the organization
or cultural community. It is possible for participants to be too strongly or
too weakly identified with a group. Too little and the group will have little
cohesion and function poorly. Too much and problems are created including conflict with other groups or cultural communities and cultural rigidity
that prevents cultural corrections of incongruities. In a pluralistic world
such as we now live in, there is a moderate level of identification and cohesion that is most adaptive for both the individuals and the organization.
In Chapter 10 we looked at the problems with different levels of cultural

ethnocentricity in a group, and found a moderate level is the best, the most adaptively effective. We are returning to that issue here.

Individual identification produces group cohesion. No identification, no cohesion. Alienation, anomie and members who are autonomous undermine group cohesion. If the members are too ethnocentric, are over identified with the group—believing their way is the only right way, perhaps God's way and cannot be changed—they become less and less tolerant of people who are not true believers. They may drive the more moderate members out. At the same time, they become intolerant of other groups to the point that only negotiations and conflict remain as ways to deal them. These kinds of overly ethnocentric, overly identified, overly cohesive groups and cultural communities are the cause of much of the conflict and many of the wars our world is experiencing today. Many are "fundamentalists" who are inflexible in their beliefs, believe all should believe as they do and that control of their societies should be in their hands. These groups will be very active in using the information incongruity handling techniques described above. They will blame their "enemies" for perceived failures and flaws in their cultures. America gets blamed for a lot of these in some fundamentalist communities. The optimal level of identification and cohesion is at the moderate level where members are tolerant of other cultures, can see what is of value in them, can work and associate with them, and are open to learn new things and correct flaws in their culture.

Being all one in a cooperative community requires constant attention to maintaining adaptive information processing that keeps the culture current and accurate, produces wholesome identification, good moderate cohesion, and organic wholeness and vitality.

The Roseto Story: The Amazing Healing Power of Social Cohesion

Cohesive communities and organizations can take many forms. The true cooperative community I've been describing is an ideal because it can continue to be cohesive while changing as needed to adapt to environmental and social changes. Thus, it can remain effective, stable, predictable and reliable for participants indefinitely. This is ideal for our health as well. In the 1960s scientists discovered Roseto, Pennsylvania, (Bruhn and Wolf: 1979) a community with a remarkably low level of mortalities from coronary heart disease that was less than half that of our American society and Roseto's neighboring communities (p. 21). After years of study of this remarkable community of Italian immigrants, the social and medical scientists concluded it was the result of Roseto's social cohesion and vitality as a cultural community. Unfortunately, this cultural community worked well only as long as it was able to maintain its Italian roots and practices. It was unable to adapt and change and so it was eventually invaded and transformed by our larger American culture and lost its cohesion and unique health benefits. The Roseto study is now a classic in the fields of social stress and social epidemiology.

Roseto grew from Italian immigrants who came to this country from Roseto, Italy in the latter years of the 19th century. The population was around 1,600 from the 1930s through the 1960s. They retained their Italian customs, lifestyle and religious practices. Bruhn, Wolf and their colleagues (1979) found:

> Widely accepted risk factors for coronary heart disease such as a diet rich in animal fat, cigarette smoking, lack of exercise, diabetes, and hypertension were at least as prevalent in Roseto as in neighboring communities (p. 21).

Their levels of serum cholesterol were the same as neighboring communities while the prevalence of obesity was actually higher in Roseto. These working class Italians could not afford to buy imported olive oil, a staple in a healthy Mediterranean diet, but had to substitute lard and other animal fats.

Other possible causes of the low death rates were also eliminated, such as ethnic factors and genetics. Italians genetically related to the residents of Roseto living in other parts of America and American Italians in general had the same coronary heart disease rates as the rest of the nation (pp. viii, ix).

Still, the death rate from myocardial infarction (heart attack) was 1 per thousand for males of all ages in Roseto, while the average for the United States was 3.5 per thousand. For females it was 0.6 per thousand in Roseto compared with 2.09 per thousand at the national level (p. viii). Most of these deaths among men were in the older age groups over 60. Clearly, Rosetans, especially younger men, enjoyed relative immunity from fatal heart attacks. Why?

> One striking feature did set Roseto apart from its neighbors ... namely its culture, which reflected tenaciously held Old World values and

customs. We found that family relationships were extremely close and mutually supportive. This cohesive quality extended to neighbors and to the community as a whole. There was a well-defined man-woman relationship in Roseto, where the man was uncontested head of the family. The elderly were cherished and respected, and they retained their authority throughout life. The atmosphere of Roseto was gay and friendly and reflected an enthusiastic and optimistic attitude toward life (Bruhn and Wolf, 1979, p. ix).

The men mostly worked in the local slate mines in the early years, then in cement, steel and similar plants in the area, while the women worked in one of the 16 small textile factories that produced blouses. They enjoyed their major annual celebration, the Festival of Our Lady of Mount Carmel, which was strongly supported and included a parade and many social activities. They had a "cornet" band that was a brass band that performed for events and provided concerts. They had 23 social clubs and civic groups and enjoyed their Churches. Seventy-five percent were Catholic and 16 per cent were Presbyterian (due to some unusual complications in getting a Catholic priest and branch in the early years of the community). Most graduate from Catholic parochial schools though public schools are available. Eighty percent of the high school graduates go on to college. This level of higher education has contributed to the transformation of Roseto and the dispersal of many of their young people to other communities with better occupational opportunities (pp. 49-66).

Rosetans during their high cohesion period had multi-stranded connections with one another: family relations, religious ties, ethnicity, common work, recreational group memberships, and their community of residence. Within the community they worked together on a variety of projects and improvements. These multi-stranded connections—which Americans also once enjoyed—are fading as Roseto transforms into a more typical American community. In America, multi-stranded relations have degraded into predominantly single-stranded connections in our increasingly individualistic society (see Chapter 7). This has also degraded our levels of cohesion and the protection from disease it provides.

Nevertheless, the study of Roseto provides us with solid scientific evidence of the benefits of social cohesion for our well-being and health. These are benefits we can expect to experience again when we establish our true cooperative organizations and communities.

The joy of being all one includes a wonderful subjective world of harmonious social rhythms and exhilarating physiological/emotional highs as the next chapter shows.

Chapter 15. The Cooperation High: The Physiology and Rhythms of Oneness

A fascination with the interplay between our physiology and our social behavior led me into stress research and generated the theme of my first book. I labeled this intimate relationship "biosocial resonation" (Moss, 1973). Our sociocultural patterns influence our physiological responses and states continually and vice versa. This includes our immediate ongoing physiological responses to whatever is happening at the moment and the generation of various common physiological states in the participants of that culture. Examples include the stress response, the physiology of excitement, joy and depression and other emotions, and the establishment of hyper-responsiveness or "tuning," such as people who "fly off the handle" and get angry at every little thing (see following sections).

When you create a cultural community, you create a physiological community as well. It might have a fast, medium or slow tempo; it may be high pressure producing Type A-like behavior or it may be relaxed and more laid-back Type B-ish. Its music may be loud, hyper and intense, or it may be soothing, mellow and harmonious. In this chapter we will see that a cooperative society produces a more healthful, stress free environment to live in and physiological states more conducive to harmonious social relations than the competitive individualistic one we now inhabit. We can experience a physiological "high," feelings of elation, joy, or energized happiness naturally without the use of drugs or stimulants. Many of us have these when we do something especially well and are delighted with it. Teachers get such a high when they have an especially good class where the students are really with them and are excited about what they are learning. Cooperative groups can make such delightful highs frequent experiences that are one of the benefits, rewards, for practicing cooperation.

First we'll look at how various cultural communities have rhythms of life and social interaction characteristic of them, inherent in their sociocultural structures. Then we'll look at the physiological patterns of group behavior as they relate to group performance.

THE RHYTHMS OF COOPERATION: INTERPERSONAL SYNCHRONY

Edward T. Hall is well known for his work on rhythms in social interaction, and "interpersonal synchrony." On group rhythms Hall (1983) said in his book, *The Dance of Life,*

> It is hard to write about rhythms in English. We don't have the vocabulary, and the concepts aren't in the culture. We in the West have this notion that each of us is all by himself in this world—that behavior is something that originates inside the skin, isolated from the outside world and from other human beings. Nothing could be further from the truth (p. 148).

Hall was particularly concerned with the rhythms that emerge in social communities as we interact with one another and enact our shared culture.

Hall found there are fundamental rhythms of social interaction inherent in the various basic sociocultural operating systems of societies. These include how fast culture members talk; do they pause after others speak before talking themselves or jump right in, even interrupting? How fast do they walk and move, how impatient, hurried or relaxed in their movements. If you set their cultural movement patterns to music would it be slow and mellow, or fast with an insistent beat? When they get together socially to dance, what do those dances look like? How are their days organized, with an easy tempo without being tied to time, or tightly scheduled with efforts to get more and more done in less and less time?

Members of a given society draw upon these inherent rhythms in producing synchrony within their groups. Our competitive individualistic culture doesn't give us rhythms conducive to harmonious cooperation. We are either doing our own thing at our own tempo, or we are competing. Competitive people tend to walk a little bit in front of others. Competitive individualists tend to have their own career or task agenda and pursue it vigorously without regard to the effect their tempo has on others. They may, for example, barge into ongoing discussions or activities, disrupting them. Sometimes, in their impatience with others, they may step in and take over, doing someone else's work themselves. They see themselves as doing it faster and better. There are speech battles. Sometimes competitive people will try to disrupt the rhythm of ongoing activities to undermine their competitors and perhaps cause them to fail. Our individualism impoverishes us in our understanding and appreciation of interpersonal synchrony and group rhythms compared with other cultures, such as the Native-Americans, Japanese and Spanish. However, we give a nod to such rhythms when we compare American communities as being fast-paced or slow-paced.

In interpersonal synchrony, in given interactions participants find ways to bring their personal rhythms and paces into synchrony. The Japanese, for example, will—often without taking thought—synchronize their breathing patterns when conversing. The Japanese and Native American cultures structure their conversations to encourage synchrony using similar tempos and practices, which include not interrupting in conversations but letting the speakers say what they want, pausing for several seconds in silence to be sure before responding. The biological anthropologist Eliot Chapple (1970, p. 46) refers to this synchronization of communication as "complimentarity." Chapple said,

> To achieve such a state, the beat or *tempo* of the two persons has to be identical. Hence, within the length of time from one pulse or beat to the next, the length of the action of one equals the length of action of the other, and vice versa.

Episodes of complimentarity are found to be "far more frequent in close friends or married couples who 'got on well.'" We Americans sometimes exhibit this complimentarity and interpersonal synchrony too. In another example, we may fall into step with each other when walking.

Hall tells us that social synchrony not only feels good, but also enhances and sometimes is essential to successfully doing the tasks at hand. When people are in synchrony they might speak of "being in the groove", of "really cooking," and similar expressions. Hall describes what it felt like when he worked with some Spanish friends in Santa Fe. "While we were building a house and were all working in close proximity, it became clear how much faster and more adept the Spanish were. It was as though our small work crew was a single organism with multiple arms and legs that never got in each other's way" (Hall, 1982, p. 149). From my point of view, these workers knew how to coordinate their house-building and had developed skills that all knew about; they could see the whole and what everyone was doing at that time and anticipate what came next.

This is another reason true cooperation is more effective in task performance than competitive individualism. The coordination and the rhythms cooperative workers utilize make it possible to do the task faster and better, and have more fun doing it.

But unfortunately, as Hall (1983) points out:

> . . . there are certain people who have a talent for breaking or interrupting other people's rhythms. In most cases they don't even know it, and how could they? After all, it's other people who are having the accidents, breaking and dropping things, stumbling and falling. Fortunately, there is the other kind of person: the one who is always in sync, who is such a joy, who seems to sense what move you will make next. Anything you do with him or her is like a dance; even making the bed can be fun. I know of no way to teach people how to sync with each other, but I do know that whether they do or not can make a world of difference in a relationship (p. 149).

In my experience, many Americans are "bargers," just barging into ongoing social interactions without regard to the processes flowing, demanding that all attention be shifted to them and whatever they are doing or saying at the moment. They are rhythm and synchrony disrupters. At a group level, an example would be basketball teams trying to upset each other's rhythm during a game hoping to produce negative consequences for the other team, such as bad passes and missed shots.

Hall is making an important point for group performances. When synchrony is disrupted, it can lead to mistakes and physical miscues like mental mistakes, stumbling, dropping, or bumbling. When synchrony is achieved, participants are more adept, speedy, and satisfied with the experience. People who cannot get into sync produce problems. For example, Hall (1983) reports that research shows that "parents who batter their children have never learned to sync with their babies" (p. 162).

Competitors can irritate and disrupt one another by unsynchronizing or refusing to synchronize their interaction patterns. They can purposely get out of step with others or walk ahead of them. The Structured Interview for assessing Type A behavior includes observing such unsynchronized behavior in verbal interactions, such as talking over the other, talking faster and emphatically, and interrupting. This is behavior considered uncouth and rude in Native American and Japanese cultures, and would be in cooperative ones as well. It definitely has a competitive flavor. Individualists just do their own thing at their own pace and generally ignore other's rhythms.

One way to determine if more cooperative behavior is occurring is looking at the level of interpersonal synchrony exhibited. One way to facilitate your efforts to create cooperative relationships with others is to pay attention to whether you are in or out of sync. Synchronicity is a seemingly small and simple matter but it is one that can open or close the door on cooperative social interactions. It certainly facilitates harmony and feelings of operating as one. Cooperative people dance life together to the same tune. Competitive and individualistic people "dance" in the same social space but to whatever tune, tempo, suits them at the moment.

I believe that a true cooperative society, more effectively and consciously than others, would use music and other devices to get people into the same rhythm, keep everyone in the tempo, and develop skills in interpersonal synchrony. For centuries work groups in many cultures used chants and working songs as they labored, especially with manual labor that needed to be coordinated. This living in rhythm with one another—this dance of cooperation—is one of the joyous payoffs for living as one cooperatively, something to look forward to each day, as Hall himself experienced.

Cooperatively orchestrating physiological patterns can give physical and emotional dimensions to the experience of oneness. Living true cooperation can give members rich emotional feelings of harmony and collective physiological highs that dramatically enrich daily life, providing continued sources of delight, excitement, and satisfying feelings of oneness and community. The psychological and physiological aspects of this oneness are also stress relieving and health enhancing.

The Physiological Dance

An exciting area of research that is bound to reveal many surprises and important insights as it progresses is the study of natural group physiology, examining the physiology of all of the group members as they interact and go about their tasks. The study of real groups in their natural settings has much to show us about the interplay between the practice of individualism, competition, or cooperation and participants' physiology while performing daily tasks. Before I retired, one of the areas of research I was considering was the impact of competitive, hard-driving, time-urgent, Type As on work-group performance, physiology, and health. Here are some examples that illustrate the physiological component of group behavior and the physiological harmony, including feelings of togetherness and shared excitement, true cooperative groups will experience and enjoy.

When groups are working well together there tends to be a convergence and covariation of their individual physiological responses while participating. Convergence means their physiological response patterns and levels converge from a variety of levels and patterns to a common one for all participants, such as common heart rate or blood pressure level or hormone levels in the blood. Covariation means that these physiological patterns go up or down at the same time and to the same degree as participants encounter experiences and challenges together. Their stress physiological patterns—heart rate, blood pressure, adrenal gland secretion levels (hormones), and the like—may activate in concerted harmony as they cooperatively engage the environmental challenges encountered.

Physiological Convergence and Covariation in Groups

It is beyond the scope of this book and unnecessary for me to provide a detailed description of the physiological and nervous system processes I will mention in this section. All that is intended here is for the reader to get a general idea of the existence of group physiological patterns and a glimpse of their consequences.

Two examples of work on group physiology that caught my attention in the early years of my research and continue to influence my thinking were William Caudill's (1958) pamphlet, "Effects of Social and Cultural Systems in Reactions to Stress" and P. Herbert Leiderman and David Shapiro's (1964) book *Psychobiological Approaches to Social Behavior.* Here are two studies reported in those publications.

Harvard Rowing Crews

Among the many examples Caudill (1958, pp. 23-24) used to illustrate sociocultural, physiological, and health pattern interactions was a study of Harvard rowing crews. Two different crews in two different years, 1953 and 1954, were studied, with several rowers on both teams. The researchers used the levels of a particular white blood cell the eosinophile as a physiological marker, among others.

One characteristic of stress responses in mammals is the increase in levels of neuroendocrine hormones that have as one—unfortunate—consequence the destruction of white blood cells. White blood cells are sensitive to stress generated hormones which can cause their cell walls to dissolve. The first medically related project I participated in as a graduate student research assistant was counting through a microscope the number of disintegrated white blood cells—lymphocytes—taken from the blood of mice being exposed to various procedures. This is a major reason people under stress are more susceptible to infections and other diseases they normally could resist. A drop in white blood cell count can sometimes be used as an indirect indicator of the presence and degree of stress a mammal is experiencing. In this example, the level of eosinophiles in each rower's blood, which dropped in response to the stress of the race, was compared.

In this example the similarity or dissimilarity in rowers' levels of circulating eosinophiles turned out to be an indicator of the degree of social cohesion and harmony of the two rowing teams during races. The two crews were studied for several weeks during their pre-race training and race situations. One could easily determine which was the winning team by nothing more than the levels and patterns of eosinophile white blood cells in the rowers during and immediately following the race. The 1953 rowing crew was a winner, while the 1954 crew was a loser. The 1954 crew exhibited wide individual variations in the level of circulating eosinophiles in both their pre-race and race responses. The winning 1953 team, on the other hand, exhibited individually variable responses during the pre-race period, but were much more uniform in their response to the race itself— their physiological responses converged. Caudill (1958, p. 24) reported that men who had been on both rowing crews felt that the losing 1954 team didn't row together as the 1953 team did and failed to achieve the necessary social integration to win. To the rowers it was obvious when they were in harmony. They reported "swinging together" in their winning races with the boat going well "almost immediately" (p. 24).

B-52 Bomber Crew

Mason and Brady (1964), in Liederman and Shapiro, reported, "We have observed a tendency in some small groups of 5 to 6 individuals for 17-OH-CS [17-hydroxycorticosterone, an adrenal cortical steroid involved in many physiological responses, including stress] levels to cluster in a rather narrow range, basally and during stress, after the group as lived or worked together for a while" (p. 16, insert mine). This is an example of physiological convergence and covariation. The covariation was their clustering together physiologically in their response to stress; their individual physiological response to the stressor from their basal level was the same.

Mason and Brady give the example of a B-52 bomber crew on a non-stop round trip flight to Argentina. This example also shows how within group role specialization can influence physiological responses, such as in those responsible. Men average a normal level of 17-OH-CS secretions of about 7 milligram per day. During flight days, the pilot, who was also responsible for handling and supervising the hazardous mid-air refueling of the bomber, had an extremely high level of 20 mg/day. The crewmen working together further back in the plane all ran a similar elevated level of about 13 mg/day (p. 17). On non-flight days these men's secretion levels were closer to the average and different from one another.

In true cooperation, I would expect cooperative task groups and others to develop a common physiological basal level when they operate together—convergence—and to covary in their physiological responses to whatever comes up, with in-group variations related to the division of labor—such as the B-52 pilot. This convergence and covariation in group members' physiology appears to considerably enhance effectiveness and feelings of togetherness and oneness.

There are ways to pull group participants' physiology into convergence, to all become the same or very similar for a time. This is a very useful thing to be able to do. And not just to win team athletic events. Human societies around the world and over centuries have discovered some of these and incorporated them into their cultural practices. They use these practices to produce a sense of oneness, of being in the same place at the same time, of focusing minds and bodies together for a variety of purposes. Some of them are familiar such as dancing together—a war dance among frontier Native Americans, or a fertility dance and rituals, perhaps—and music, such as singing while marching and working. Religions use songs, chants and rituals to get worshipers spiritually in tune with each other and presumably with their deity. The howling together of the wolf pack before hunting caribou described in Chapter 4 serves a similar purpose. Scientists call this "group entrainment."

Producing Group Entrainment: Dance, Music, Rituals, and Trances

Entrainment refers to the process of synchronizing biological processes and rhythms among people in social interaction through environmental stimuli (Lex, 1975, including p. 208; Chapple, 1970, including pp. 29, 46). Group neurophysiological entrainment may be mild and short-lived, moderate, or so strong it can disrupt normal physiological and brain functioning. The latter may produce behavior observers would call being possessed or having a vision. Entrainment can affect biorhythms such as our circadian rhythms (24 hour sleep-awake cycle) and female menstrual cycles. Co-eds living in college dorms have been found to converge toward similar menstrual cycle periods, for example.

The most commonly affected physiological systems are our sympathetic or parasympathetic nervous systems (or in extreme situations, both), related endocrine glands such as the adrenal gland, and certain brain waves. The sympathetic and parasympathetic nervous systems are the two components of our autonomic nervous system. This system controls a great many of our basic biological functions. In stress the sympathetic nervous system produces what is often call the "fight or flight" response, with the adrenal gland producing "adrenalin." Many of us are familiar with these stress responses. The parasympathetic nervous system helps produce the "relaxation response" to the stress fight or flight excitation.

Entrainment may produce excitement and arousal or relaxation and peaceful calm depending on the group activity, the desired goal, and the physiological processes involved. Excitation, for example, can be produced by rhythmic dancing, flashing lights, and music, including beating drums, shaking rattles, shouting and singing, and clapping hands that can produce physiological convergence and entrainment of the sympathetic nervous system and of brain waves and activity among the participants; in some cases it can lead to trance states. The intense evangelical charismatic religious services that produce trances, talking in tongues, "possessions," and ecstasy use such devices.

Group meditation techniques, on the other hand, often produce parasympathetic nervous system and brain wave entrainment. The use of a single word such as "om" or "um" spoken aloud repeatedly and in rhythmic harmony with the other participants can dampen left brain rational and detailed activity in the participants favoring right brain synthetic and more holistic activity and giving the mediators feelings of oceanic oneness with the universe.

These group neurophysiological entrainment experiences are valued and sought by many people in many societies. Virtually all societies—as far as I can tell—provide and engage in practices that produce entrainment or physiological convergence temporarily in gatherings of participants. These experiences can be very important in producing and maintaining feelings of identification with a particular society or sub-culture such as a church or the Woodstock Nation feeling among rock fans.

I would imagine that most readers have had such experiences in their churches, at patriotic gatherings, at concerts, or in other activities such as dances. Unfortunately, sometimes drugs and alcohol are used to attempt to reach these states. Doing it naturally without addictive substances is best.

Participants frequently interpret these altered and group entrained neurophysiological states as higher order experiences, especially of spiritual and religious significance. In religious or spiritually based groups, these experiences can provide endorsements or "proof" of the power and validity of the culture and its teachings and practices: "the Spirit was with us today."

In other cases, these entrainment techniques may be used to produce reduced inhibitions and sexual arousal as expressions of ecstasy: some cultures' fertility rites and loud, crowded, intense, nightclub dancing are examples. Entrainment can also be used to arouse anger, aggression, and vengeful emotions, such as war dances, soldiers' chants and shouts before battle, and fan pep rallies and competitive shouting and cheering frenzies at athletic events. The turning of soccer fans into a destructive mob is an extreme example.

In light of the benefits for group cohesion and worker coordination provided by physiological convergence and entrainment, the practice of some Japanese businesses of singing the company song and doing rhythmic calisthenics and other exercises together before work—often disparaged by individualistic Americans—makes sense.

AUTONOMIC NERVOUS SYSTEM "TUNING"

Normally, our sympathetic—excitation—system and our parasympathetic—relaxation—system activate when excitation or relaxation are appropriate. However, sometimes the intense and frequent activation of one or the other can change it so that it responds when it shouldn't. A parasympathetically tuned person may seem depressed, passive, uncaring, hard to get going and lacking energy. In social stress we are especially interested in the sympathetic fight or flight response. If one is exposed to highly stressful environments for a period of time, the sympathetic nervous system changes so that it takes less of a social situation to trigger it. It becomes "hyper-responsive." Sympathetically tuned people, for example, often respond to situations inappropriately with anger. They may exhibit free-floating hostility just waiting for something, anything, to set them off.

As an example, cats and dogs, as well as humans, normally respond to being petted, caressed, and stroked with their parasympathetic nervous system, relaxing and in the case of cats purring. However, a sympathetically tuned cat or dog, perhaps as the result of mistreatment or need to constantly defend itself, does not respond to petting with the normal or balanced animal's parasympathetic response, but with a sympathetic one. When this sympathetically tuned animal is petted it will more likely respond with impatience and try to escape, or with anger, perhaps biting. A sympathetically tuned human may respond similarly to efforts by others to be affectionate, and show offense at being touched (Gellhorn and Loofbourrow, 1963, pp. 89-116; Moss, 1973, pp. 114-116).

I once did a study of an exaggerated startle response among some people of Maine called locally "jumpers" (Moss:1968). They were the source of considerable amusement and sometimes inconsiderate harassment. Their startle responses were often spectacular and sometimes triggered by "friends" and co-workers to produce the most mayhem, such as when carrying dishes or standing on the edge of a dock. I suspect they were victims of sympathetic nervous system "tuning." Our competitive society frequently produces ideal conditions to produce sympathetic tuning in us. I suspect that such tuning under lays much of the "road rage" and similar outbursts of anger we Americans' experience. I also believe sympathetic tuning is an element in

Type A coping response patterns and both are a product of our hard-driving efforts to succeed in America's intense competitive individualistic culture.

Making the paradigm shift from competitive individualism to cooperation will eliminate most of the sympathetic tuning generated by our current society and the problems that result.

Michio Kaku, an acclaimed physicist and author, took a futurist's look at the social challenges our rapidly evolving technology likely will create for us in his book, *Hyperspace* (New York: Anchor/Doubleday, 1995. p. 292).

The supply of energy is a primary determinant of a civilization's technological development. In the framework Kaku is using, we are currently a Type 0 civilization. Kaku said:

> To reach Type I status requires a remarkable degree of social cooperation on a planetary scale. Aggregates on the order of tens of hundreds of millions of individuals are necessary to exploit the resources of uranium, internal combustion, and chemicals. However, aggregates on the order of billions are probably necessary truly to harness planetary resources. Thus the social organization of a Type I civilization must be very complex and very advanced, or else the technology cannot be developed.

> By definition, a Type I civilization requires a cohesive social unit that is the entire planet's population. A Type I civilization by its very nature must be a planetary civilization. It cannot function on a smaller scale.

Chapter 16. Is Business on the Brink?

THE HISTORICAL TREND: FROM CONTROL-ORIENTED TO MORE COOPERATIVE ORGANIZATIONS

What I've been calling the "dominance hierarchy" style of organization generated by competition has been the dominant form of company organization during our industrial period. As Edward Lawler III, director of the Center for Effective Organizations at the University of Southern California and widely read author on management, (1992) points out, "The oldest, best-established approach has been referred to as top-down, pyramidal, hierarchical, mechanistic, and bureaucratic, but perhaps it is best described as the *control-oriented approach*" (p.25, emphasis as per original). Lawler traces the roots of the now traditional control-oriented approach to Max Weber, the classical late 19th and early 20th century sociological theorist who examined the rationalization and bureaucratization of modern organizations—with considerable ambivalence—and to Frederick Winslow Taylor's infamous "scientific management," also in the late 19th and early 20th centuries in America. "Scientific management" involved a division of labor into simple, repetitive tasks that could be routinized and taught to uneducated workers. Maximizing workers efficiency by detailed study of the best and fastest way to do the jobs was the goal. "Historically, the term *well managed* has been applied to organizations that have strong leadership at the top and that execute the traditional control model of management better than other companies do," according to Lawler (1992, pp. 11-12, emphasis as per original).

Our industrial period got rolling as a product of the Civil War and with the spread of the railroads in the following years, flourishing in the first half of the 20th century. It included innovations such as Henry Ford's assembly line and used a work force heavily populated for many years by poorly educated immigrants. Taylor's scientific management worked well and sometimes produced tremendous gains in productivity. In the 1920s, when Alfred Sloan transformed General Motors by introducing the multidivisional style of organization, the traditional control-oriented hierarchy model of corporation management "had grown to maturity and was the driving force behind the American economy" according to the economist Jeremy Rifkin (1996, p. 93). At the apex of power for the traditional control-oriented industrial model of management in the late 1950s and early 1960s, the level of productive accomplishment was very impressive as five hundred giant American corporations produced half of our nation's industrial output and nearly a quarter of that of the noncommunist world (Rifkin, 1996, p. 94). The control-oriented approach to management still predominates in America (Lawler, 1992, p. 27).

Attacks on this traditional American multi-level dominance hierarchy bureaucracy style of management began to emerge in the late 1950s and early 1960s by organizational specialists and academics in books such as *Personality and Organization* by Chris Argyris (1957), *New Patterns of Management* by Rensis Likert (1961), and *The Human Side of Enterprise* by Douglas McGregor (1960). "They pointed out that even the best organizations were significantly underperforming because of the way they organized and treated people. They went on to argue that much higher levels of performance were possible if organizations used participative management approaches," according to Lawler (1992, pp. 13, 14). It was the dehumanization of workers by our rational, control-oriented bureaucracies that troubled Max Weber too (Coser, 1977, pp. 230-234).

Beginning in the late 1950s and 1960s Toyota developed "lean production", a management innovation that was adopted widely in Japan, eventually proving a serious challenge to American businesses. Rifkin (1996) observed:

> The Japanese form of lean production starts by doing away with the traditional managerial hierarchy and replacing it with multi-

skilled teams that work together at the point of production. In the Japanese lean factory, design engineers, computer programmers, and factory workers interact face-to-face, sharing ideas and implementing joint decisions directly on the floor... Under the new system of lean production, the factory floor becomes in effect the research and development laboratory, a place where the combined enterprise of everyone in the production process is utilized to make "continual improvements" and refinements in the production process and the final product (p. 97).

That's exactly what a cooperative company would do.

The "continual improvements" are the result of the practice of "kaizen," mentioned earlier in Chapters 4 and 11 and elaborated in a following section. "Workers from every department are invited to take part in the design of new cars." Called "concurrent engineering," it is

based on the principle that everyone affected by the design, scale-up, production, distribution, marketing, and sales of a new automobile should participate as early as possible in the development of a new car to ensure that each department's specific needs and requirements are taken into consideration and to help pinpoint potential trouble spots before full-scale production is set (p. 97).

Studies have shown that 75 percent of the product's cost is determined at the conceptual stage, so if planners can get it right there, the company can greatly reduce costs, repairs, and adjustments later on.

According to Rifkin (1996), a study of American auto companies found that their manufacturing equipment was inoperative 50 percent or more of the time, while the Japanese auto companies were down less than 15 percent of the time. In addition to the reasons described above, this was because in Japan the work teams are given great latitude over the production process and if a machine breaks down or there is a bottleneck—such as not enough parts—the workers fix it themselves. They don't have to notify supervisors who go through the hierarchical process to get technicians to the machine (p. 98).

This management style, compared with American style mass production, uses half the human effort in the factory, half the manufacturing space, half the investment in tools, half the engineering hours to develop a new product in half the time. It also requires less than half the inventory on site, and this all results in fewer defects. In a comparison of a General Motors manufacturing plant with a Toyota one, Rifkin (1996) reported that Toyota "took 16 hours to build a car in 4.8 square feet of work space per vehicle per year, with .45 defects per car." At the GM plant, "it took nearly thirty-one hours in 8.15 square feet with 1.3 defects." And Toyota used half the labor (p. 100).

The lean production approach also produces employees "well versed in a number of tasks on the production floor" with individual workers having "a far better understanding of the overall manufacturing process—knowledge that can be used effectively within team settings to pinpoint problems and make suggestions and improvements." And, "to assist workers in seeing how their work fits into the larger production process, Japanese companies provide employees with access to all computerized information generated by the company," Rifkin (1996) reported (p. 98). Decision-making is pushed as far down the managerial ladder as possible so as to be closer to the point of production. Rifkin points out that the Japanese emphasis on working with the process makes them well suited for adapting and adopting the new rapidly evolving technologies.

These Japanese businesses as described by Rifkin are practicing a form of cooperation as I've been defining it and it is exciting and encouraging to see. Their culture teaches group centeredness, which gives them a big advantage and head start in mastering cooperation. They demonstrate effectively that cooperation works and out performs competitive dominance, control-oriented hierarchy forms of organization. Their productivity reinforces my conviction that cooperative societies will produce whatever is needed in half the time, or less, using fewer people and resources than our current competitive capitalistic market economy using control-oriented bureaucracies.

However, according to Lawler (1992, p. 14) it wasn't until the 1980s that American managers became receptive to new management approaches such as participative management being developed in America and the Japanese cooperative model. The motivation was American companies were losing out to competitors in other countries, and worse, they were losing out to foreign competitors who were building plants and buying companies in the United States. The Japanese were manufacturing automobiles, televisions, and other products in the U.S. with American workers with an efficiency and quality that surpassed our native corporations.

Concurrently, "traditional thinking about what kind of management approach can provide competitive advantage was significantly shaken by several books that appeared," Lawler (1992) said (p. 13). These included

William Ouchi's (1981) *Theory Z*, Thomas J. Peters and Robert H. Waterman's (1982) *In Search of Excellence*, James O'Toole's (1985) *Vanguard Management*, and Rosabeth Moss Kanter's (1985) *Change Masters*. "These books argued that competitive advantage can best be achieved not by doing the old management better but by adopting new and innovative management approaches that are more effective at organizing and managing people" (p. 13). These books along with the clear evidence of the superiority of Japanese management practices provided strong incentives for the American business community to change.

The failure of billions of dollars invested in computer technologies to produce dramatic improvements in productivity was another blow. The failure was due to outmoded organizational structures that weren't able to accommodate the technology. American businesses then had great difficulty making adaptive changes, and still do (Lawler and Worley, 2006). Despite all of this, participative management and the more cooperative Japanese model, while accepted as part of main stream business organizational practices, are far from replacing the entrenched control-oriented bureaucratic hierarchies.

From my point of view, the current situation is very encouraging. We have good working practices that contain elements of cooperation in one form or degree of maturity or another. Cooperation is already working its way into our American culture. It is proving its worth. Now if we can awaken Americans to the obsolescence of competition and individualism as basic cultural operating systems and the marvelous benefits to be gained by adopting cooperation as our culture, we are on our way. There is no need to fear cooperation as an unknown; we have real-life experience with it already in some of our businesses. There is also no need to get in a big rush, these fundamental changes take time.

RENSIS LIKERT'S PARTICIPATIVE GROUP MANAGEMENT AND MANAGEMENT BY GROUP OBJECTIVE (MBGO)

Likert's fresh perspective on management and organizations published in the 1960s came from years of research experience in which he observed a wide array of organizations and found repeatedly that the most effective companies in the long run used similar approaches to management. This approach he called "participative group management" and came to label it "System 4." Likert's work demonstrates the power of working together as coordinated groups and being more group-centered compared with working independently in a competitive individualistic environment.

System 4, Participative Group Management

While Likert described what would later be called System 4 in *New Patterns of Management* (1961), it was in his following books such as *The Human Organization: Its Management and Value* (1967), and *New Ways of Managing Conflict*, written with Jane Gibson Likert (1976) that his familiar tables and charts itemizing in detail the characteristics of organizations he labeled "System 1, System 2, System 3, and System 4" appeared by name. These four different styles of organization represent a continuum from what I've been calling dominance hierarchies, Lawler called control-oriented organizations, and Likert called System 1 organizations, to Likert's newly appreciated and defined "participative group" organization labeled System 4. Likert identified System 1 as "exploitive authoritative," System 2 as "benevolent authoritative," System 3 as "consultative," and System 4 as "participative group." (See for example, Likert, 1967, p. 14.) Likert characterizes these four management systems in considerable detail, with a great deal of empirical support and practical findings in his various books for anyone wishing more information. I will focus on the heart of his conceptualization of the more cooperative participative group management approach. This material was taken from *The Human Organization: Its Management and Value* (1967, 14-26). I am presenting these properties in a somewhat different order than Likert did and comparing only System 1 and 4 for brevity.

Decision Making

Likert emphasized that in System 4 organizations the decision-making process is a group process and this encourages teamwork. Participative groups are able to share and utilize complete and accurate information, are more aware of problems within the organization, especially at lower levels, and make use of good technical and professional knowledge found anywhere in the organization. The group decision processes tend to push decisions to the place in the organization where information is most adequate or pass the relevant information to the place where the decision must be made. Participation in the decision-making process helps motivate them to engage constructively in the implementation of those decisions.

In contrast, in exploitive authoritarian System 1 organizations decision making is based upon information that is the least accurate of the four management types. Decisions are not made on the lower hierarchical levels where accurate information, including professional and technical information, exists. Instead decisions are made at the top with only partial and inaccurate information, with no or only partial awareness of problems, and only the professional and technical knowledge people at their high level posses. Decisions are made man-to-man rather than as groups that include those most involved and thus do not motivate workers to are to carry out the decisions. In fact, System 1 decision-making processes usually yield adverse motivations that lead workers to unenthusiastically implement decisions or even sabotage them (pp. 20, 21).

Goal Setting or Ordering

The System 4 organizations use participative group processes to set goals for the groups' respective areas of stewardship. They set high goals that all in the organization, including all levels of the hierarchy, accept and pursue without being ordered to do it. The employees' engagement with the organization sometimes leads to groups at lower levels pressing for higher goals than those endorsed by the top level managers. System 4 organization employees accept and implement their goals both overtly and covertly (pp. 21, 22).

At the System 1, exploitive authoritative, end of the continuum, orders are issued and "high goals" are set and pressed by top management. But these goals and orders are covertly strongly resisted by subordinates ordered to pursue them who often make only an appearance of accepting them.

Control Processes

In participative group System 4 organizations the feelings of responsibility for one's own performances, for the organization and for its processes are likely to be shared throughout the organization. There are strong social expectations and incentives for all participants to obtain complete and accurate information with which to guide their own behavior, that of their work group, and the relationships between their work group and others in the organization. Consequently, in System 4 organizations information and measurements reported tend to be complete and accurate. There is widespread sharing of responsibility for review and control of the organization with "lower units at times imposing more rigorous reviews and tighter controls than top management." "Informal and formal organization are one and the same; hence all social forces support efforts to achieve [the] organization's goals" (pp. 22-23).

By contrast, in System 1, exploitive authoritative organizations, the interest and incentive to control, along with the capacity to exercise it, are all concentrated at the very top of the hierarchy. The organizational dynamics produced induce lower level participants to distort and falsify information that consequently is "usually incomplete and inaccurate," and to generate informal organizations that oppose the goals of the formal organization.

Performance Characteristics

In participative group System 4 organizations productivity is excellent, with low turnover and absenteeism. Using quality control and inspection techniques "to help workers guide [their] own efforts," "members themselves will use measurements and other steps in efforts to keep losses to a minimum," (p. 24). The participative group management approach ideally produces behavior similar to that of true cooperation, where the experts working in task groups "on the line" practice quality control routinely.

In exploitive authoritative System 1 organizations productivity is mediocre, with high levels of turnover and absenteeism, scrap loss and waste are "relatively high unless policed carefully," and quality control and inspections are necessary for policing workers' performance.

Character of Motivational Forces

In System 4 organizations economic compensation, setting goals, improving methods, and appraising progress are all achieved through group participation. As a consequence, personnel accept responsibility and are motivated to achieve the organization's goals because of "favorable, cooperative attitudes throughout the organization" including "mutual trust and confidence."

The exploitive authoritarian System 1 organization uses "fear, threats, punishment, and occasional rewards" to motivate, generating considerable hostility and conflict between the top tiers of the hierarchy and those on the bottom (pp. 14-16).

Looking at true cooperative organizations for comparison, competitive triumph over others and individual aggrandizement and advancement are not tolerated, desired, or available in cooperative social systems. One works for the common good and group-centered goals versus individual goals, including the adaptive survival and benefit of the organization as an organization. Participants identify with the organization or community and benefit from the emotional and psychological rewards of being accepted and a part of something bigger, finer, and more meaningful than self-centered competitive individualism offers. Trust and confidence in others and their competence is fundamental to cooperation. The organization takes care of them materially and rewards their contributions with approval, money, and material rewards.

Communication Process

In participative group System 4 managed organizations, communications are wide open, up and down the hierarchy, initiated at all levels, between any and all groups and individuals, with little distortion and great accuracy. This is of course one of the sources of adaptive effectiveness and success in System 4 organizations, as well as in true cooperative ones.

In System 1 organizations there is comparatively very little interaction and communication around the organization. As a rule, information is initiated at the top of the hierarchy and handed down. There is little or no upward communication of information, and when there is, it tends to be distorted and inaccurate, according to Likert. This necessitates creating spy systems, suggestion systems, and similar devices by the high level managers in order to inform themselves of what is going on (p. 16-18).

Wide-open and continual communications throughout the organization or community about everything, including how the social system is doing adaptively, are fundamental to cooperative social systems. Anything that undermines or distorts these communications undermines the adaptive effectiveness of the social system.

Interactional-Influence Process

System 4 organizations produce "extensive, friendly interaction with [a] high degree of confidence and trust," a great deal of "cooperative" teamwork throughout the organization, with employees enjoying a substantial amount of influence on their departments (pp. 18, 19).

System 1 organizations have "little interaction and always with fear and distrust, "with no cooperative work interactions, and with subordinates and lower levels of the organization having no influence on their work units or departments.

Clearly, Likert's System 4 companies are heading toward cooperation. Integrating all of the elements of a true cooperative system would enhance and advance these organizations, especially if they consciously eliminate internal competition and individualism, minimize hierarchy and learn to use their culture as an adaptive tool.

The Law of the Situation

In his discussion of cross-functional teams to help defuse interdepartmental competition Likert (1975) makes an important point: "What Mary Parker Follett called the "law of the situation" and the "authority of facts" becomes the major source of directions. Instructions from supervisors become minimal" (p. 52). This is true of cooperative organizations wherein the task groups are constantly keeping track of the environment, what is going on in the organization and responding accordingly. Cooperative organizations are not interested in opinions or competitive company "politics."

However, trying to produce more cooperative self-managing participative groups within a competitive individualistic company culture can produce problems. For example, Scott Fisher, one of Likert's colleagues, explained to me (2005) that these groups need continued supervision because they can sometimes go "renegade" if not watched carefully, and turn against management and the organization, pursuing their own internally developed agendas.

In another effort to deal with the internal competition and pursuit of individual goals within companies based on our culture of competitive individualism, Likert and Fisher introduced group goals.

MANAGEMENT BY GROUP OBJECTIVE (MBGO)

In their 1977 article, "MBGO: Putting Some Team Spirit into MBO," Rensis Likert and M. Scott Fisher point out that management by objective (MBO), a style of management that has been widely used in American business and other organizations for many decades, can lead to internal competition to the detriment of the organization. Likert and Fisher (1977) said:

> With MBO, managers relate to each of their subordinates as individuals. All interaction is *person to person*. Consequently, subordinates frequently strive to achieve their own objectives while disregarding whether their colleagues achieve theirs. Even worse, the evaluation and reward process of MBO can cause each work group member to

avoid cooperating with, and giving help to, other group members. Because each person's achievement is compared with the relative success of the other members, if they do well, his work is likely to be seen less favorably. If they do poorly, his work will be seen more favorably.

Thus work group members may even act so as to contribute to the poor performance of their colleagues. This kind of behavior is clearly contrary to the best interests of the firm and adversely affects its success. In fact, many firms have found peer competition among work group members so costly they have abandoned MBO (pp. 40-41, emphasis as per original).

Likert and Fisher have just described classical competitive individualistic behavior. That's what you should expect from a competitive individualistic company culture.

Turning this around and trying to create cooperative work groups without changing the basic cultural operating systems to cooperative is essentially futile from my perspective. That is the problem with all of Likert's participative group models from my point of view, they are not consciously set in cooperative company cultures, which they must be to fully flourish and be trustworthy. Competition and individualism will eventually worm their way into any social practices undertaken within that cultural environment.

Likert and Fisher suggested management by group goal objective (MBGO) as an alternative that could eliminate the internal adversarial competition between individuals generated by MBO. Their solution was to insert an element of true cooperation, a group goal endorsed by the work group. Care would have to be taken here that what is actually produced is not the shared individual goals of individualistic mutual-aid, or the alliances among competitors in competitive mutual-aid. To be cooperative, the group goal must relate to the functioning and adaptation of the group as a social system. If participants see this as the best way to advance their personal careers or to out-compete and get ahead of others in the company, it is just the same old competitive individualism rather than cooperation.

"With MBGO, managers and their subordinates act as teams in setting objectives and evaluating performance in achieving them. Thus interaction is between the manager and all the subordinates who report to him or her in *group* problem-solving sessions," Likert and Fisher reported (1977, p. 41, emphasis as per original).

In true cooperative organizations the task groups' goals are derived from the dynamic organizational goals and consensus, and are set by the organization's adaptive needs. The task groups do not set the groups' goals except as ongoing situations and changes require, and then according to what are best for the organization as a whole. Group interaction in true cooperation focuses on deciding on a particular course of action and involves the use of members' expertise and information to determine what is best; this is not a democratic operation to set goals that all members individually can endorse.

There is no evidence that Likert was trying to create cooperative organizations as I'm defining them. However, the ongoing interaction patterns described by Likert and Fisher (1977) for MBGO broadly fit those of a true cooperative organization:

> They also help to create an atmosphere of cooperative teamwork. Work group members are motivated to help each other by sharing the workload and by sharing new insights and better strategies for accomplishing desired results. If one member of the work group is temporarily overloaded, a colleague can easily pick up part of the load to ensure organizational success and avoid breakdowns. There is no need for precise definitions of responsibility, which eliminates fear and the desire to protect ones "turf" from encroachment by others. Only broad, general assignments are required because of the cooperative relationships among work group members. Moreover, each cycle of objective setting and evaluation reaffirms the area of individual responsibility of each member of the group and reemphasizes the need for each to feel responsible for the success of the entire group's efforts (p. 41).

Over the years many companies have adopted participative group management and MBGO. However, Fisher (2005) informed me that it sometimes failed for a variety of reasons, including lack of top management understanding and support, internal competition at the company and in at least one case a handful of "participative" workers conspired in the theft of products. Bruce Gibb (2009) reminds me that another reason these efforts fail is because the compensation systems are based on the existing hierarchy, the higher up you are the more you are paid. This produces resistance to changing to the flatter participative management organization. Still, participative group management has become an important component of business and organizational literature and practice. The adoption by American business people of Likert's model and those like it—such as Lawler's model described in the following chapter—is a great encouragement because it shows that American business people are capable of changing directions from the traditional control-oriented hierarchy, adopting more cooperative paradigms, and working to improve and apply them, if slowly. Just the direction we need to be heading.

Here we have a few more trends in business heading toward true cooperation. First we will examine the work of Edward Lawler III, and then Japanese management practices in America.

LAWLER'S HIGH INVOLVEMENT ORGANIZATION

Edward Lawler III, like Rensis Likert, is a major researcher and theorist in business management. His work continues the developing focus on improving business's performance by taking care of employees and giving them satisfying work, incorporating them into the information and decision making networks, and providing supportive work conditions. He is also looking at ways to make businesses more adaptive and responsive to environmental changes as organizations. He is a professor of management and organization in the Graduate School of Business Administration at the University of Southern California, where he is the director of the Center for Effective Organizations. In his 1992 book, *The Ultimate Advantage: Creating the High-Involvement Organization*, he draws upon and reviews years of research and work by many professionals on job enrichment, work teams, various quality oriented initiatives (e.g. quality circles and Quality Work Life efforts), compensation patterns and related management issues. From all of this and his own extensive research and experience with businesses he developed a model that he calls the "high-involvement organization" that contains many elements of true cooperation.

Lawler's extensive writings show how his ideas and techniques evolved and are applied to different issues. For example, the term "high-involvement" organization is replaced by the "new logic" corporation in his book, *From the Ground Up: Six Principles for Building the New Logic Corporation* (2000). In one of his most recent books, *Treat People Right! How Organizations and Individuals Can Propel Each Other Into a Virtuous Spiral of Success* (2003), Lawler has much to say about compensation patterns, hiring the right people, training, competencies, and getting people in the right place with meaningful work. We will look at cooperative elements in the organization of businesses he is recommending with Christopher G. Worley in their 2006 book, *Built to Change: How to Achieve Sustained Organizational Effectiveness.*.

WORK DYNAMICS

Lawler distinguishes between what he has labeled the "control-oriented approach" and the commitment or "involvement-oriented" approach to management and organizational structure. His (1992) high-involvement model of management places an "emphasis on few levels in the hierarchy, seamless organizations, quick adaptation and change, lateral work relationships, and the responsibility of organizations to create meaningful and satisfying work" (p. xiii). He also emphasizes the value of giving all individuals in the organization, including those at the lowest levels, more information, power, and rewards (p. xi). This style of organization moves us closer to cooperation and has many similarities with true cooperation.

The working dynamics of high-involvement work teams fits closely with cooperative groups' dynamics. Lawler (1992) said,

> Organizations should be structured so that individuals at the lowest level in the organization not only perform work but also are responsible for improving work methods and procedures, solving problems on the job, and coordinating their work with that of others. Employees also can and should be expected to operate without a controlling supervisor (p. 30).

And, "the involvement oriented approach argues that employees should be given general missions and philosophies as guides for their behavior and then allowed to respond to the customer [or environment in true cooperation] as they see fit" (p. 35, insert mine). The high-involvement approach "emphasizes dealing with new situations at a low level and empowering employees to solve problems as close as possible to where they occur" (p. 37). This permits the organization to dramatically reduce its hierarchy of control levels, flattening its hierarchy. It also requires more lateral communication and coordination between work teams.

HIGH-INVOLVEMENT ORGANIZATIONS ARE STILL YOUNG AND GROWING

Lawler (1992) points out high-involvement organizations are comparatively new and are not yet mature or as widely accepted as the "control-oriented" approach. Lawler (1992) observed, "those organizations that have moved in this direction are still learning how to use the approach" (p. 45). This is not yet a mature management and organizational style. Among the "host" of small and medium sized companies that had implemented the high-involvement approach at that time were W. L. Gore, Donnelly Corporation, Herman Miller Furniture, and Nucor Steel. Donnelly Corporation (or Donnelly Mirrors as it was known locally) and Herman Miller Furniture, both in Michigan, were frequently mentioned when my cooperation group (see acknowledgements in the Preface) and I asked local business people to identify more cooperative companies. Among the larger companies are Motorola and Xerox (p. 45).

Lawler described the variety of high-involvement work teams and organizations. They range in size and scope from small work teams assigned a coordinated task such as on an assembly line, to more creative work teams developing new products and solutions, to larger work teams dealing with a major, more or less self-contained, chunk of the company's product or services, to mini-enterprises operating as nearly autonomous business units with their own bottom line and clientele, to essentially free-standing divisions of several hundred employees.

While production teams have been around a comparatively long time, "the practical knowledge about how to actually operate managerial and white collar teams is still in an embryonic stage" (p. 118). He notes that Likert suggested organizations could be made up of overlapping participative groups so that the entire structure was made up of overlapping teams. Nevertheless, according to Lawler, in 1992 in most organizations the work teams approach is still limited to the direct production of goods and services, with most teams used only at the lowest levels. Both Likert and Lawler have created models of participative group management for the whole company. Now, however, organizations based totally on teams or participative group management are rare (p. 114). Still, we can learn a great deal and take encouragement from what has been accomplished so far.

Creating the fully cooperative business organization is a continuing challenge. Lawler (1992) said:

> Only recently ... have writers been concerned with the broader organizational design and systems issues that arise when an entire organization is managed with the involvement oriented approach. Advocating participative supervision and advocating creation of involvement-oriented organizations are significantly different.... The latter ... requires the creation of new work systems, policies, procedures, practices, and organizational designs—in effect, the creation of a new type of organization (p. 31).

In his book *Built to Change,* Lawler with co-author Worley (2006) focuses on such an organization.

APPROACHING THE TRUE COOPERATIVE ORGANIZATION

Reading business management books, I am continually amazed at the astounding amount of effort, ingenuity, intensity, and plotting and planning required for businesses to stay successful in modern America's (and the world's) competitive capitalistic market place. Most of it fails. According to Lawler and Worley, peaking and fading is common. In the early 1980s *In Search of Excellence* (Peters and Waterman, 1982) identified a number of companies that were then excellent performers. But by the late 1980s many of those companies were already no longer excellent performers. Inability to change adaptively to the business environment is common. Of the original Forbes 100 in 1917, only 29 made the list in 1987. Even so, those survivors earned a return that was 20 percent less than the market. Of the list of companies in the 1957 Standard and Poor 500, only 74 remained in the list by 1997 (Lawler and Worley: 2006, pp. xiii, xiv). Those that survived were not great performers. It takes an enormous amount of effort to change modern American business organizations dramatically as the world evolves, and few succeed. Lawler and Worley (2006) give many examples. They observe that it is far easier to create a new start up business organized to fit the new environment than it is to change the old ones.

Clearly, there is great need for the development of more adaptive organizations in the American business community, and Lawler and Worley (2006) address this need in their book, *Built to Change.* It is encouraging that their vision of a more adaptive organization is tending strongly toward the true cooperative model. Adding their recommended organizational components to Lawler's high involvement practices comes quite close. Among the cooperative elements considered is focusing on the changing environment, which in this case is the customer and eliciting continual customer feedback on how the company's efforts are working. They emphasize the importance of hiring competent people who are bright and energetic; people who enjoy pursuing solutions, innovations and improvements. Appropriate rewards for quality performance and success are required. Lawler and Worley also recommend organizing the company around tasks with a fluid organization that shifts smoothly as the necessary tasks change, typical of cooperative organizations. Employees are expected to develop multiple competencies in order to contribute when and where needed. Rigid organization with clear and fixed lines of communication and decision making and detailed job descriptions are gone. Minimal hierarchy is used (pp. 90-93). The importance of keeping a new "built for change" organization independent from the larger, older organization it is part of or from other conventional American businesses in order to protect it from "infection" is emphasized (p. 107). As I've mentioned, this requirement turns up again and again whenever we look at developing cooperative organizations within our competitive individualistic society. As Lawler and Worley summarize:

> This means creating an organization that encourages experimentation, learns about new practices and technologies, monitors the environment, assesses performance, and is committed to continuously improving performance (p. 21).

This fits our description of a cooperative organization. It is clearly advocating what I am calling with Gardner (interlude above) the self-renewing organization or society. Still missing, however, is the use of culture as a coping tool, a dynamic working consensus, and group centeredness.

One intriguing technique being used in businesses to create and maintain a common culture and community is what its author, Bruce Gibb, calls the "camp mode". This is one way to develop a dynamic consensus that evolves with the company's experiences and that guides the task efforts of the employees.

THE CAMP MODE METHOD OF CONSENSUS BUILDING

In Chapter 5 we learned from Holldobler and Wilson (1990) that "the highest level of the ant colony is the totality of its membership rather than a particular set of superordinate individuals who direct the activity of members at lower levels" (p. 355). In human cooperative organizations, the whole group-centered membership working together as one produce and operate a dynamic cultural consensus and set of common goals that are used to produce a division of labor and task groups to engage the environment adaptively and produce what the organization needs. It is the total cooperating membership that operates the organization.

Bruce Gibb (2001, 2003, 2009), a widely respected organizational psychologist and development consultant, has successfully created in a number of companies and organizations what he has labeled the "camp mode" or "community." This works in tandem with an organization's normal hierarchically organized work mode.

Gibb (2003) draws this insight from tribal behavior.

> The archetypical image of the community mode is a tribe conversing, sharing information, feasting and celebrating their accomplishments, learning from their failures, telling their myths and genealogies, acknowledging the legends of their ancestors, participating in rites and rituals, etc. This brings a sense of identity as a community, the knowledge of belonging, a feeling of commitment, and a sense of ownership (p. 108).

For companies it is a time to discuss problems and disappointments and generate solutions, to relive and celebrate successes, to make plans and set goals, and to generate a fresh consensus. The camp mode meetings can help produce and maintain the group-centeredness so important to cooperative organizations. With a refreshed consensus and new or renewed common goals the employees are ready to return to the task mode and carry out their plans. They take with them a realization that they are a dynamic community working together for a common objective that will benefit them all.

A typical example is a total-plant or organization meeting where everyone has a voice and all participate in analysis of current operations, create a common vision and make plans. This meeting is followed by mini-camp meetings for each work group to plan to achieve the overall goals set at the camp meeting. These are followed by quarterly departmental camp meetings and total organization meetings twice a year. Thus organizations rotate back and forth between the camp mode and the hierarchically organized work mode. This comes as close to having the entire membership operating the organization as we are likely to get short of full cooperation.

Gibb has used this technique successfully to create and/or develop a variety of organizations of various sizes including six Greenfield plants in Mexico, Spain, Portugal, Hungary, Thailand and India (2003, p. 110).

JAPANESE MANAGEMENT PRACTICES IN AMERICA

Rehfeld, in his 1994 book *Alchemy of a Leader: Combining Western and Japanese Management Skills to Transform Your Company*, draws upon his years of experience with the Japanese as a top manager with Toshiba and Seiko. His understanding of some of their unique cultural practices, so different from our own, offers a fresh perspective along with suggesting some concrete social patterns we can use in our efforts to understand and create true cooperative organizations.

The Japanese culture is not a pure cooperative one but it has more co-operative elements than ours' does. Their culture was shaped by a very different history from ours, and by a unique ecological/geographical environment. While many of their particularly Japanese cultural expressions will be of little use to Americans, their centuries of life in a crowded island habitat has produced a more cooperative culture. They have learned to focus, of a necessity, on the good of the group, organization, or society. One of their major advantages is they are a group-centered, group-oriented people, which is one of the basic components of cooperation.

Rehfeld (1994) agrees with Likert, Lawler, and many others that our "Western-style top-down authoritarian management" doesn't work. He also has found that efforts to adapt the Japanese consensus-style management don't work well in America. Reaching consensus takes too long and is frequently too difficult in our individualistic and competitive country. If you ask a group of competitive individualists to agree on anything, you will frequently have problems, and any agreement reached is often tentative. Rehfeld recommends a collaborative management style derived from his synthesis of Japanese and Western management practices (p. 3). I believe that a cooperative company built upon a cooperative culture with a consensus on both the culture of cooperation and common group goals from the start will have little trouble operating with and maintaining a consensus. Especially if doing so is a condition of continued employment.

I mentioned earlier the Japanese practice of focusing on the task at hand and letting the process of solving it unfold at its own pace. As Rehfeld (1994) said, "there is more emphasis on completing human transactions in the most productive manner rather than holding to some predetermined schedule" (p. 9). This is the cooperative way. The American way is to be clock driven, with deadlines set for completion and often schedules for various phases to be accomplished. The cooperative way is to take as long as it takes to complete the task as thoroughly and effectively as possible.

KAIZEN

Kaizen has received a great deal of attention in America and Rehfeld (1994) calls it "the single most important management tool I've encountered" (p. 23). However, he also concluded that because of its deep roots in Japanese culture it is not easily understood or implemented in the United States. Rehfeld characterizes Kaizen as a "process of continual improvement" in which many small steps and improvements produce over time continual advancement and adaptive evolution of the organization. One does not go for the huge, "home run" idea or suggestion, but pays attention to all the little things. These cumulative changes help keep the company abreast of changes in the environment, such as market demands, and responsive to customer and other requests.

As the Japanese practice it, kaizen requires that every effort be thoroughly analyzed for ways to improve performance next time, including criticism of each member's performance by the group. American's find this constant negative mutual self-criticism unacceptable, but when "tempered with appropriate amounts of praise and appreciation," Rehfeld has found that Kaizen "can be a very effective management tool" (p. 24).

Rehfeld said he was often told by his Japanese colleagues, "mistakes are the mother of invention" because in Kaizen when employees make a mistake they quickly admit it but "do not bother to explain it," instead, "they focus on the countermeasures they plan to take to remedy the problem" (p. 25). They fix the problem, not the blame. "For the Japanese, to blame someone within the company for a failure constitutes a failure by the person placing the blame. Pointing a finger at someone else is considered lazy, at best, and shows a basic incompetence, the inability to work with others," Rehfeld reported (p. 82).

Rehfeld found the contrast between American's "natural reflex" "to find a scapegoat" to blame, flavored with "whispered insults in the hall," versus the Japanese efforts to work together with the person(s) or group(s) who made the mistake to find out what went wrong and fix it, with no blame attached, could not be more stark (p. 81). The Japanese managers do not threaten dismissal as a rule; instead they recognize that failure is generally a complex thing and not a problem of one individual. The biggest mistake is not to admit a mistake as been made, preventing the resolution of the underlying problem. The Japanese practice of Kaizen, coupled with their

strong and multistranded relationships with others within their companies, makes it easy to take small, exploratory, chances and deal with the
inevitable mistakes. This can be very helpful during trial-and-error explorations of alternative solutions.

Kaizen focuses employees' attention on the *process*, not the end product. It leads to constant improvement of the process that constitutes what
the work group is actually doing (p. 28, pp. 33-36). All social behavior is
a process, and focusing on improving that process is the essence of social
transformation. It also requires and produces much greater awareness of
the social processes the group is enacting. It is essential to the fundamental cooperative group goal of constantly improving the match between the
social structure and the ever changing environment. Rehfeld feels Americans are too focused on the end product and do not pay much attention to
the process. I would agree with that, and expect this Kaizen focus on the
constant assessment and improvement of the process of group task performance in cooperative groups.

Kaizen also focuses attention on the group's goals. "Taking the spotlight
off the individual and putting it on the group makes it easier for people to
feel comfortable about admitting mistakes at every step and reporting them
to management right away" (p. 29). To this end, the group provides itself
with a considerable and continuous flow of information about how it is
doing. Rehfeld (1994) said:

> When you go into a Japanese company, for example, you find charts
> and graphs posted all over the place, measuring every business, man-
> ufacturing, sales, and management activity. Every department seems
> to have its own set of charts and graphs, which are updated regularly
> and which serve as barometers of the group's performance. In most
> cases, the workers and employees themselves create these charts,
> not some corporate communication department (p. 29).

Kaizen as the Japanese practice it includes individuals and groups making suggestions for consideration. Americans often have little confidence
these suggestions will ever benefit them and are less likely to make them. In
cooperation the improvements are made by those responsible for that task
area as they are recognized—on the run. A suggestion box is not needed.

Interpersonal Relationships, Company Identification, Wa, and Giri

The Japanese are far more sensitive than are most American companies to the building and maintaining of quality relationships with employees, suppliers, and customers, and with building a strong, trusting, loyal, identification of employees with the company. The Japanese put the preservation of trusting relationships between their workers, customers, and suppliers before profit, before getting the "best deal," meaning cheapest price. Relationships, trust, familiarity, and expectations of continued secure relations in the future are sought.

Wa

It is common to hear workers for Japanese companies say, "I belong to Toshiba," or "I belong to Sony," according to Rehfeld (1996, p. 53). This identification with the group or organization is a must in true cooperation. As Rehfeld emphasized, "What the typical 'Lone Ranger'-style of [American] business person needs to know is that only teams can compete with other teams. Westerners too often approach business like an individual sport" (p. 54, insert mine). When it comes to interpersonal relations and group-centeredness, Rehfeld places the United States and Japan at opposite extremes, with everyone else—other countries and cultures—in between (p.55).

The cohesion of Japanese work teams has been referred to as "group ego." Rehfeld said, "I've seen it at work many times. Employees who possess this group ego derive genuine pleasure out of the group's accomplishments." Rehfeld warns, "Good managers need to ask themselves not only if their product is better than what the competition offers. They also need to ask themselves if their team is as good, as tight, and as group-oriented as it can be" (p. 55). We've probably all heard of the Japanese saying, "the nail that stands up gets pounded down." To individualistic Americans this sounds repressive and dehumanizing. But Rehfeld places it in the context of Japanese efforts to build community and group identity, pointing out that it "reflects the Japanese preoccupation with enhancing the work process within the group rather than lionizing any one individual worker" (p. 84). Or, we might add, allowing one egocentric individualist to do his or her own thing at the expense and diminishment of all the others while undermining the quality of their group's functioning. This group-centeredness is a critical lesson Americans must learn. I have found it rare in America, no doubt in major part because it is anathema to both individualism and internal competition.

The Japanese put an enormous amount of effort into building relationships in their businesses. They do many things to establish deeper interpersonal relations, understanding, and comfort with each other including playing golf together, drinking together, going to the hot springs together, and getting "belly to belly" with each other, and never talking business (Rehfeld, 1996, p. 57). They want to know the whole person. Getting to honest, inside relationships with the whole person is called "honne". They want to know about the employee's home life and personal interests. "Simply showing an interest in an employee's personal life is a powerful way for a manager to convey status to that person" (p. 60). Most of the informal socializing necessary to build these relationships happen after work, though lunch and some short interactions during the day offer opportunities. Many Americans would balk at this, preferring to keep their personal life private and remain uninterested in other's lives.

Cooperative companies will likely have a good deal of this. How much depends upon how the participants feel about sharing their outside lives. A cooperative society would have a lot of this as participants know each other as whole people and are all one.

Giri

The norms of reciprocity used to be much stronger in America. If someone did you a favor, it was expected that you would eventually return that favor and be available to provide assistance if asked. Norms of reciprocity are important tying strands in holding communities together and making them mutually beneficial. Our increasingly self-centered individualism and competitive nastiness have rotted the fabric of our reciprocity network, isolating us from one another. The Japanese, on the other hand, as our opposites in these matters, continually work to maintain such norms of reciprocity, which they call "giri." "Giri" has a rich meaning not directly translatable, but includes "a range of obligation" or "indebtedness to others," and is nearly always a positive force in social relations according to Rehfeld (p. 67). In Rehfeld's (1996) words:

> Giri is the result of all Japanese relationship-building. It is that palpable, yet intangible, sense of personal honor, the "I can't do that to so-and-so because we have giri between us" attitude, or, "of course I'll come in and work on Sunday to help my colleague, with whom I have a relationship built on giri." The goal of Japanese manager and

worker alike is to build and maintain giri, a pattern of honorable interactions as widely as possible (p. 68).

Related to giri are "on," "omoiyari," and "enryo," all of which do not translate easily into English. "On," apparently, is an element of giri—or vice versa—and arises when gifts, kindnesses, and the like are bestowed without calculation on others, and is a sense of obligation to return such a beneficial act (p. 190). "Omoiyari" places the needs of others first; practitioners anticipate other's needs and provide them without being asked. "Enryo," which "involves considering others by restraining one's own desires," includes avoiding making unnecessary or too many requests of others (p. 189). All of these practices together produce a kindly and considerate social environment, one of great value to participants, one worth working to preserve, contributing to devotion and loyalty to the company. Such practices and other-oriented thinking, or something very similar, I expect to be present in true cooperative organizations and communities. They are the exact opposite from individualism's self-centered focus, acting for oneself without regard for others, and adversarial competition's continual conniving to exploit, undermine, and deflate others. Rehfeld (1996) found, "relationship building is perhaps the most compelling and satisfying part of doing business Japanese-style" (p. 70). And as a result he reports, "I've come to have little use for criticism aimed at individual personalities" (p. 82).

Rehfeld discusses many more useful Japanese management practices, but this sample is enough to give us some insight into how cooperative companies and societies will operate. It shows the direction that our cooperative social evolution is taking. And there is plenty of evidence that these Japanese practices work better than our competitive individualistic ways do. Taking these lessons on cooperation from the Japanese to heart and adapting them into sociocultural practices that we are comfortable with, can greatly hasten our creation of cooperative companies and organizations.

We can see that there are trends in business that are heading toward cooperation and can provide pathways toward the transformation of our society that we need at this time. They give us experiences and existing organizations we can build upon. However, none of these management practices produce cooperative social systems in America as I've defined them. Fully cooperative companies and societies will still be substantially different and a major advancement in our human social evolution. It is time for Americans to stop tinkering and get on with it.

The prominent economist Lester C. Thurow in his book *The Future of Capitalism* (N.Y.: Penguin, 1997, pp. 253-255), concluded:

> Societies need some overarching goal toward which everyone can be working to create a better world. In the past such visions came to those who believed in socialism or the social welfare state....Neither socialism nor the social welfare state points to a road that might be traveled to build a better collective future that will include the unincluded.... To work, democracy needs a vision of utopia—a route to a better society—a vision of what it is that transcends narrow sectarian self-interest.... In the end democracy rests on consent but does not create it, assumes a degree of compatibility among its citizens but does not work to make it true....

Chapter 17. Goodbye to Our Old Civilization, And Not a Moment Too Soon

Cooperation will start small and spread gradually throughout our society, probably taking many generations. Two to three hundred years for a complete transformation may be required. As the process unfolds, changes in the structure of society will be gradual but profound. In this and the next chapter I use one possible form of true cooperation for illustration. Since we humans have never produced a cooperative society like the one I've been describing, I have to make theoretical assumptions and there will be places where we just won't know what it will be like until we get there. In this chapter I provide an overview of how many familiar social patterns and roles will be gone in a mature cooperative America. It provides a contrast that is helpful in imagining a pure cooperative society.

The first thing time travelers from our times into a fully cooperative America in the future would notice is the abundance, and the ease with which it is provided. (For an insightful and entertaining imagined time travel into a more cooperative America written in the 19th century, enjoy the classic: *Looking Backward: 2000-1887*, by Edward Bellamy.) In our cooperative future, far less time is spent providing the necessities and luxuries of life than in our current society. The quality of the products is of the highest and enjoyed by all who are cooperating. The comfort, leisure, and material wellbeing of this new world without poor, hungry or unattended sick people are readily apparent.

Our time traveler then searches in vain for many social patterns and institutions. Familiar occupations and services are gone. Economy, government, education, even leisure pursuits are different.

GONE IS THE COMPETITIVE CAPITALIST "FREE-MARKET" ECONOMY

A fully mature cooperative society or civilization has no need for money. Some variations of cooperation and less developed cooperative societies may use some money or markers of exchange such as credit cards—as Bellamy's imagined future society did. With the distribution of goods and services handled differently—as shown in the next chapter—and since cooperative societies reliably provide everything every cooperative participant needs for their survival and well-being for their entire life, there is no need for our money economy based institutions. There will be no banks, no stocks and bonds, no financial institutions, no credit card companies.

Because cooperative people are always provided for as one of the functions of the cooperative society there is no need to accumulate anything. No need to prepare for an uncertain future. So there is no need for savings and investments; no need to acquire large amounts of material goods; no need for insurance of any kind; no need for retirement programs; no need for "social security" benefits. The function of cooperative societies is to make the uncertainties of life a human community or society must contend with more secure and predictable; to deal with them as a rapidly adapting information-processing social system. This is vastly more efficient and beneficial and successful than leaving it up to individuals or their families to survive as best they can or up to entrepreneurs to maybe come up with a solution, typical of our current American society.

This eliminates a huge number of current companies and organizations and their occupational roles. No bankers or tellers or underwriters, no insurance agents, no stock brokers, no financial advisors or commentators on TV shows or in financial papers, no printing of money, and no administrators for the huge financial bureaucracies required now. People now employed in these occupational roles will then be freed-up to work on providing the necessities and adaptive information, solutions, and innovations that constitute a cooperative society's daily work.

As we work our way through this list, it will become clear that there will be a lot of people available for a lot fewer "jobs" in a cooperative society. The cooperative society handles this by requiring less work of each participant than is now the case. I imagine that a 20 hour work week—or less—will be plenty to provide for all that a cooperative society living in abundance requires. What will cooperative people do with the extra time? Lots of things, as the following chapter illustrates.

There will be no need or concern for constant expansion of the economy, for eternal economic growth. That is a product of our competitive capitalistic market economy, and has nothing to do with effective cooperative adaptation to our ever-changing environment. How much a cooperative society produces is decided by the needs of the participants and the cooperative social system. A cooperative society produces what is needed when it is needed and stops when that need is filled. The workers move on to other needs and tasks.

There are no competing companies duplicating essentially the same products and services at high cost, while also trying to maximize profits and sometimes minimizing the quality of the products to the degree they can "get away with." Consumers now are often overwhelmed with the huge variety of choices, such as in toothpaste, shampoos and other hair care products, cold and flu remedies and the like. This is true of many products including cars, electronic gadgets, "apps," insurance plans, and more. There is a type of stress called a "surfeit of positive choices" that can result. People can't decide which to chose and often don't have the information necessary. This wasteful competitive over-kill and flooding of the market will be gone. There will be no attempts to exploit our biological properties or weaknesses such as with unhealthy foods that cater to our "sweet tooth" or our delight in "salty treats." There will be no production of "status symbol" products that prove we are "winners" and better than others.

Cooperative societies have one task arena for each and all of the goods and services produced. There is one "car company," for example, that makes whatever motor vehicles are required at the highest level of quality, constantly refining and evolving these as adaptation requires. There is one food task arena that takes care of the food supply from growing and manufacturing it to delivery. There will not be dozens of "brands" of food products. The food will be of much higher quality. There will be no shopping malls, no multiplicity of grocery stores, clothing stores, drug stores, and so forth.

The elimination of competitive manufacturing companies and retail outlets, again, dramatically reduces the number of "jobs." All of that duplication and waste is gone. In addition, there will be no sales, marketing, advertising, and related occupations and companies, and no unions.

We've already commented upon the elimination of economic inequalities and stratification with the abandonment of competition and the adoption of cooperation in Chapter 8. There will also be no financial booms and busts to ruin our life-long efforts and no related financial insecurities. No depressions or recessions. There is no financial arena for these to occur in. Instead, there will be just ongoing adaptive security and predictable abundance. That is a huge difference a future traveler will likely both marvel and rejoice to discover.

Truly, our current economy requires an extraordinary amount of people, effort, money, and resources to do rather inefficiently and unpredictably what a cooperative society could do faster, better, and way cheaper.

GONE IS THE ADVERSARIAL HORROR OF COMPETITION

As a social stress researcher, this is one of the components of our current American society I will be happiest to see go. Competition imposes adversarial battles upon people who would get along just fine without them. There is no adaptive benefit to the arbitrary adversarial combat inherent in internal, within group, competition, especially compared with cooperation. Dividing the world into a few winners who have most of everything, also-rans with some benefits, and losers with little of anything does not serve people or societies well. Competition creates a desperate race that is never won. Those currently in the lead must constantly watch over their shoulders, watching out for their determined competitors pounding hard right behind them. Winning and the joy of success may be snatched from you by malicious competitors. The constant efforts to defeat each other include cheating, conniving, betrayal, and efforts at destroying others self-esteem and confidence. These latter include attempts to destroy your reputation with lies and false witness, insults, put-downs, trash talk, embarrassing revelations, fault finding real and maliciously imagined. Think of a national political campaign here. And what of the "losers" who live a marginal life without the satisfaction of a rewarding career or occupation? Competition includes efforts to dominate and control others from spouses to multinational corporations. This is precisely the kind of arbitrary control sometimes bordering on tyranny our founding fathers hoped to escape with our new democratic government. All of this adds up to a churning cauldron of social and psychological stress generating mental and physical illness prolifically. From my point of view, it has got to go, for our very health and well being. And go it all does in a cooperative society, into the dustbin of history. Now why did we ever do that?

With that dark and dreary world jettisoned, we will be amazed at how contented, joyous, peaceful, healthful and bright life can be. It will also be much easier to get things done. Everyone will be working together for the benefit of all rather than being artificially divided into intense, warring groups trying to get it all and block other's access to any. Without these adversarial battles our interpersonal relations are cleansed of all the insults, put-downs, mean-minded fault finding, vengeful responses to vengeful responses, the need for constant vigilance and so forth. A visitor to the future will be delighted at the warm and friendly relations, the lack of defensiveness, the compassionate and kindly concerns, and joy in sharing information, successes, experiences and gifts. The consensus eliminates most disagreements and arguments and competing goals, values and beliefs.

Social stress is a general risk factor that influences the frequency of just about every disease you can name. The reduction in illness in general, such as we witness when smoking is banned, is worth the effort in itself. Add to it the distress, discontent, depression, and other emotional drains that competition and individualism produce and you see why I'm anxious to get "from he'ah" "to the'ah."

GONE ARE INDIVIDUALISTIC DEMOCRATIC DECISION MAKING PATTERNS
AND GOVERNMENTS

As we have observed in many places in this book, our individualistic democratic form of government and the practice of decision by majority vote was a major paradigm shift and a big step up the ladder for human social evolution. We and our ancestors helped make it a reality and enjoyed its many benefits and improvements over the older more tyrannical forms of government. But we have out grown both our individualism and the democratic decision making patterns and government we produced. Time to move up the ladder once again.

Our political system was designed to deal with the kind of people we Americans are utilizing the elements our culture provided (see Chapter 7). In a true cooperative society, our consensus, group centeredness, and common group goals focusing on continual adaptation to our changing environment builds the decision-making right into the culture. What do we do in a given situation? Cooperation either has the adaptive answer already in its culture or a process for discovering it through research and trial and error testing. Taking a majority vote of the population on what to do would look ridiculous to cooperative peoples. What's that got to do with adaptation? Actually, not much. So the decision making and problem solving in cooperation is much faster, adaptively focused, made by experts working on the line—the point the society connects with the environment—to solve problems as they emerge. There will be no committees, no legislatures, no hierarchies to go up and down for decisions, few meetings, no votes, and no need for social structures to do this. Decisions are made much faster at the level where they will be enacted and are much more effective.

Consequently, there will be no democratic government in a cooperative society. No socialist, communist, aristocratic, theocratic, plutocratic or military or dictator dominated governments either. No government as we think of it at all. There is no need for one since cooperative communities operate from a consensus. Gone will be the gargantuan processes and procedures of our government for making decisions in the midst of a sea of differing opinions and goals. Our courts can take decades to come to a decision, with all kinds of legal wrangling going on, and costing thousands even millions of dollars. Our various branches and locales of government exist to wade through complex decision making processes that again can take months and years. And then, once a decision is made, competitors may begin actions to change it through the courts or the same legislative or other government offices. America has tied itself in knots when it comes to decision making so that the *process* is what we do, millions of us, day in and day out. The end product is often an anticlimax, and irrelevant to the common good. All of this and all of the organizations and occupations that go with it will be gone in cooperation. No courts, legislatures, lobbyists, government organizations and employees, politicians, ineffective enforcement agencies for the laws, interest groups and so on. Another huge contribution of people and talents to the cooperative society's adaptive efforts is the result.

All of the entitlements we now struggle to finance and control and all of the bureaucracies to handle them will also be jettisoned. All the government provided civic works will be handled by cooperative task groups and we won't need governments to provide sewers, water, garbage collection, roads and so forth.

Our competition hides from us how much consensus we already have and prevents much greater levels of consensus from developing. We are too focused on the artificial battle with our adversaries that competition has imposed upon us to see the lurking consensus among us. With competition pulled out of America, these arenas of consensus and the cooperative relations they can generate are revealed and developed.

In cooperative societies, misbehavior and the treatment of serious miscreants are handled firmly and according to procedures and punishments already in place in the culture. Everyone knows what is going to happen. But the emphasis is nearly always on restoring the deviant to the harmony of the cooperative community. At the same time, with no poverty, everyone provided all they need, and no money to steal and nothing to spend it on if they did, the motivations for many forms of crime are drastically reduced.

It's amazing how many occupations we democratic Americans have created to deal with—and sometimes legitimize—our conflicts and disagreements. It is good to remember, as the economist Lester Thurow (1997) points out, "Democracy, if one means everyone voting, is a very new social system and has not yet proven that it is the 'fittest' political form available" (p. 267).

GONE IS OUR EDUCATIONAL SYSTEM AND LONELY PARENTHOOD

Our existing educational system and its unions and social structures will be missing from our cooperative society. How education might be handled cooperatively is described in the next chapter. It is a community affair without age graded classes and possibly without school buildings and with different curricula from what we currently use. Education and socialization of our people now is a hit and miss disorganized activity. There are no or ineffective efforts to match our socialization and education programs with the needs of our society and with jobs and positions needing trained and skilled people. Consequently, there are serious mismatches between the training and areas of specialization offered and what businesses, communities and others need. (The problems of "fit" were examined in Chapter 13.).

With the elimination of our competitive and democratic social practices, we will also be able to eliminate one of the continuing distractions and burdens of our existing educational system. That is the pressure from society to solve many of our social problems through our schools; making the schools both educators and agents for politically mandated social change.

Our parents need assistance socializing their children and helping them deal with the vicissitudes of growing up in a complex world. Some parents do very well, some not so well, and all can use guidance and support. It will all be handled completely differently in a cooperative society. America has tried to fix these problems, believing correctly that no child should be left out or behind in the socialization and training process for life. But our competitive individualistic educational system and socialization practices work against too many of our children and young people. The huge waste of human lives and talents common in America today will be gone. A cooperative society would raise children as a coordinated community effort, with all involved in the teaching of values, norms and skills (see Chapter 13). More on how this will be done in the next chapter.

No More Fragmented Health Care

A key political football in our society is health care. As a medical sociologist I can tell you that none of the various efforts we use, such as fee-for-service or pre-paid programs, private and/or government insurance, preventive versus acute care medical programs and the organization of health care delivery, such as our hospitals, clinics, and emergency rooms, are working as thoroughly and effectively as we need. And they never will as long as we approach health care using a competitive individualistic culture. In a cooperative society there will be no medical insurance, no Medicare and Medicaid, and no need for them. No competing drug and other medical treatment and equipment providers duplicating efforts and charging high prices. No one will be financially wiped out by a serious health problem. There will be no private practice. The fragmentation of health care services that require patients to run from building to building and specialist to specialist, consuming huge amounts of our collective time and energy will be gone. Too often Americans simply don't know how to navigate our complex health care system for their maximum benefit. The exploitation of our needs by greedy competitive companies will be a bad dream. The smooth integration of medical science, development of new drugs and treatments and medical care delivery will be routine in cooperation. A unified and tested body of medical knowledge will eliminate many areas of diagnostic confusion and treatment error. More details on how a cooperative health care system would operate are provided in the following chapter.

No Charity

There will be no charity. Believe it or not, charity is to a considerable measure a competitive product. It is what successful competitors give to mollify those they have defeated and keep them from revolting. It is what those "winners" high on the economic stratification ranking give to those "losers" on the bottom. It was bread and circuses for the common people in the Roman Empire. In being charitable the competitive givers gain status, approval, from their peers and perhaps society. We honor Andrew Carnegie for his free public libraries and other charities, for example, but he was a ruthless competitor and exploiter of his workers, practicing Social Darwinism. There are, of course, in our society, benevolent people and organizations, such as some of our churches that provide humanitarian aid because that is their cultural belief. But there is no charity within cooperative societies because there is no need for it. Everyone receives everything they need for their survival and well-being routinely. Competition produces the need for charity. The biblical adage that the poor are always with us applies to competitive individualistic societies but not to cooperative ones. Cooperative societies take care of everyone as a matter of course, training them for productive roles and providing for all of their needs in abundance and with ease.

No Professional Competitive Sports

Individualism produces recreations that are individualistic, such as some hobbies and crafts. Competition produces competitive recreations such as the competitive sports and games we enjoy so much. Cooperation will produce its own cooperative recreations. We will have to wait and see what these are but I would imagine they will include participatory activities wherein the "players" cooperatively solve some engaging task such as outdoor survival challenges or produce something such as artwork. They may have their own noncompetitive games or perform together such as neighborhood music groups or play performance groups. In the late 70s and early 80s, Terry Orlick explored more cooperative games—"challenge without competition"—including those played in more group-centered and cooperative "primitive" societies. I played some of these with my college students in my classes on cooperation and with nursery children around 2 years of age and they enjoyed them. Some of these suggest what cooperative games might be like.

I imagine that, while some playful competitive contesting and games may be played in a fully cooperative society, for the most part our current competitive sports industry will be gone. There will be no professional competitive sports leagues with all of the bureaucratic organizations, arena constructions, promotion and advertising services and very expensive players and coaches. For an analysis of the contribution to the extreme distortions of our economic distributions produced by our professional competitive athletics, along with our business CEOs and others, take a look at Robert Frank and Philip Cook's (1996) insightful: *The Winner-Take-All Society.*

No More Frenzied Mobs of Obnoxious Reporters

One of the hallmarks of a true cooperative society is that it establishes open communications channels available all of the time to everyone that keeps them informed of what is going on. There is also the single body of correct information available anytime one wants to know what the state of the art is of any scientific or other activity. There is no need for press conferences and the news media to provide up-to-date information, including disasters, exciting developments and the like. The task people working those arenas will describe what is happening and what is being done. "Interviews" with key people will be routine. I doubt that there will be the rather nosey curiosity about others personal lives that we see in our current society. For one thing, everyone lives pretty much the same lifestyle, no rich and famous living wildly extravagant lives above everyone else. Celebrities are a product of competition and will be gone in cooperative societies. There will be no "news media" as we now know it, and no paparazzi and their celebrity watching publications and shows. Because there is consensus there will be no "pundits" and commentators expressing opinions on the various competing "issues" of the day, no panels of debaters arguing with each other that take up so much media coverage today. In a fully cooperative society there is nothing to argue about, strange as that may seem to vigorous competitors. The focus is on the adaptive challenges being faced and progress on their cooperative solution. So, gone will be the multiple

TV channels, commercials, cable and disc companies, multiple newspapers, and all of the bureaucracies involved in their production, no reporters. Just how a cooperative society will use the wide-open communication channels we will have to wait and see, especially the entertainment dimension. Probably there will still be recordings and live and televised performances of music, dance, plays and other entertainments.

AN END TO RIGIDITY

Competitive individualism fosters battles for control over jobs, organizational "turf," bodies of information, the flow of money and so forth that produces rigidity in our social organizations. Job security trumps adaptive changes that might cost current incumbents their livelihood and social status. This rigidity backfires in the long run by preventing adaptive changes that are necessary for the survival and continued effectiveness of the organizations. Cooperative organizations are constructed to be rapidly adapting and information processing and are constantly making adaptive changes and refinements to their culture and social processes. Participants expect their roles to evolve and change, but that they will always have a role, a place to be somebody, and cared for. They have no fear of change and in fact anticipate it.

THE END OF "LEADERSHIP"

Among the holy-on-highs of competitive individualism in America is the glorious individual who gets the haloed label "leader," or "entrepreneur," as well as "hero," "soloist," "prima donna," "top gun," "star," and many others. These roles glorifying and ranking one person above all others are not found in true cooperation. The group is the acting unit in true cooperation not individuals, so such individual glorifying labels simply don't apply. American business literature is loaded with volumes on "leadership." Such books would be considered bizarre in a cooperative economic environment. For example, the Japanese find our form of "hero" leadership disrupting and obnoxious. John Rehfeld (1994) in his book *Alchemy of a Leader* on the Japanese approach to business, whom we met in the last chapter, said:

> In the West, a leader is usually someone with a strong ego, often with a kind of charisma that allows the person to take charge, make decisions, and assume responsibility without being bothered by more mundane things, like consulting with subordinates. This kind

of charismatic leader would flounder in most Japanese companies, destroying essential harmony and team spirit (p. 177).

The Hutterites also take a dim view of our American-style leadership and refuse to place aggressive, assertive, and controlling people in their leadership roles, as we saw in Chapter 3. Prominent business writer Edward Lawler III (2006), whom we met in the last chapter observed: "The reality is that most heroic leaders fail in their attempts to change organizations. Study after study has shown that most would-be saviors are unsuccessful in producing significant organizational change" (p.16)

No Free Riders

There will be no free riders in cooperative organizations or communities. Competition encourages people to get something free for nothing if they can. Steal other's ideas or inventions and use and market them yourself. As one American inventor said, "Invention is one percent inspiration and 99% litigation." It encourages letting others do the work but sharing in the credit and benefits. It includes being lazy and being taken care of. Parasitism is an enthusiastically pursued adaptive pattern in nature and human societies. It includes competitively dominating others and making them do your work for you. Anything that permits a person to meet their survival needs without contributing to the community that produces and provides for those needs is free riding. Many criminals are free riders. Our American welfare rolls are occupied by both needy people and clever free riders.

In cooperation, every effort is made to engage all of the participants in the cooperative enterprise. This includes finding a place where there is a good fit between the participant and the social roles of the organization or community. People with limitations, such as the handicapped, are treated with respect and trained to do what they can, and given a meaningful place to be somebody. But free riding cannot be tolerated. Free riders gum up the operation of cooperative communities, often creating "dead spots" where needed work is not done. This makes the community much less effective and drains resources wastefully. They are a burden without benefit. In cooperation, the group and its members come first. Individuals who are disruptive and destructive have no claim on the cooperative community and no place. Their actions are a form of aggression against the community. Cooperative communities take responsibility for their cooperating members; they are not responsible for free riders and their survival or well being.

No doubt we will think of other competitive individualistic patterns that will disappear as well and good riddance for the most part. Obviously, eliminating all of these competitive individualistic American sociocultural patterns means the end of most of America as we know it. And that is, of course, the point. We need a new form of civilization, a new cooperative culture. It is also obvious that we cannot make such wholesale changes over night, even if we wanted to. It will take time to experiment with true cooperation and get good at it and let it spread through our society, transforming us as it does. In good time—many generations—the old American competitive individualistic society will melt away, its going hardly noticed, as we enthusiastically embrace our next level of social evolution: a fully cooperative society.

The next chapter gives us a general overview of what a cooperative society would be like and tries to give a glimpse of the rich emotional experience that awaits us as we take part in this magnificent adventure of major social transformation and advancement of the human condition.

Chapter 18. All One in a Break-Out, Self-Renewing Cooperative Society

The Vision

Some vision of a better society, a better world, a heavenly world perhaps, has been a nurturing dream throughout our human history. A sweet sense of hope to brighten difficult times and give courage flowed from these visions. Our visions whisper we are special beings, so much nobler and finer and more powerful than we appear now, destined for a more exalted existence. But nearly always we imagine the source of the desired transformation will come from somewhere else, outside of us and our societies, a place of great power and sometimes of justice, goodness and glory. From the gods, from a messiah, from the reincarnation of great souls, from aliens, from powerful spiritual forces from the earth or from the heavens, from the rare alignment of heavenly bodies and their energies, from somewhere ... out there ... will come our transformation to a miraculous people, the people we were always meant to be.

As varied as these dreams are, for the most part they envision a more co-operative world of peace, compassion, benevolence and abundance, a world of enlightenment, beauty and wisdom. Often it is a world of rich connections between people, perhaps spiritually, mentally, or through ESP, making us all one. Even our popular novels often embrace these visions (see for example, Dan Brown's 2009 novel *The Lost Symbol* in which science is on the brink of helping us develop a powerful shared consciousness). While some of these visions require us to become "worthy" by living according to pre-scribed principles, most of the visions I know about do not require us to do a whole lot. The wonderful outside source transforms us and our world like a fairy godmother with a magic wand. Is there a little bit of the lazy free-rider in some of the dreamers of our visions? Or perhaps they lack faith in human beings to do better on their own; to pick themselves up by their bootstraps and transform their societies to match their dreams.

Another possibility is these visions have been guiding us all these centu-ries toward a better society. They are reference points for our earthly jour-ney. It is possible that we have reached the point in our social evolution where the power to make our dreamed transformation is at last within our collective grasp, contained in our current societies, just waiting to be turned on, to be enacted, to be lived. The Hutterites believe so and are showing a good effort to create their vision of heaven on Earth. Other American com-munal utopians gave it a try in the 19th century; their failures were discour-aging but were also informative trials and errors. Have we been collectively struggling toward our visions all along and arrived at the threshold of the Promised Land without realizing it? Are we covered with dust, low on food and water, exhausted from the journey, our eyes glazed, still putting one pioneering booted foot in front of the other, not yet seeing that we are *here*?

I believe that is the case. I also believe we are going to have to do the work, to grunt and puff and sweat to make it happen. Our vision is not going to drop into our lap from outer space, we are going to have to become worthy of it by the "sweat of our brows," by creating it ourselves. We've worked hard to accomplish marvelous things many times in our existence. This we can do as well; it is well within our capacities. We are by all ac-counts a young species just coming into its own. Perhaps we knew in our hearts all along, if vaguely, where we were headed, proclaimed in different voices and songs by our visionary teachers in every era.

You have learned a lot about cooperation from this book. I've shown you work group cooperation among the proximity fuse scientists, communal cooperation among the Hutterites, biosocial cooperation among the euso-cial ants and termites, trends toward cooperation in business management, and shown you the fundamental tools available to us all that are used to construct any cooperative social system of any size.

Still, "the proof is in the pudding." I'm the kind of scientist that doesn't accept "proof" of a hypothesis or finding until it proves its worth in actually predicting and explaining phenomena, and in solving real problems and producing effective results. Until we can successfully fly rockets we can't be sure our rocket science and technology are correct. Until we produce cooperative social systems, we can't be sure we've got it right or have the complete picture. The next step is to go to trial and error efforts to build cooperative families, companies, organizations and societies. As we try out our current understanding of cooperation we are bound to learn a great deal and fill in lots of gaps. As we enrich our body of knowledge about cooperation we will move closer and closer to a pudding proof. Once we get it, we can much more rapidly and confidently spread the information and techniques and hasten our transformation to a cooperative society.

Separate books could be written providing details for how to operate a cooperative family, particular small and large businesses according to what they produce, various societies, or a world-wide civilization. This chapter offers an overview of one possible cooperative American society. It pulls together the many qualities and components presented in earlier chapters. You can imagine along with me. Each of you understands the basics now and can visualize a cooperative society using your experiences and cultural background. It would be interesting to compare our various models; there could be all kinds of useful insights worth sharing.

In the Palm of Your Hand

Let me give you a brief description of our possible cooperative society you can hold in the palm of your hand for reference. Then we'll look at some details.

The dynamic consensus on culture, the common group goals, the group centeredness and social dynamics of true cooperation make society an organic whole. It operates as a functioning unit without internal competing interest groups or personal agendas. This eliminates the need for government and economies as we know them to organize our interactions—make up the rules—and resolve differences and decide courses of collective action.

The cooperative society is organized into task groups. Providing everything humans need to survive and prosper is the daily activity. Each of the adaptive needs of humans is assigned a task group. These include for food, shelter and buildings, education and training, health, transportation, communications, provision of power (electricity and others), basic services such as sewers, water, roads, garbage, recycling and the like, distribution of products, conservation and research and development. Each task group takes care of everything related to that arena (examples follow). Every participant is provided routinely everything they need "for free" for their lifetime. They are entitled to this complete care because they are competently performing the specialized tasks for which they have been trained. There is no need for money or credit cards. Needed goods and services are delivered or provided directly to each participant.

The culture of the cooperative society is constantly tested and modified to keep it accurate and effective. All participants are kept informed and taught new skills as required. Expanding the collective intelligence, the shared body of knowledge, is enthusiastically pursued.

Overall, the cooperative society is vastly simpler and more streamlined, more effective, uses far fewer resources, takes much less of participants' time and energy to operate, and is more fun, exciting, secure and satisfying to experience than our current American society.

LIVING IN A COOPERATIVE SOCIETY

THE WONDER OF ONENESS

For individualists, before you were paying attention only to your own goals and little social world; now you have to keep track of what is going on in the whole social system and your ever-changing role in it to accomplish common group goals. You have to use group goals, rather than personal ones, to guide your behavior all day long. Learning to care about the social system as a social system and all of your cooperative companions requires opening up your brain to a much larger and more complex and dynamic world than individualists are accustomed to. We'll have to start small, with just small groups or companies until we get the hang of it. The positive consequence network of the cooperative social system is going to be especially troublesome for individualists to accept and master. It all requires setting aside individualists' self-centered selfishness and short sightedness for a whole new self-image and persona.

It could get a bit mind boggling at first. However, the rewards make it worth it and the improvement in quality of life that offers realistic optimism about the future can be very seductive. Becoming cooperative brings us home to our natural habitat of community. Humans are happiest in a group, a group of people "like me" where they belong and can snuggle into community life contentedly and safely. We already live in consensus with millions of other people who share our various cultures. The cooperative consensus is just bigger in scope and superior in content. Having your awareness opened wide to a bigger more exciting and rewarding and inclusive life can be breath taking. The sense of being part of a great and powerful whole that is so much bigger than our tiny little self, that oceanic feeling of oneness, is one of humankind's most prized experiences. It is a high that is daily enjoyed in true cooperation because that is the way the cooperative world is. It's worth hopping out of bed in the morning for.

THE COOPERATIVE INTELLIGENCE: LET SOCIETY DO IT

Another major change in cooperative societies is that the cooperative process makes the decisions for us using the best information and with our collective good in mind. We can relax and turn our attention to other things as our task groups provide us with the best of everything reliably and with integrity.

Cooperative societies operate with a cooperative intelligence. This intelligence takes all of the individual intelligence, knowledge and skills that are constantly advancing and evolving and orchestrates them together and operates with the resulting whole. Knowledge and skills are of central importance to cooperative societies and a major focus of attention and effort. To constantly adapt to the changing environment requires complete and up-to-date information about everything. Pursuing new information about how the world works, testing existing knowledge and social processes, and making the resulting correct information part of the dynamic consensus is a major activity in cooperative societies. And there is one and only one body of shared information.

It is the cooperative society that is the unit of action here, not individuals. It is the cooperative society that "decides" everything for the adaptive benefit of the society as a social system and for the benefit of each individual. Making sure every participant has access to this information and their lives are governed by correct understandings is paramount.

The idea that part of society should con the other part out of their money with false information and gimmicks would dumfound cooperative peoples

... why on earth would you do such a thing? A cooperative society would look askance at the huge number of "watch dog" organizations required in America from *Consumer Reports* type magazines and websites to government organizations to protect us from dangerous products, commercial cons, provide true evaluations of products and services and so forth. In our competitive individualistic society every individual must fend for him or herself, getting consumer education, researching each purchase and action alone, trying to choose between multiple competing products and services with incomplete and misleading advertising, looking out for scams, cons and cheats, watching out for hidden contract clauses or behind the scenes manipulations that take advantage, sort through multiple conflicting positions and opinions, all before finally we take a deep breath, choose, and hope for the best. Anxiety, stress and fatigue accompany these continuing efforts.

Our competitive capitalistic market economy was never created with the benefit of the consumer in mind, but rather the benefit of the producer, the business people, the money people and the capitalists that own it. Why would anyone want to live in such a brutally dangerous and misleading society that doesn't give a hoot about you except as a source of money? Cooperation dumps all of this into the trash bin of history, where it belongs. In cooperation, it is the society's responsibility to see to it that everyone gets what they need and of the best quality as a societal function. The individual doesn't have to make all of these difficult decisions in the midst of a minefield, but enjoys the benefits as a reward for their constructive role fulfillments creating and enacting the society's social systems.

Cooperation creates a highly intelligent and well-informed community operating as a whole looking after itself and all its participants, rather than requiring each participant to fend for himself or herself as best they can in a mostly hostile environment. This cooperative intelligence is at the heart of everything cooperative societies do, including their task organization and performances.

WHAT ABOUT RELIGION?

Our religions express our cultures. For example, our Christian religions are based upon the individualism of our larger society. Bellah et al. (1985) call it "biblical individualism." It is the individual that must find his or her way into heaven by good deeds, repentance of sins, learning the doctrine of the religion and committing themselves to Christ and His service. Local congregations are collections of individuals attempting to build an ethical, mutually supportive, and spiritual community, primarily using individual-istic mutual aid. Still, many of these religions encourage cooperative values and more cooperative practices, as I've mentioned above.

It is difficult to anticipate what will happen to our current religions as the world transforms into a cooperative society. One possibility is that the cooperative society becomes a tolerant home for a variety of our current and some new religions. Another possibility is that our religions shift from in-dividualism and/or competition based belief systems to cooperative-based ones, still maintaining their history, values, and practices but modified. Or our world religions could meld together, blending their best qualities, and letting out-moded portions float away on the breeze. Then we would have a "super religion," so to speak, to guide us and as a memento of our past histo-ries. Most likely, over generations of cooperation, we will gradually evolve a new religion or religions firmly grounded in cooperation while satisfying our spiritual desires and needs. Cooperation is uniquely suited to form the core of a world-wide religion embracing all of us in a common, compassion-ate, community (see the final interlude at the end o this chapter). At the very least, a cooperative society gives us the opportunity to practice what most of our world religions preach.

The classical sociologist Emile Durkheim in his book, *The Elementary Forms of Religious Life* (New York: The Free Press, 1954), observed that some-times people worship their own societies. The power and capacities of soci-ety are so much larger and grander than most individuals can easily grasp or comprehend that they make their society divine in their efforts to visualize them. Unaware of what they are doing, they celebrate their societies in the deities they worship and the things they hold sacred. (See also Coser, 1977, pp. 136-139.) Could this happen in a cooperative society? I'm not suggesting it should, only that it could.

A fully cooperative society would express many of the higher values and visions that religious people have dreamed of for centuries. These include a community of compassion, benevolence, integrity, and peace; an ethical and moral community producing people with integrity; a community of oneness enjoying unity in values and purpose; a community of mutual abundance and wellbeing. The physiological and rhythmic patterns of cooperation can produce the "highs" of some "spiritual" experiences. The "oceanic feelings of oneness" that characterize some religious experiences also characterize some cooperative community experiences.

Is cooperation going to give us the spiritual and religious home so many have sought for centuries? Is it the finishing piece our existing religions require to fully express their gospel stories, their visions for a "perfect" human community? This will be one of the fascinating stories to watch unfold as our cultural paradigm shifts.

AND ART?

What about the arts? Cooperation is an expressive form of society with people used to sharing and communicating many things. They are used to experiencing "aha" moments, "spiritual" highs, oceanic feelings of oneness, and being attentive to all kinds of things in the environment. They are well educated and refined. I expect they will use the arts to express their joy, their delights, and the beauty around them, as well as other emotions and experiences. I expect they will find aesthetic bliss, as do many Americans, in many arenas besides art, such as good food, colorful gardens, the many dimensions of nature, the charm of our family and friends and so on. I imagine the classics in music, art and literature will continue to be classics and be added to.

Cooperative societies give participants leisure time to pursue artistic interests that many frustrated would-be American artists have to forgo to earn a living and raise a family. I imagine the cooperative society will find avenues to display and perform these artistic expressions to the shared delight of all. I also expect cooperative people to form more neighborhood musical and play performance groups, such as string quartets for their own pleasure as well as others. I would expect the arts to be expressed in fashions, architecture, the products cooperative people use and so forth. They have the time and talent to do that.

Cooperative arts will include artistic works that capture the lives of groups as groups and specialties, expressing the group-centered experience that goes beyond individualistic views. I have often heard that scientists and professionals such as medical doctors see all kinds of beautiful things in their work that they cannot express. It would be wonderful to have artists who can do that for the good of the profession or group and the larger society wishing to know what that world is like. No doubt cooperative artistic works will produce the emblems, anthems, and symbols of the cooperative world.

Organization by Task

Cooperative organizations and societies are organized around the tasks that must be accomplished in order to reach the common group goals. The goals are broken down into their component task areas and then into each task area's component tasks and so forth down to the specialized group that will do the actual work. The task areas are operated by competent, well trained people, with the most competent available coordinating and evaluating the work at any given moment. Larger tasks are broken into ever smaller ones as needed, changing when and as needed. Coordinating responsibilities are not a fixed role but fall to whoever is the best qualified to handle the current activity and then passed along, flowing through the group of cooperative workers as required. There are no fixed role/job definitions, but rather arenas of task responsibility and competence. All are trained in multiple competencies and skilled in organizing cooperative actions on the run as situations unfold. There is no controlling hierarchy, although some coordination/facilitation specialists may be occasionally utilized.

Cooperative societies operate as a fluid whole in unity. The division of labor is built upon the task designations with the understanding they can be changed and refined at any time as adaptation requires. Participants are expected to have multiple competencies so they can move to where the action is and help where there is temporary need. Remember that the cooperative society is the tool of the participants to assure their survival by maximizing their successful and rapid adaptation to changes and conditions in the environment. It is a task cooperative people engage in with enthusiastic commitment.

There will be ongoing tasks inherent in our survival including providing food, clothing, shelter, transportation, communications, health care, waste recycling and disposal, harmonizing with the natural environment, research, education, energy, appliances and tools, resources and raw materials, and so forth. There will also be important and often recurring temporary tasks such as harvesting foods, dealing with accidents, catastrophes and major weather related problems including floods and hurricanes that require immediate mobilization.

New task areas can be expected to emerge as the cooperative society grows and develops and our world evolves. Distribution of the products of the various task areas is directly to the consumer, individual or organizational. Each task area produces what is needed by the society at that moment and no more. When the needs are met, attention and activity turn to other areas. There is no use for money as a means of internal exchange in this cooperative model; money and related financial task areas have been eliminated.

Let's take a few of the permanent task areas as examples of the cooperative organization. Let's begin with food.

Food

Those specialists responsible for our food would decide which foods to produce, grow them, preserve and deliver them, and recommended recipes and cooking procedures. Quality prepared meals would be available as well. Only high quality healthful foods would be produced and portions and nutritional values are constantly assessed in meals and foods available. No doubt there will still be treats and chocolates and other delights. The food may be delivered directly to homes or be picked up for free at attractive local distribution centers. You just walk in and take what you need. It will always be there so no need to "load up." No doubt there will be the equivalent of restaurants serving a wide variety of foods as well. All free, just go in and order as you please. I expect cooperative people to be delighted with life and enjoy living it to the fullest, including enjoying their food. They will also be appreciative of their abundance and refined in their behavior, eating wisely and amounts that are healthy.

Some farm and food labor problems—such as food harvesting and processing—our current society handles with cheap, sometimes illegal, immigrant labor are tied to our competitive capitalist profit-oriented market pressures. In a cooperative society, the food belongs to everyone. Since the necessary labors leave lots of "free" time in cooperative societies, the community is able to mobilize rapidly large work forces to hand harvest fruit and vegetables as part of their community efforts. A cooperative community could make it a great time for celebration of the harvest and reaffirmation of community solidarity. Less desirable and skilled jobs such as in food processing plants would likely be handled on a rotating basis so that no one works in those jobs for long, or as age-cohort tasks assigned temporarily to younger people as they grow up. Waiters and waitresses may also be age-cohort related jobs (This was Bellamy's suggestion in *Looking Backward.*)

Transportation

We sometimes see technology as the production of devices which we then use. We overlook the degree to which our technology is shaped by our cultural patterns, and that technology would take different forms in different cultures. Transportation is an example. Our romance with our personal automobile is an individualistic cultural pattern. From an adaptive point of view, the personal automobile and the long distance truck are poor transportation solutions. They cost too much and are inefficient. The gridlocks looming on our highways and byways are a product of our individualism. We have the technology to move lots of people and goods lots of places without producing gridlock or even long waits.

In a cooperative society, transportation would be coordinated by specialists in that task area. They would make decisions concerning the best way to transport people and products and see to it from planning, to manufacturing of the vehicles, to scheduling and loading and unloading, and maintenance. They would take into account heavy travel times and accommodate them. They realize that getting people—all competent specialists of great value to the community—to their destinations is critical for adaptive effectiveness of the whole society.

I believe cooperative societies will opt for very pleasant mass transit that practically coddles riders. I remember the early days of the railroads when they were luxurious with large reclining seats, domed observation cars, elegant dining cars, lounges, and a smooth, scenic ride. We can add internet connections and other modern comforts and amenities. And it's all free, just hop on. The buses, subways, and "trolleys," could also be made much more pleasant, comfortable, and omnipresent. Those needing special attention could call up for a van ride to their destinations or a mass transit terminal. Shuttles would be everywhere. In a cooperative society, participants would welcome the chance to visit and get the "news of the day" with their neighbors, who are all doing things of importance to all, as they ride. There would not be the aloof separateness our competitive individualism produces among passengers in our society. Routes would be determined by need and not profit or competition. Smaller routes would have smaller vehicles, but they would not be abandoned. If many want to travel by plane on the holidays, ways are provided to make it happen. Again all for free, just reserve a seat.

Over the generations it will take to make America fully cooperative, housing patterns would be altered to maximize effective mass transit. I expect that cooperative societies will house people close to where they work to make it easier to get to work and socialize with coworkers. People may walk to their work and enjoy a relaxed community with sidewalk cafes and the like. There would be no rush hour traffic.

You might still have a family or personal car. More likely, there will be a neighborhood garage with cars residents can borrow for the day—for free. But there will likely be regular delivery services available for many things as well. Few people will need a personal automobile to get the transportation they require.

Health Care

Health care is a very broad topic reaching into just about all of the others, as it should, including food, shelter, and education. Social stress is one of my greatest personal concerns. At last the heavy burden of increased disease susceptibility, stress produced diseases, depression, anger and discontent, disruption of relationships, uncertainty and anxiety, reduction in alertness and decision making and in quality of life generated by the stressfulness of our current society will be gone. Out cooperative society will have shucked off most of the endemic sources of social stress bedeviling us: competition and individualism. Health care will be free and operated by a single task area set of specialists, coordinated around each community's health needs. Health care specialists are trained according to the need.

I imagine that the neighborhood health clinic will become the main contact and entry area for community members. Each clinic would be responsible for the health of those in their area. The clinic would be a mini-hospital and pharmacy that provides preventive care, regular checkups, out-patient surgeries, takes care of any health issues that come up and follows up to make sure drugs are taken and other directions are followed. It would contain a collection of specialists determined by the health care task group to be the most appropriate for the health needs and usual health problems of that population. Health care givers are all among the most competent available and establish friendships with their user population. Social and psychological counseling and therapy would also be handled by the clinic. If you feel unwell or emotionally troubled by current events in your life or need guidance to community resources the neighborhood clinic is your first—and always free—stop. Regional hospitals for more serious health problems would receive patients from the local clinics.

Health care programs including education would be provided for various work groups and age cohorts at work or at school and over public communications channels such as TV and the internet. There would be a consensus on the proper health care patterns, drugs to be used, technologies and their applications and so forth among the cooperative participants. The discovery, development and distribution of medical advances and new drugs would be clean and fast, unhindered by economic and political constraints that block or delay too many advances now. All of a patient's records are kept in one place providing full knowledge of what medications are being taken, personal conditions such as allergies, and medical history for the use of health care specialists. I imagine there will be many more highly competent specialists at the current nurse practitioner and physician's assistant level than is now the case. Medical training would be streamlined and ongoing. Ongoing medical research would be a major effort in a cooperative society.

Education, Socialization, and Training

Socialization of young people is a community project in which all take part. This is possible because of the consensus and the positive consequence network built into cooperative societies. I believe the family will still be a primary social unit of cooperative societies. Parents are assisted as needed and are trained in the proper socialization techniques mentioned in earlier chapters. Children are considered community citizens and are watched over to make sure they are properly cared for and safe. Exactly how this will work we can only imagine but likely there will be socialization/education specialists who work with children, perhaps in neighborhood training facilities or schools, to help them develop needed knowledge and skills and to discover each child's potentials and talents. Education will be much more fluid and community based, focusing on developing future citizens and competent specialists. Students would advance at their own pace in various subjects, working with others at that level, regardless of age. Working in the community with real responsibilities will be part of their upbringing starting from a young age. These tasks meet community needs and help children see how society works and introduces them to many of the people they will live their lives with and develops their social skills. They can be such things as baby sitting, yard work, cleaning, simple constructive projects, food harvesting, and many more, especially as their talents are developed and training progresses.

As talents emerge, young people are trained to develop those talents and for particular specialties that need those talents. The training process gradually moves the young person into their adult roles. People are trained for roles that need filling and are guided into those roles. There is a "job" for everyone, and everyone has a job. It will be job of great value to the community and gives the person a place to enact their self, to be somebody, with joy and pride. The abundant "free time" cooperative people enjoy provides opportunity for individuals to explore topics and other task arenas of interest to them. Great effort is expended to make good matches between social and occupational roles and individuals and their talents and capacities. This includes lifelong training and sometimes moving into other roles or even other task areas as life unfolds.

The rebellious adolescent goes the way of the competitive individualism that creates and fosters it with its values of independence, disrespect for authority, and go your own way. In cooperative societies, young people look forward to and enjoy their gradual integration into society and in learning many things, especially operating as one community.

At this time I'm not sure what role schools will play, or TV or the internet in the education of young people. Cooperative societies are very open and transparent in their information exchange, so people are constantly exposed from an early age to whatever is going on in that society and grow up having these activities explained to them and experiencing some of them first hand. Education may be more focused on specific information content and skills with students being whoever needs that training at the moment regardless of age or other demographic characteristics. People will be training at their own pace and capacity. Boys fast in math and slow in language mastery would be taught with others at their common pace. Remember, in cooperation competence is a fundamental requirement for participation, and for positive self-images and high self-esteem.

Among the contrasts between our current American society and world and a cooperative America and world-wide civilization will be the normative level of individual education, developed skills, and capacity to track complex sociocultural processes. Currently, the bulk of humans on Earth have nowhere near the training, understanding, and capacities required for routine daily cooperative participation in our emerging high tech, Information Age civilization. Too many, for example, have no or inadequate understanding of what a culture or social system are or the skills to work with them.

Sex and Population

How will sexual behavior be handled? We'll have to wait and see. I can imagine a variety of possibilities, but I would be guessing. I doubt that cooperative societies' sexual practices will be "Puritanistic" and cold. Cooperation is a joyful culture that engages in life with enthusiasm. But it will be a socially responsible enthusiasm.

In my personal observations, one of the most common and unnecessary tragedies in life is children born too soon to unprepared parents with all of their lives permanently impaired as a consequence. The proportion of children born out of wedlock and raised by single parents is alarmingly high and getting higher (ranging from a high of over 70% to around 50% to a low of 23% in various American demographic populations). The current often irresponsible, self-centered, sexual behavior of many Americans will be remembered with astonished horror by future cooperative societies. It is a tragedy that so many of our young people do not receive good training and guidance in their sexual activities so that the lifelong results are healthy, satisfying, and adaptive. Problems with our American reproductive and sexual behavior are evidence of the inadequacy of our competitive individualistic society to guide these critical and most elementary human processes adaptively.

Cooperative societies will pay attention to the fit between their population size and the environment. Currently, over population is a major problem world-wide, straining natural resources, destroying needed natural habitat and eliminating species at an alarming rate. Producing greater harmony between ourselves and our natural environment will guide our cooperative reproductive patterns, ensuring we do not overrun the Earth and destroy our home.

Research

Cooperative societies' goal of effective environmental tracking and adaptive responses requires extensive and ongoing research. Research of all kinds from basic to applied to innovative inventions are pursued. There is constant effort to expand the knowledge base of the culture, to improve current techniques, and to understand emerging problems that indicate changes in the environment or inadequacies in existing knowledge or technologies. This effort will be housed in research centers containing allied and interdependent sciences and technologies. The best and brightest are working together on problems—not racing against each other in competition—and information is freely shared as it emerges. No need to wait for publication or conferences. Trial and error testing is continual and modified on the run as results emerge and suggest the next step. Young trainees are included and develop their competencies helping and observing as well as being instructed.

One Body of Correct Information

Attending to the cooperative society's single, ever evolving body of correct information is a major task arena. All other task arenas depend upon, draw from and contribute to it. Keeping it accurate, current, coherent, free from incongruities, well organized and easily available to all requires constant effort. Alerting the relevant task groups, such as research, that there are problems that need more information or conflicts needing empirical testing and then monitoring progress is part of the task group's responsibility. The constant testing, and refining of this information is a focus of cooperative societies. If there is a question, empirical testing is pursued until it is answered.

This is one of cooperative societies' greatest accomplishments and gifts to its participants: maintaining a single complete and accurate body of information accessible to all upon demand. It is the cooperative version of Google but without competing versions and subjective opinions and sly ads. This is where you go to find out the nature of things. It includes what science knows to this point, areas of research being pursued, history, encyclopedia, dictionary, medical information, guidance on everything under the sun from planting tomatoes to cleaning bugs off your car to making nutritious meals and when the next eclipse of the sun will be.

In the past various groups, often "professionals, controlled bodies of information and charged for teaching others or using it for their benefit. That is already changing with the creation of the internet. Accurate information is becoming constantly more accessible to anyone with access to a computer connected to an internet server. This is one of the most important developments in our Information Age: making information a community property available to all. This shared body of knowledge is at the heart of the cooperative society's power. It contributes to a dynamic consensus on "what is" that guides cooperative decisions and actions.

Constant Information Communication: What's Happening Now

The information communication task area uses all of the communication technologies, including television, the internet, handheld devices, printed material, and telephones to keep the population abreast of what is happening, what changes are being made, what associated changes are required by various task areas, and who is involved. This includes recent scientific and technological developments. It would include things of interest, entertaining, and just charming and fun novelties. This is what people will largely be talking about with one another during their day. All participants will be contributing to this information flow concerning their own task role assignments and what is happening with them.

There are no "opinions" expressed, no judgments and debates of the accuracy or value of the material, no gleeful revelations of private misbehavior, no gossip, and other topics that delight competitive individualists. Current and updated information on what is happening is the primary content. Information on tasks, especially difficult ones, cooperatively accomplished, are of special interest. Problems, failures, new information, are processed and reported as well. Everybody knows everything all the time in cooperative communities. This is necessary for the highly coordinated rapid cooperative responses and task performances that shift to where the action is as needed that characterize cooperative societies. Cooperation is a tuned-in lifestyle.

Simplifying and Standardization

Because of the consensus and absence of competition, cooperative societies will have standardized technologies. The electronics devices, computer programs and operating systems, internet devices, building codes, tools, and so forth will be produced by the responsible task area in cooperation with all others and will all be the same and compatible. The forms to be filled out will be standardized and simplified and familiar to all, and there won't be many of them. Those responsible, including writing new computer programs, will be the best, the most competent people the cooperative society can produce. Their work is constantly updated and refined. Changes, such as program updates, are made for the population for free. When something is working well, it is used. The constant modifications of technology and computer programs for no other reason than to increase or maintain sales and profits blessedly will be in the past.

Stay Tuned

While it would be fun to speculate, I think we will have to wait for co-operative societies to emerge to see what clothing fashions they favor, housing and furniture designs they use, and, as mentioned the previous chapter, the details of their recreations and entertainments. All of these will have a consensual and communal flavor with no effort to advertise one's self, to pursue self-aggrandizement, or make a personal "statement."

AND THE LIVIN' IS EASY

The good news is that we are launching into a major social transformation that is going to lead us into a fundamental sociocultural paradigm shift of greater proportions than anything we've experienced before and with very positive consequences. In many ways this new culture is the expression of the good in our human societies that has been perking and bubbling for a long time. In other ways it will be like stepping through a veil into a new world that has never existed before for which we have little prior experience. It goes beyond even our dreams and visions for a better world. It will be exciting, exhilarating, eye-opening and full of "aha!" experiences. Best of all, it will be a world of peace and companionship and plenty where the livin' is easy.

For our final comment on the coming world of cooperation we turn to the marvelous mythologist Joseph Campbell in the following reflection.

A NEW WORLD WITH NEW MYTHS AND LEGENDS

Bill Moyers and Joseph Campbell, a renowned scholar of mythology, engaged in an epic conversation about myth that produced twenty-four hours of film, a six-hour, widely watched and acclaimed PBS television series, and a book: *The Power of Myth* (N.Y.: Anchor , 1991). Moyers said,

> The last time I saw him [Campbell] I asked him if he still believed—as he had once written—'that we are at this moment participating in one of the greatest leaps of the human spirit

---

to a knowledge not only of outside nature but also of our own deep inward mystery.'

He thought a minute and answered:

'The greatest ever' (Campbell, 1991, p. xix).

Campbell feels, as Rollo May (see Chap. 7) and I do, that we are in a period of social transformation for which our old myths are increasingly inadequate. Both Campbell and I see our transformation producing a worldwide society. We require new heroes and myths capable of helping us comprehend who we are becoming and our relationships with each other and the world. Adds Campbell (1991), "What all the myths have to deal with is transformations of consciousness of one kind or another. You have been thinking one way, you now have to think a different way" (p. 155).

Campbell identifies several components of the new understanding and world view he feels we must embrace:

1. A realization that we are all one and that we must pursue a common purpose as a single power.

2. A greater understanding of nature and our place in it.

3. A realization that the highest order of human development produces compassion.

4. Service to others and the community.

All are components or goals of true cooperation. Our yet-to-emerge transforming myths, aiding us in our move to a cooperative culture, will, indeed, need to embrace these components.

Commenting on our current condition, Moyers said:

> When you think about what people are actually undergoing in our civilization, you realize it's a very grim thing to be a modern human being. The drudgery of the lives of most of the people who have to support families—well it's a life-extinguishing affair. To me, that's the curse of modern society, the impotence, the ennui that people feel, the alienation of people from the world order around them.

Campbell called it a "sociological stagnation" "that evokes nothing of our spiritual life, our potentialities, or even our physical courage—until, of course, it gets us into one of its inhuman wars."

We need new heroes and myths because our society must have "constellating images to pull together all these tendencies to separation, to pull them together into some intention." "The nation has to have an intention somehow to operate as a single power" (Campbell, 1991, pp. 160-163). The adoption of the culture of cooperation, with its common group goal of rapid adaptation to the changing environment for the benefit of all will provide this "intention."

Unfortunately, as Moyers perceptively noted, "The history of Western culture has been the steadily widening separation of the self from society. 'I' first, the individual first" (Campbell, 1991, p. 105). We are going in the opposite direction from the one Campbell, and I, advocate. Looking at tribal cultures, Campbell (1991) shows us some of what is missing in our current society:

> Society was there before you, it is there after you are gone, and you are a member of it. The myths that link you to your social group, the tribal myths, affirm that you are an organ of the larger organism. Society itself is an organ of a larger organism, which is the landscape, the world in which the tribe moves. The main theme in ritual is the linking of the individual to a larger morphological structure than that of his own physical body (p. 90).

What a comfort such myths would be for us in our jumbled and confusing times.

Campbell believes "the only myth that is going to be worth thinking about in the immediate future is one that is talking about the planet, not the city, not these people, but the planet, and everybody on it" (p. 41). This is precisely what the culture of cooperation does, it is the perfect content for new myths embracing and celebrating our oneness as a society, as humans on Earth, and as living, adapting creatures of nature. Campbell discusses Black Elk, the famous Sioux visionary. Black Elk saw his tribe in a vision as one hoop and all other "nations" as hoops. In his vision Black Elk "saw the eventual cooperation of all the hoops, all the nations in grand procession" (p. 110-111). The blending of all hoops into one worldwide one, yes, here is an element of our vision for the future.

This oneness generates companionship and compassion. Discussing Schopenhauer, Campbell (1991) said, "our true reality is in our identity and unity with all life." "So when Jesus says, 'Love thy neighbor as thyself,' he is saying in effect, 'Love they neighbor because he *is* yourself'" (pp. 138-139). He is an integral part of the society, the whole, that you are identified with and dependent upon. Campbell tells us that, "The big moment in the medieval myth is the awakening of the heart to compassion, the transformation of passion into compassion" (p. 143). Compassion is the one thing that turns the human beast of prey into a valid human being, Campbell concludes (p. 144). As we become one in a cooperative community and learn to take others' roles feeling sympathy, empathy, and compassion, we at last achieve the dreams of centuries of myths.

This yearning for a new paradigm, new myths, new societies expressed by May, Moyers, and Campbell articulate the malaise of our society and our times. We now have the means to banish our malaise and its sources and give ourselves peace. We have the answer: it is the culture of cooperation. Cooperation will, indeed, massively and decisively transform the human condition and our quality of life. It will create ongoing harmony everywhere, between humans and between society and nature. It produces compassion with all living things, appreciation for all things, and a profound, functional, conceptual and emotional oneness. How do we get to this wonderful Utopia? It's no longer a mystery, true cooperation is no longer a stranger, the path is clear.

Bibliography

Argyris, Chris. *Personality and Organization.* New York: Harper Collins, 1957.

Arrington, Leonard J., *Great Basin Kingdom: Economic History of the Latter-Day Saints, 1840-1900.* Lincoln Nebraska: University of Nebraska Press, 1966.

Baldwin, Ralph B. *The Deadly Fuze: The Secret Weapon of World War II.* San Rafael, California: Presidio Press, 1980.

Bellah, Robert N., Richard Madsen, William M. Sullivan, Ann Swindler and Steven M. Tipton. *Habits of the Heart: Individualism and Commitment in American Life.* Berkeley: University of California Press, 1985.

Bellamy, Edward. *Looking Backward: 2000-1887.* New York: Houghton Mifflin (The Riverside Press Cambridge) 1926.

Bruhn, John G. and Stewart Wolf. *The Roseto Story: An Anatomy of Health.* Norman Oklahoma: University of Oklahoma Press, 1979.

Catton, Bruce. *Michigan: A History.* New York: W. W. Norton, 1976.

Caudill, William. "Effects of Social and Cultural Systems in Reactions to Stress," Memorandum to the Committee on Preventive Medicine and Social Science Research, Social Science Research Council Pamphlet #14, June, 1958.

Chapple, Eliot D. *Culture and Biological Man: Explorations in Behavioral Anthropology.* New York: Holt, Rinehart and Winston. 1970.

Chesney, Margaret A., and Ray H. Rosenman, (Eds.), *Anger and Hostility in Cardiovascular and Behavioral Disorders.* Washington: Hemisphere, 1985.

Cochran, Gregory, and Henry Harpending. *The 10,000 year Explosion: How Civilization Accelerated Human Evolution.* New York: Basic Books, 2009.

Coser, Lewis A. *Masters of Sociological Thought.* 2nd Edition, New York: Harcourt Brace Jovanovich, 1977.

Daly, Herman E. *Beyond Growth: The Economics of Sustainable Development.* Boston: Beacon Press, 1996.

De Waal, Frans. *Good Natured: The Origins of Right and Wrong in Humans and other Animals.* Cambridge, Mass.: Harvard University Press, 1996.

Diamond, Jared. *Guns, Germs, and Steel.* New York: W. W. Norton, 1997.

Dielman, T. E., A.T. Butchart, G. E. Moss, R. V. Harrison, W. R. Harlan, W. J. Horvath. "Psychometric Properties of Component and Global Measures of Structured Interview Assessed Type A Behavior in a Population Sample." *Psychosomatic Medicine.* 49:458-469, 1987.

Durkheim, Emile.*The Elementary Forms of Religious Life.* New York: The Free Press, 1954.

Eisenberg, Daniel. "A Theater Very Near You: A glut of fancy new megaplexes could spoil the happy ending for the big movie-house chains," *Time.* September 13, 1999, p. 40.

Fisher, M. Scott. Personal communication. March, 2005.

Frank, Robert H., Philip J. Cook. *The Winner-Take-All Society: Why the Few at the Top Get So Much More Than the Rest of Us.* New York: Penguin, 1996.

Friedman, Thomas L. *The World Is Flat: A Brief History of the Twenty-First Century.* New York: Farrar, Straus and Giroux, 2006.

Gellhorn, Ernst, and G. N. Loofbourrow. *Emotions & Emotional Disorders: A Neurophysiological Study.* New York: Hoeber Medical Division/Harper & Row, 1963.

Gibb, Bruce. "Myths, Legends, and Lore and Cultural Evolution," *Organizational Development Journal.* Volume 21, Number 3, Fall 2003, pp. 103-110.

Gibb, Bruce. "Organizational Leadership Structure: The Camp Meeting," unpublished manuscript, 2001.

Gibb, Bruce. Personal communication, February, 2009.

Guarneri, Carl J., "Brook Farm and the Fourierist Phalanxes: Immediatism, Gradualism, and American Utopian Socialism," in Donald E. Pitzer, Ed., *America's Communal Utopias.* Chapel Hill: The University of North Carolina Press, 1997, pp. 159-180.

Hall, Edward T. *The Dance of Life: The Other Dimension of Time.* Garden City,

New York: Anchor Press/Doubleday, 1983.

Hesse, Hermann. *Steppenwolf.* New York: Bantam, 1969.

Hiestand, Michael. "Golf courses find rough; Glut of layouts forces creative marketing" *USA TODAY.* Tuesday, January 19, 1999, p. 1C.

Holldobler, Bert, and Edward O. Wilson. *The Ants.* Cambridge, Mass.: Belknap Press of Harvard University Press, 1990.

Hostetler, John, and Gertrude E. Huntington, *The Hutterites in North America: Case Studies in Cultural Anthropology,* Series Editors: George and Louise Spindler, 3rd Edition. Fort Worth: Harcourt Brace, 1996.

Huntington, Gertrude E., "Living in the Ark: Four Centuries of Hutterite Faith." in Donald E. Pitzer, Ed. *America's Communal Utopias.* Chapel Hill: The University of North Carolina Press, 1997, pp. 319-351.

Infield, Henrik F. *Utopia and Experiment: Essays in the Sociology of Cooperation.* New York: Frederick A. Praeger, 1955.

Johanson, Donald, and Blake Edgar. *From Lucy to Language.* New York: Simon and Schuster Editions, 1996.

Kanter, Rosabeth Moss. *Change Masters: Innovation for Productivity in the American Workplace.* New York: Simon & Schuster, 1985.

Keirsey, David, and Marilyn Bates, *Please Understand Me: Character and Temperament Types.* Del Mar, California: Prometheus Nemesis Book Company, 1984.

Kemmis, Daniel. *Community and the Politics of Place.* Norman, Oklahoma: University of Oklahoma Press, 1990.

Kephart, William M., *Extraordinary Groups: The Sociology of Unconventional Life-Styles.* 2nd Edition. New York: St. Martin's Press, 1982.

Kinkade, Kat, *Is it Utopia Yet? An Insider's View of Twin Oaks Community in Its 26th Year.* Ann Arbor, Michigan: Cushing-Malloy, 1997.

Kohn, Alfie. *No Contest: The Case Against Competition.* Boston: Houghton Mifflin, 1986.

Kraybill, Donald B. and Carl F. Bowman, *On the Backroad to Heaven: Old Order Hutterites, Mennonites, Amish, and Brethren.* Baltimore: The Johns Hopkins University Press, 2001.

Lawler, Edward E., III. *The Ultimate Advantage: Creating the High-Involvement Organization.* San Francisco: Jossey-Bass, 1992.

Lawler, Edward E., III. *From the Ground Up: Six Principles for Building the New Logic Corporation.* San Francisco: Jossey-Bass, 2000.

Lawler, Edward E., III. *Treat People Right: How Organizations and Individuals Can*

Propel Each Other Into a Virtuous Spiral of Success. San Francisco: Jossey-Bass, 2003.

Lawler, Edward E., III, and Christopher G. Worley. *Built to Change: How to Achieve Sustained Organizational Effectiveness.* San Francisco: Jossey-Bass, 2006.

Leiderman, P. Herbert, and David Shapiro, (Editors). *Psychobiological Approaches to Social Behavior.* Stanford, California: Stanford University Press, 1964.

Lex, Barbara W., Private communication, photocopy, "The Neurobiology of Ritual Trance," draft of a revision of "Physiological Aspects of Ritual Trance," *Journal of Altered States of Consciousness.* 2 (2): 1975, pp. 109-122.

Likert, Rensis. *New Patterns of Management.* New York: McGraw-Hill, 1961.

Likert, Rensis. *The Human Organization: Its Management and Value.* New York: McGraw-Hill, 1967.

Likert, Rensis. "Improving Cost Performance with Cross-Functional Teams," *The Conference Board RECORD.* Vol. XII, No. 9, September, 1975, pp. 51-59.

Likert, Rensis, and Jane Gibson Likert. *New Ways of Managing Conflict.* New York: McGraw-Hill, 1976.

Likert, Rensis, and M. Scott Fisher. "MBGO: Putting Some Team Spirit into MBO," *Personnel,* Volume 54, No. 1, January-February, 1977, pp. 40-47.

Malinowski, Bronislaw. *Argonauts of the Western Pacific.* New York: E. P. Dutton, 1961.

Mason, John W., and Joseph V. Brady. "The Sensitivity of Psychoendocrine Systems to Social and Physical Environmnet," in Leiderman, P. Herbert, and David Shapiro, (Editors). *Psychobiological Approaches to Social Behavior.* Stanford, California: Stanford University Press, 1964.

May, Rollo. *The Cry for Myth.* New York: W. W. Norton, 1991.

McCullough, David. *John Adams.* New York: Touchstone/Simon & Schuster, 2001.

McGregor, Douglas. *The Human Side of Enterprise.* New York: 1960.

Mead, Margaret (Ed.). *Cooperation and Competition Among Primitive Peoples.* Gloucester, Mass.: Peter Smith, 1976. (originally pub. by McGraw-Hill, 1937; Revised Beacon edition, 1961; cited volume recent printing.)

Mithen, Steven. *The Prehistory of the Mind: The Cognitive Origins of Art, Religion and Science.* London: Thames and Hudson, 1996.

Moss, Gordon E. "The 'Jumpers" of Maine: A Sociological Appraisal," *The*

Journal of the Maine Medical Association, Volume 59, No. 6, 1968, pp. 117-121.

Moss, Gordon E. *Illness, Immunity, and Social Interaction: The Dynamics of Biosocial Resonation.* New York: Wiley-Interscience/John Wiley, 1973.

Moss, Gordon E. "Biosocial Resonation: A Conceptual Model of the Links Between Social Behavior and Physical Illness," in Z. J. Lipowski, Editor. *The International Journal of Psychiatry in Medicine: Current Trends In Psychosomatic Medicine:1.* Volume 5, Number 4, Fall, 1974, pp. 401-410.

Moss, Gordon E. "Identification and the Curve of Optimal Cohesion," in George Haydu, Ed. *Experience Forms: Their Cultural and Individual Place and Function.* 1979, pp. 209-240.

Moss, Gordon E., T. E. Dielman, Pamela C. Campanelli, Sharon L. Leech, William R. Harlan, R. Van Harrison, and William J. Horvath. "Demographic Correlates of SI Assessments of Type A Behavior." *Psychosomatic Medicine.* 48:546-574, 1986.

Mowat, Farley. *Never Cry Wolf.* New York: Bantam, 1979.

Murcray, Colin, Private communication, August, 2009.

O'Toole, Jack. *Forming the Future: Lessons from the Saturn Corporation.* Cambridge, Mass.: Blackwell Publishers, 1996.

O'Toole, James. *Vanguard Management.* New York: Doubleday, 1985.

Orlick, Terry. *The Cooperative Sports & Games Book: Challenge Without Competition.* New York: Pantheon Books, 1978.

Orlick, Terry. *The Second Cooperative Sports & Games Book.* New York: Patheon Books, 1982.

Ouchi, William. *Theory Z: How American Business Can Meet the Japanese Challenge.* Reading, Massachusetts: Addison-Wesley, 1981.

Peters, Thomas J. and Robert H. Waterman, Jr. *In Search of Excellence: Lessons from America's Best-Run Companies.* New York: HarperCollins, 1982.

Phillips, Kevin. *Wealth and Democracy.* New York: Broadway Books, 2002.

Putnam, Robert D. *Bowling Alone: The Collapse and Revival of American Community.* New York: Touchstone/Simon & Schuster, 2000.

Rehfeld, John E. *Alchemy of a Leader: Combining Western and Japanese Management Skills to Transform Your Company.* New York: John Wiley, 1994.

Reid, T. R. *Confucius Lives Next Door: What Living in the East Teaches Us About Living in the West.* New York: Vintage Books, 2000.

Rifkin, Jeremy. *The End of Work: The Decline of the Global Labor Force and the Dawn of the Post-Market Era.* New York: Tarcher/Putnam, 1996.

Samuelson, Robert J. "Close to the Lunatic Edge," *Newsweek*, April 21, 1997, p. 53.

Sherif, Muzafer. "Experiments in Group Conflict," in *Scientific American*, 195 (5), 1956, pp. 54-58.

Sherif, Muzafer, O. J. Harvey, B. Jack White, William R. Hood, and Carolyn W. Sherif. *Intergroup Conflict and Cooperation: The Robber's Cave Experiment.*" A Publication of the Institute of Group Relations. Mazafer Sherif, Director, The University of Oklahoma, Norman, Oklahoma, 1961. The University Book Exchange.

Sherif, Muzafer, and Carolyn W. Sherif. "Chapter 11, In-Group and Intergroup Relations: Experimental Analysis," in Muzafer Sherif and Carolyn W. Sherif. *Social Psychology.* New York: Harper & Row, 1969, pp. 221- 266.

Thurow, Lester C. *The Future of Capitalism.* New York: Penguin, 1997.

Tindall, Blair. *Mozart in the Jungle: Sex, Drugs and Classical Music.* New York: Atlantic Monthly Press: 2005.

Tocqueville, Alexis de. *Democracy in America*, Volume II. trans. Henry Reeve. London: Saunders and Otley, 1840.

Turnbull, Colin M. *The Mountain People.* New York: Touchstone (Simon & Schuster), 1972.

Van Munching, Philip. *Beer Blast: The Inside Story of the Brewing Industry's Bizarre Battles for Your Money.* New York: Times Business/Random House, 1997.

Westrum, Ron. *Sidewinder: Creative Missile Development at China Lake.* Annapolis, MD: Naval Institute Press, 1999.

Westrum, Ron. Private communication, December 5, 2002.

Wheatley, Margaret. *Leadership and the New Science: Learning about Organization from an Orderly Universe.* San Francisco: Berrett-Koehler.

Whitman, Walt. *Leaves of Grass; and Selected Prose.* New York: The Modern Library, 1950.

Will, George. "Our Age of 'Social Autism'," Ogden Standard-Examiner, November 20, 2005, p. 7A.

Williams, Redford. *The Trusting Heart.* New York: Time Books, 1989.

Wilson, Edward O. *Sociobiology: The New Synthesis.* Cambridge, Mass.: Belknap Press of Harvard University Press, 1975.

Wilson, Laura. *Hutterites of Montana.* New Haven: Yale University Press, 2000.

Wright, Ronald. *An Illustrated Short History of Progress,* Toronto: House of Anansi Press, 2006.

INDEX

A

Adversarial competition, 1, 20, 132, 139, 148, 158, 171, 245, 258, 264
Alienation, 11, 215-216, 218, 293
Anomie, 215-216, 218
Approval, 31-32, 51, 95, 195-202, 204-205, 243, 269
Art of associating together, 103-105, 165
Astor, John Jacob, 136-137
Autonomous group involvement, 218
Autonomous man, human, 109

B

B-52 bomber crews, 230
Baldwin, Ralph B., 36, 38-40, 42
Barber, Benjamin R., 145
Bell Labs, 12
Bellah, Robert N. , 27, 109, 114-119, 121-122, 128-129, 133, 138, 185, 280
Biblical individualism, 115-117, 129, 185, 269, 280
Bitch goddess of success, 138
Blumer, Herbert, 209-210
Boom-bust cycles, 84, 104, 131-132, 140-142, 264
Break-out society, 10-11, 275

C

Camp mode, 4, 189-193, 251-252
Campbell, Joseph, 292-295
Capitalism, 132-133, 135-138, 143-144, 153, 259
Chimpanzees, 73, 75-76, 78, 112
Civic Individualism, 116-118
Cohesion, 54, 102, 113, 151, 173-174, 182, 190, 199, 204, 207-209, 213-220, 229, 232, 256
Colonial invertebrates, 63, 66
Communal utopias, 10, 43
Communes, 9
Compassion, 111, 131, 275, 281, 293-295
Competence, 31, 41, 45, 52, 64-66, 68, 87-88, 91, 96, 140, 150, 152, 157-158, 175, 181-182, 201, 211, 243, 283, 288
Competition, 1, 3, 7, 9, 11, 15, 17-25, 27-28, 32, 42, 51, 54-55, 62-63, 71, 79, 86, 91-93, 97, 108, 112, 118, 125, 127, 129, 131-135, 138-140, 143-145, 148-149, 151, 156, 158, 171, 183-189, 191, 193, 195, 197, 201, 213, 228, 235, 239, 244-246, 256, 258, 264-265, 267, 269-270, 272, 281, 285-286, 290-291
Competitive mutual aid, 22-25, 28, 62, 70, 72-73, 79, 82, 111, 213
Consequence network, 31, 32, 52, 138, 196, 197, 204-207, 278, 287
Control-oriented organizations, 240

Made in the USA
San Bernardino, CA
24 April 2018